JONESY™

BOYLE • HUMPHRIES • PEER

VOLUME THREE

BOOM!
BOX™

JONESY Volume Three, September 2017. Published by BOOM! Box, a division of Boom Entertainment, Inc., 5670 Wilshire Boulevard, Suite 450, Los Angeles, CA 90036-5679. Jonesy is ™ & © 2017 Sam Humphries and Caitlin Rose Boyle. Originally published in single magazine form as JONESY No. 9-12. ™ & © 2016, 2017 Sam Humphries & Caitlin Rose Boyle. All rights reserved. BOOM! Box™ and the BOOM! Box logo are trademarks of Boom Entertainment, Inc., registered in various countries and categories. All characters, events, and institutions depicted herein are fictional. Any similarity between any of the names, characters, persons, events, and/or institutions in this publication to actual names, characters, and persons, whether living or dead, events, and/or institutions is unintended and purely coincidental. BOOM! Box does not read or accept unsolicited submissions of ideas, stories, or artwork.

BOOM! Studios, 5670 Wilshire Boulevard, Suite 450, Los Angeles, CA 90036-5679. Printed in China. First Printing.

ISBN: 978-1-68415-016-8, eISBN: 978-1-61398-687-5

DEDICATED TO
THE REAL JONESY
♥ ♥♥ SAM

DEDICATED TO
BRENDAN
♥ ♥♥ CAITLIN

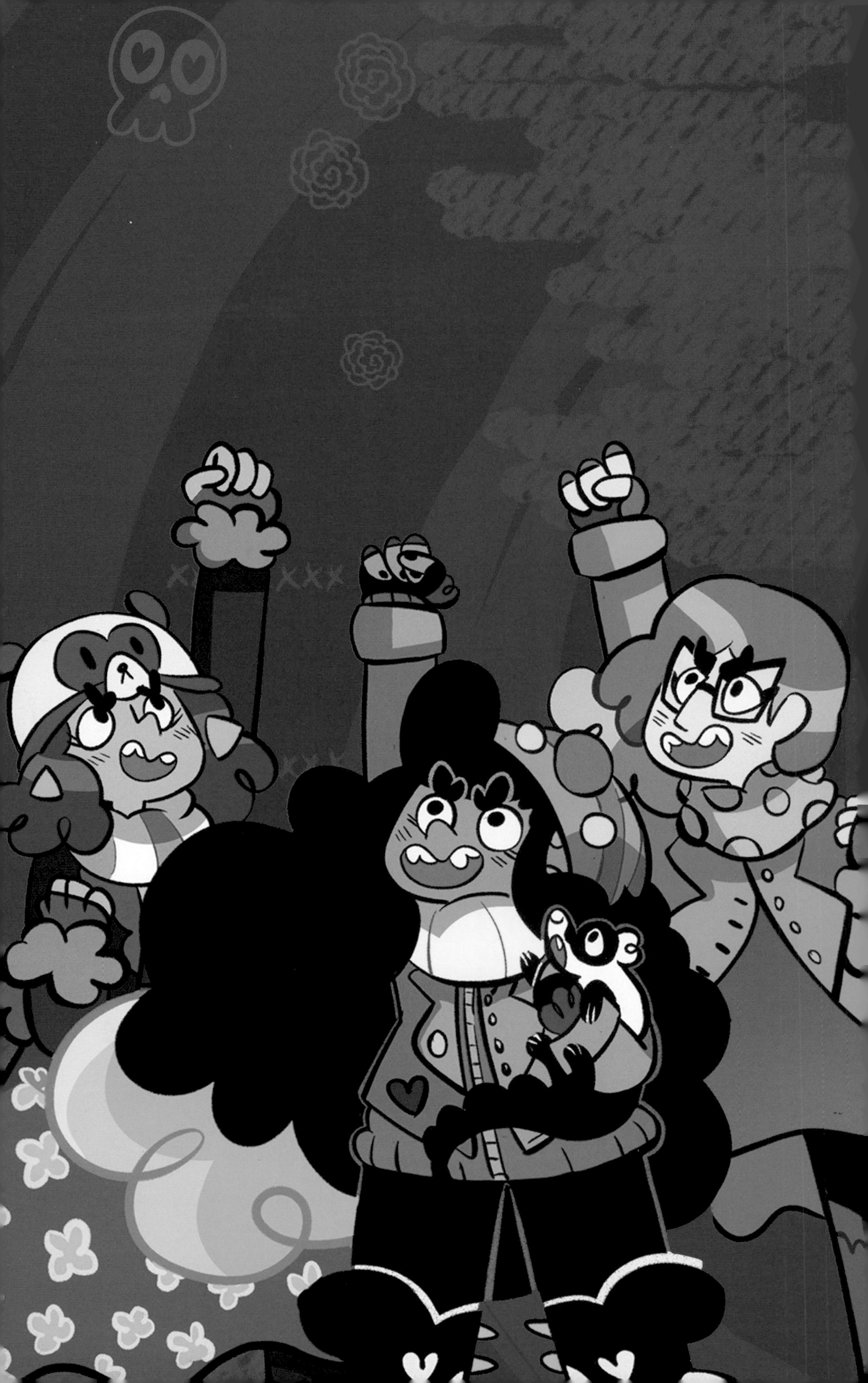

BY
CAITLIN ROSE BOYLE
& SAM HUMPHRIES

WITH COLORS BY
BRITTANY PEER

LETTERS BY
COREY BREEN

COVER BY
CAITLIN ROSE BOYLE
WITH COLORS BY BRITTANY PEER

DESIGNER
KELSEY DIETERICH

ASSISTANT EDITOR
MATTHEW LEVINE

EDITORS
JEANINE SCHAEFER &
SHANNON WATTERS

CHAPTER ONE

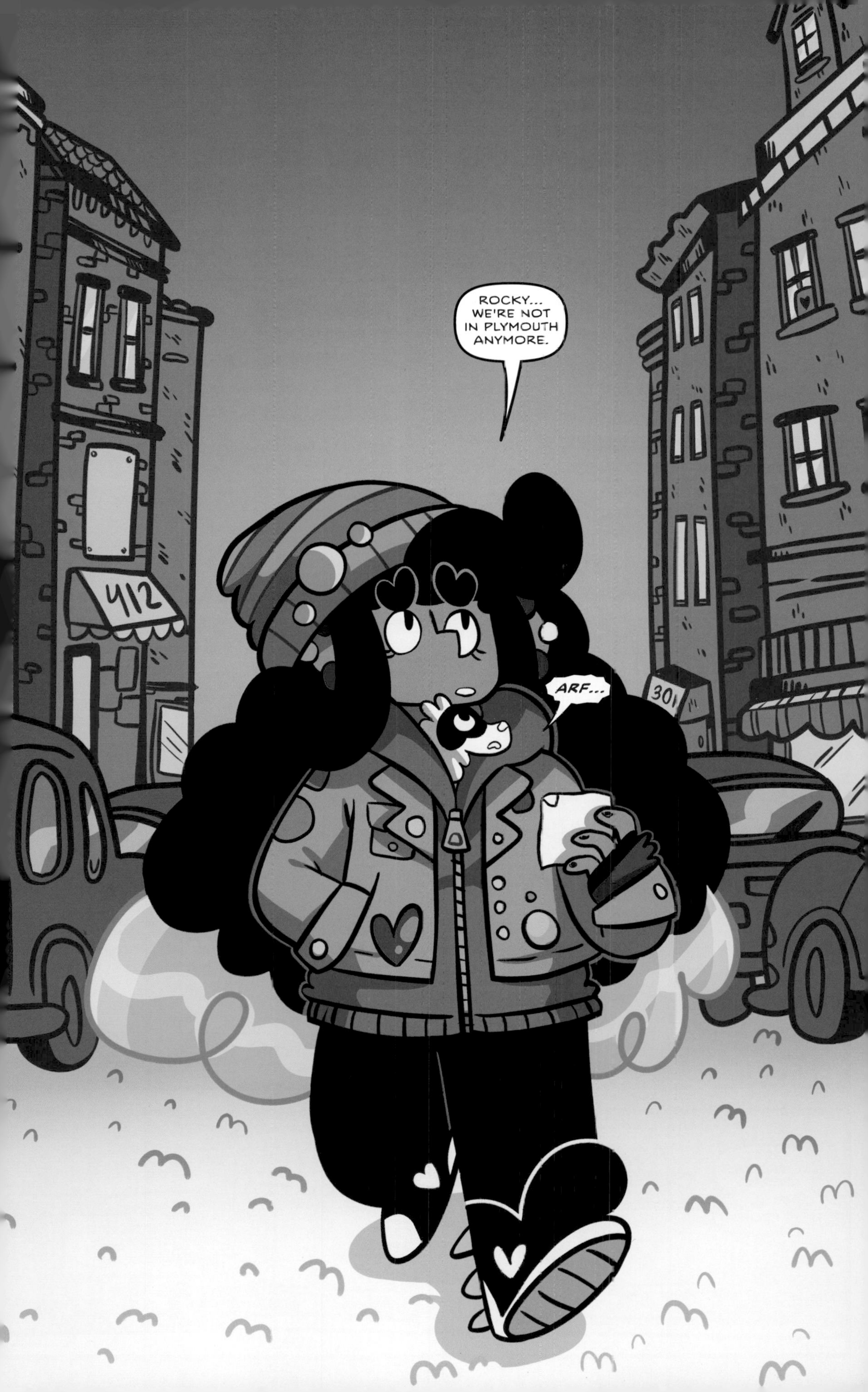
412
ROCKY... WE'RE NOT IN PLYMOUTH ANYMORE.
ARF...
301

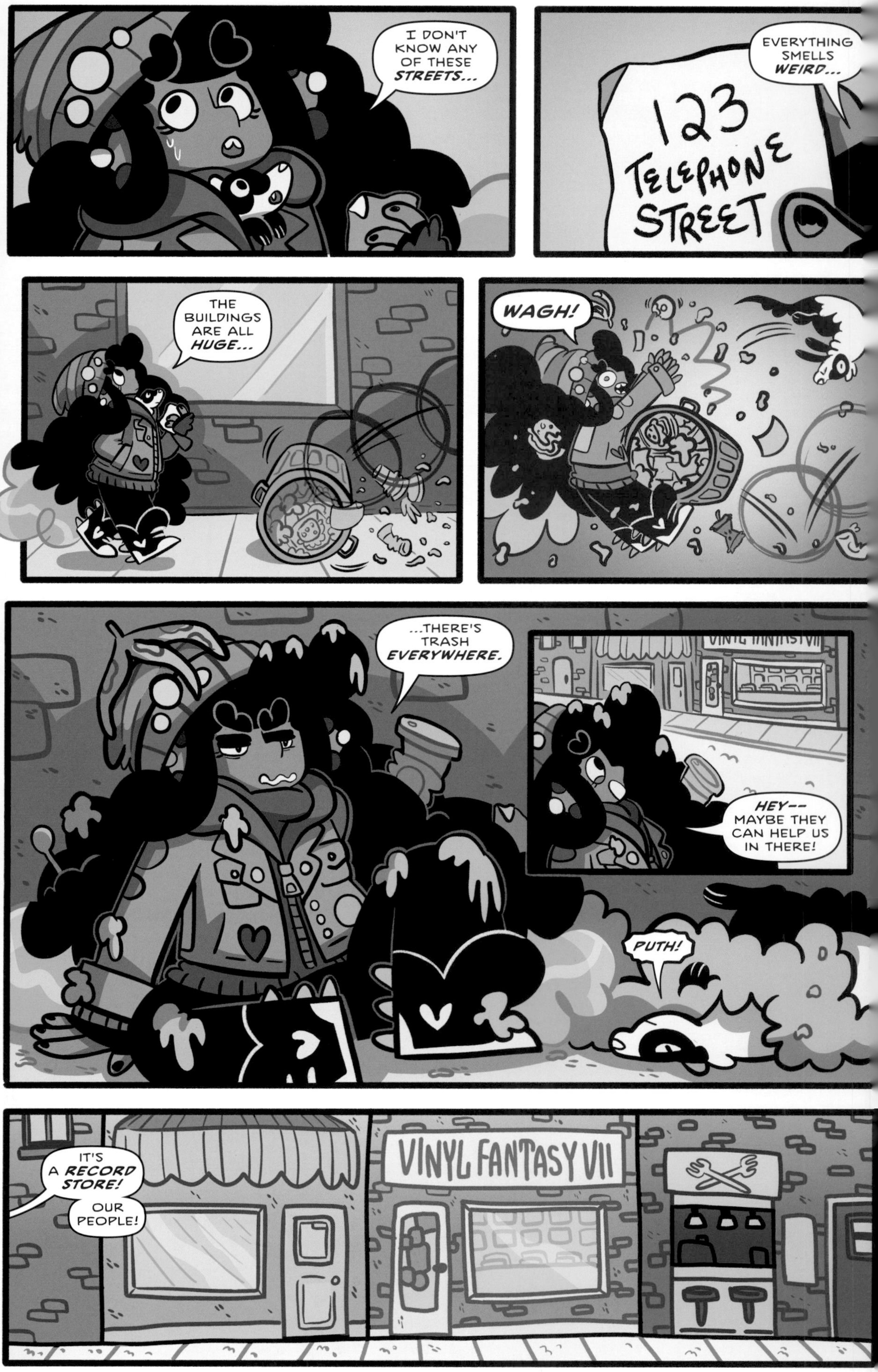
I DON'T KNOW ANY OF THESE STREETS...
EVERYTHING SMELLS WEIRD...
123 TELEPHONE STREET
THE BUILDINGS ARE ALL HUGE...
WAGH!
...THERE'S TRASH EVERYWHERE.
VINYL FANTASY VII
HEY-- MAYBE THEY CAN HELP US IN THERE!
PUTH!
IT'S A RECORD STORE!
OUR PEOPLE!
VINYL FANTASY VII

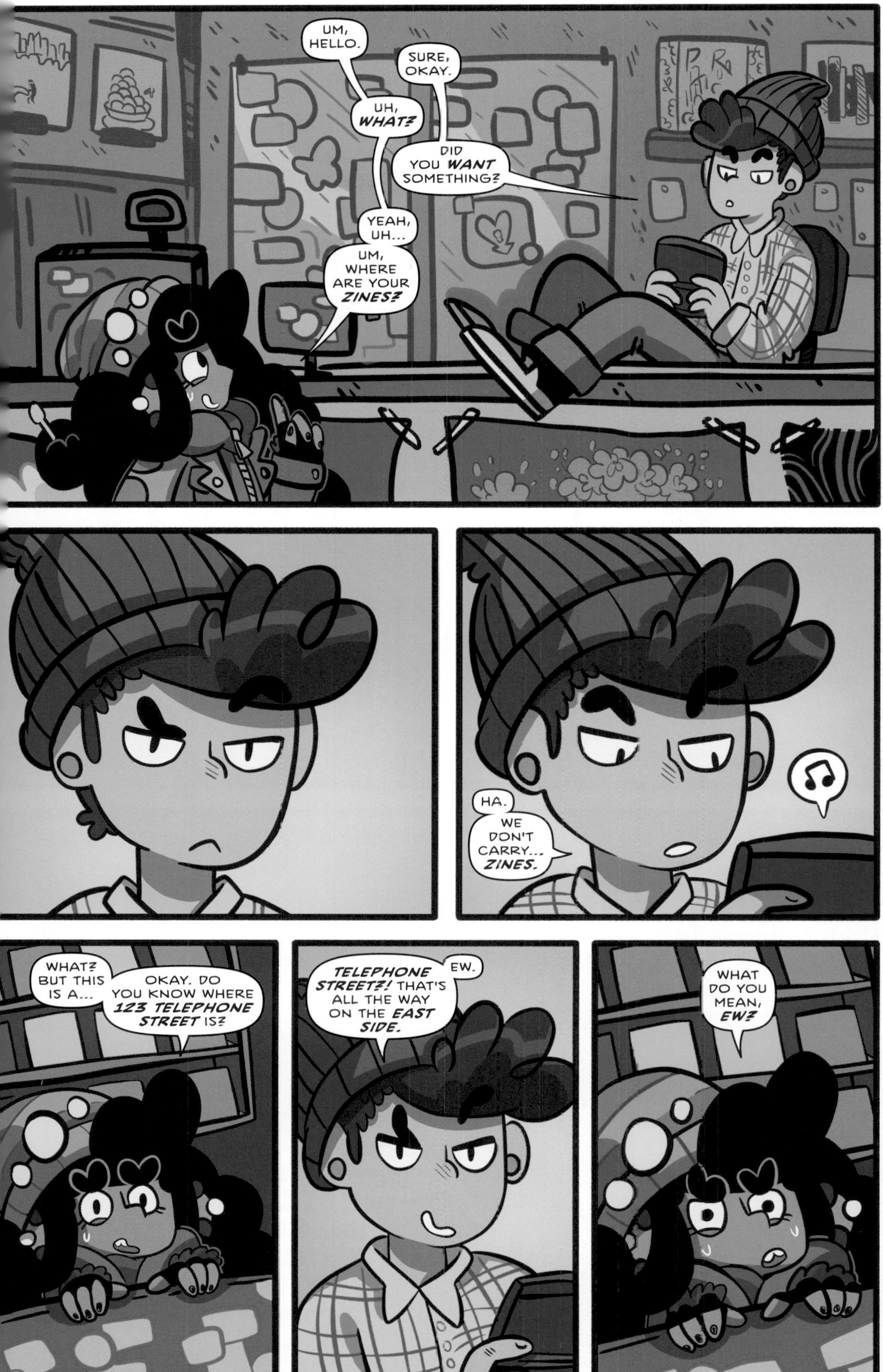
UM, HELLO.
SURE, OKAY.
UH, WHAT?
DID YOU WANT SOMETHING?
YEAH, UH...
UM, WHERE ARE YOUR ZINES?
HA.
WE DON'T CARRY... ZINES.
WHAT? BUT THIS IS A...
OKAY. DO YOU KNOW WHERE 123 TELEPHONE STREET IS?
TELEPHONE STREET?! THAT'S ALL THE WAY ON THE EAST SIDE.
EW.
WHAT DO YOU MEAN, EW?

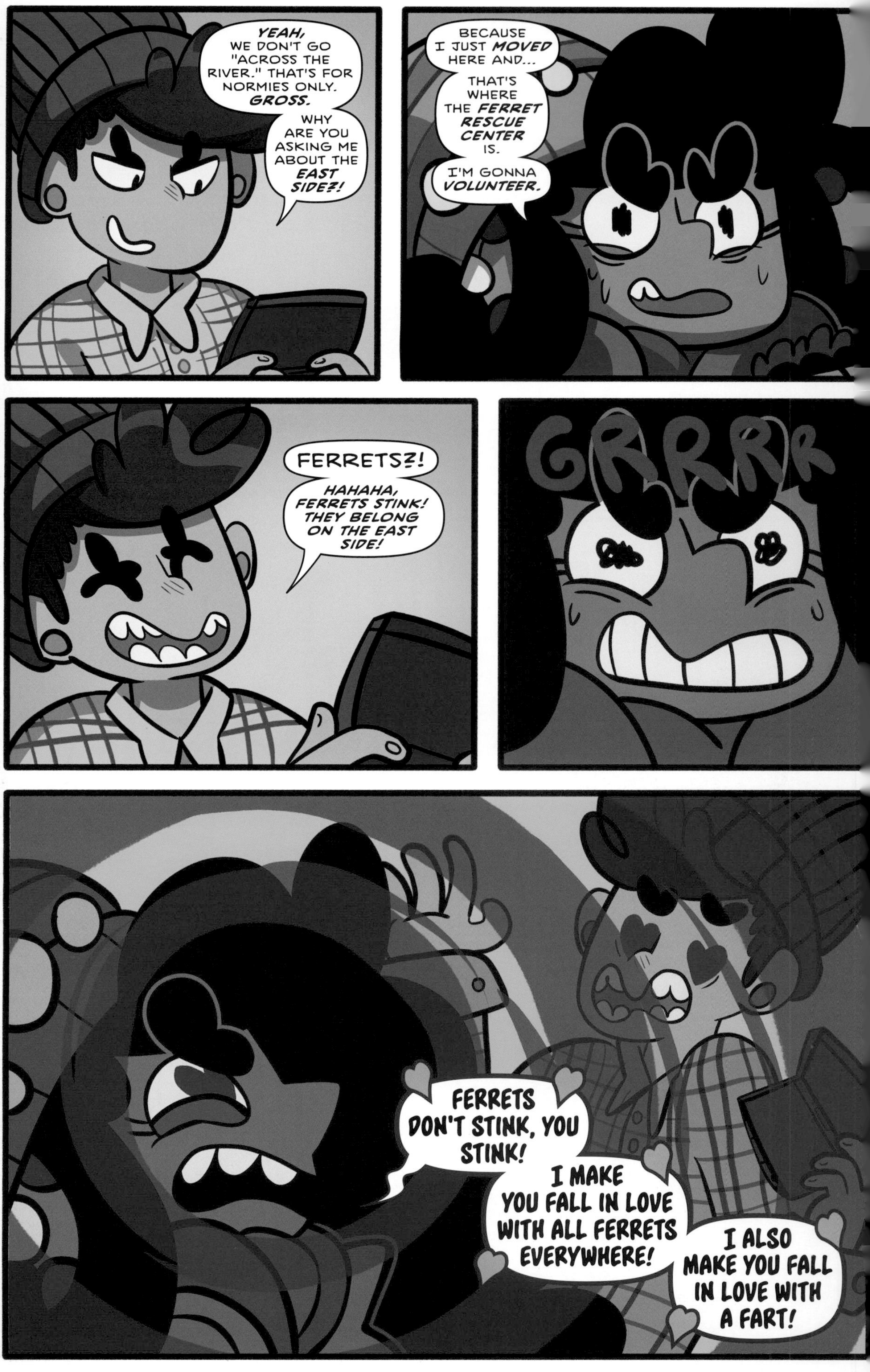

YEAH, WE DON'T GO "ACROSS THE RIVER." THAT'S FOR NORMIES ONLY. GROSS.
WHY ARE YOU ASKING ME ABOUT THE EAST SIDE?!
BECAUSE I JUST MOVED HERE AND...
THAT'S WHERE THE FERRET RESCUE CENTER IS.
I'M GONNA VOLUNTEER.
FERRETS?!
HAHAHA, FERRETS STINK! THEY BELONG ON THE EAST SIDE!
GRRRR
FERRETS DON'T STINK, YOU STINK!
I MAKE YOU FALL IN LOVE WITH ALL FERRETS EVERYWHERE!
I ALSO MAKE YOU FALL IN LOVE WITH A FART!

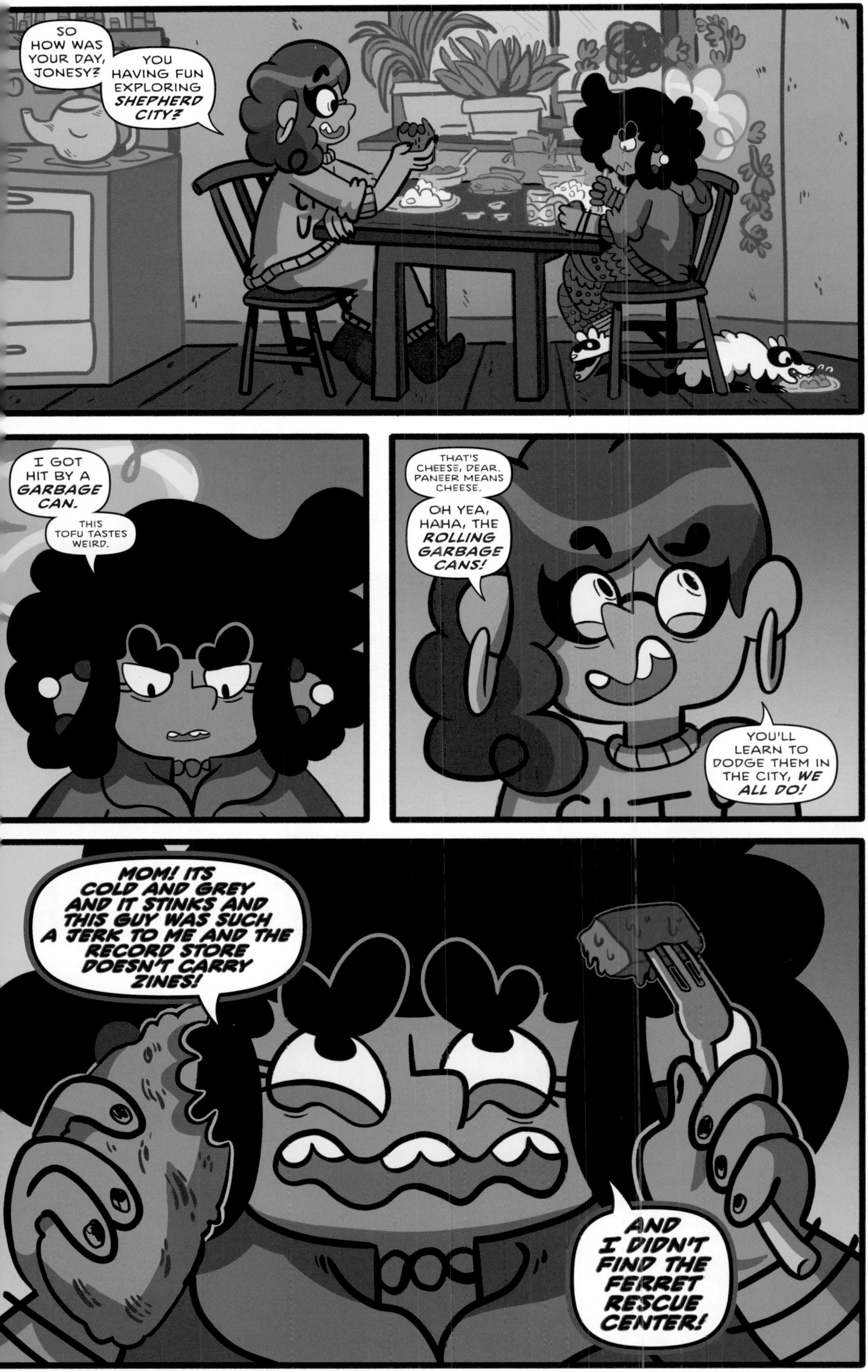
SO HOW WAS YOUR DAY, JONESY?
YOU HAVING FUN EXPLORING SHEPHERD CITY?
I GOT HIT BY A GARBAGE CAN.
THIS TOFU TASTES WEIRD.
THAT'S CHEESE, DEAR. PANEER MEANS CHEESE.
OH YEA, HAHA, THE ROLLING GARBAGE CANS!
YOU'LL LEARN TO DODGE THEM IN THE CITY, WE ALL DO!
MOM! ITS COLD AND GREY AND IT STINKS AND THIS GUY WAS SUCH A JERK TO ME AND THE RECORD STORE DOESN'T CARRY ZINES!
AND I DIDN'T FIND THE FERRET RESCUE CENTER!

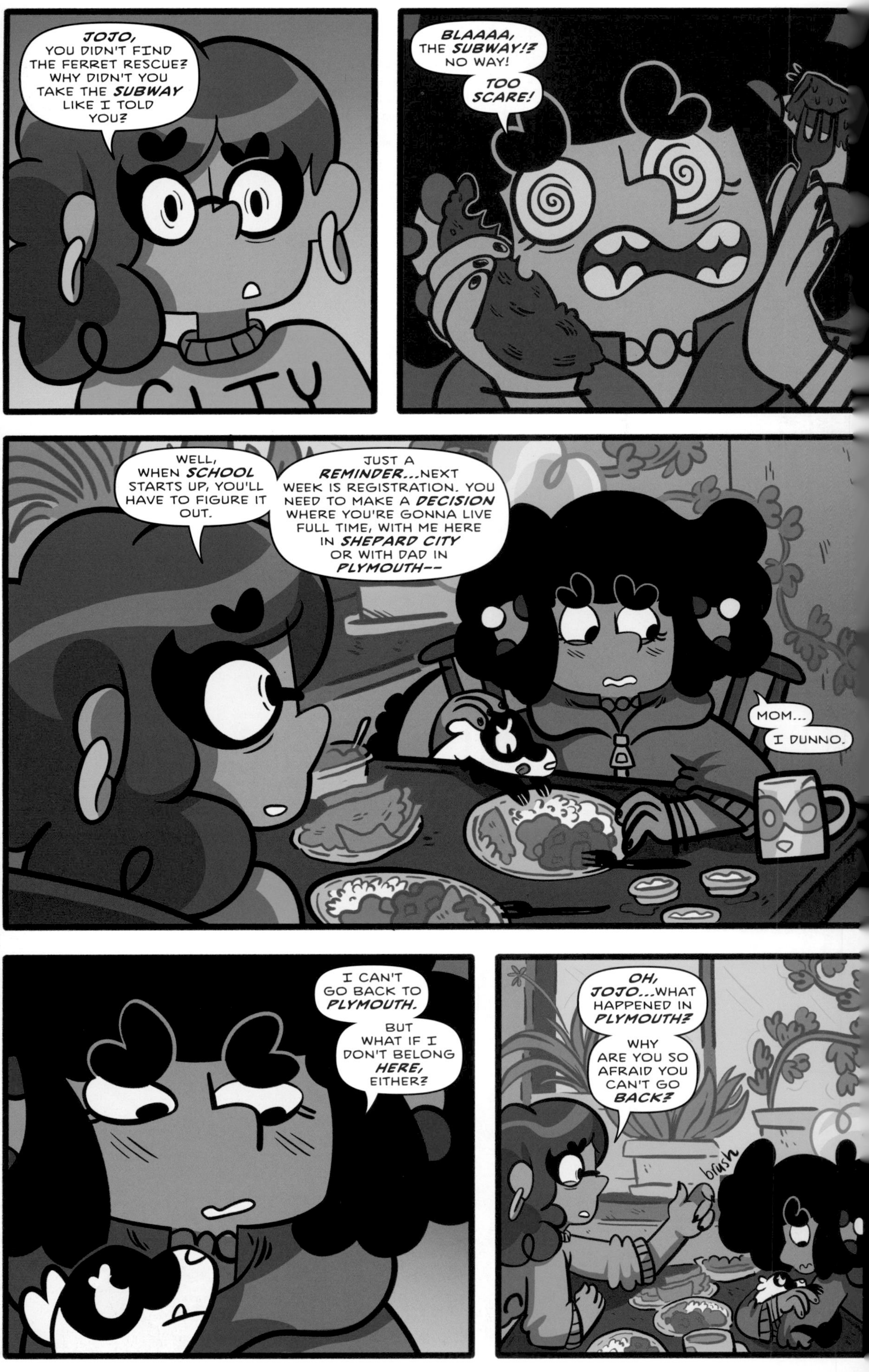
JOJO, YOU DIDN'T FIND THE FERRET RESCUE? WHY DIDN'T YOU TAKE THE SUBWAY LIKE I TOLD YOU?
CITY
BLAAAA, THE SUBWAY!? NO WAY!
TOO SCARE!
WELL, WHEN SCHOOL STARTS UP, YOU'LL HAVE TO FIGURE IT OUT.
JUST A REMINDER...NEXT WEEK IS REGISTRATION. YOU NEED TO MAKE A DECISION WHERE YOU'RE GONNA LIVE FULL TIME, WITH ME HERE IN SHEPARD CITY OR WITH DAD IN PLYMOUTH--
MOM...
I DUNNO.
I CAN'T GO BACK TO PLYMOUTH.
BUT WHAT IF I DON'T BELONG HERE, EITHER?
OH, JOJO...WHAT HAPPENED IN PLYMOUTH?
WHY ARE YOU SO AFRAID YOU CAN'T GO BACK?
brush

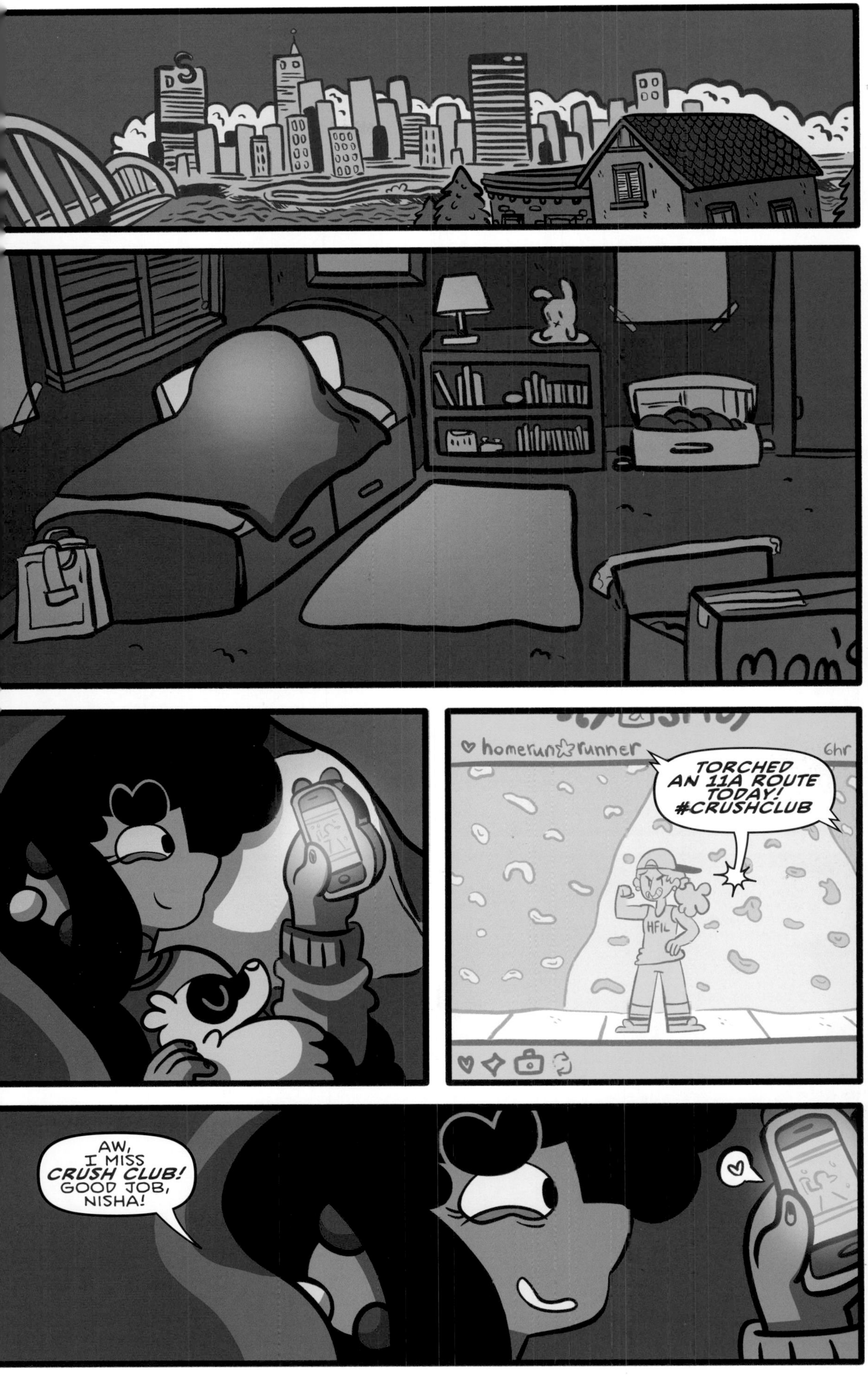
homerun☆runner
6hr
TORCHED AN 11A ROUTE TODAY! #CRUSHCLUB
HFIL
AW, I MISS CRUSH CLUB! GOOD JOB, NISHA!

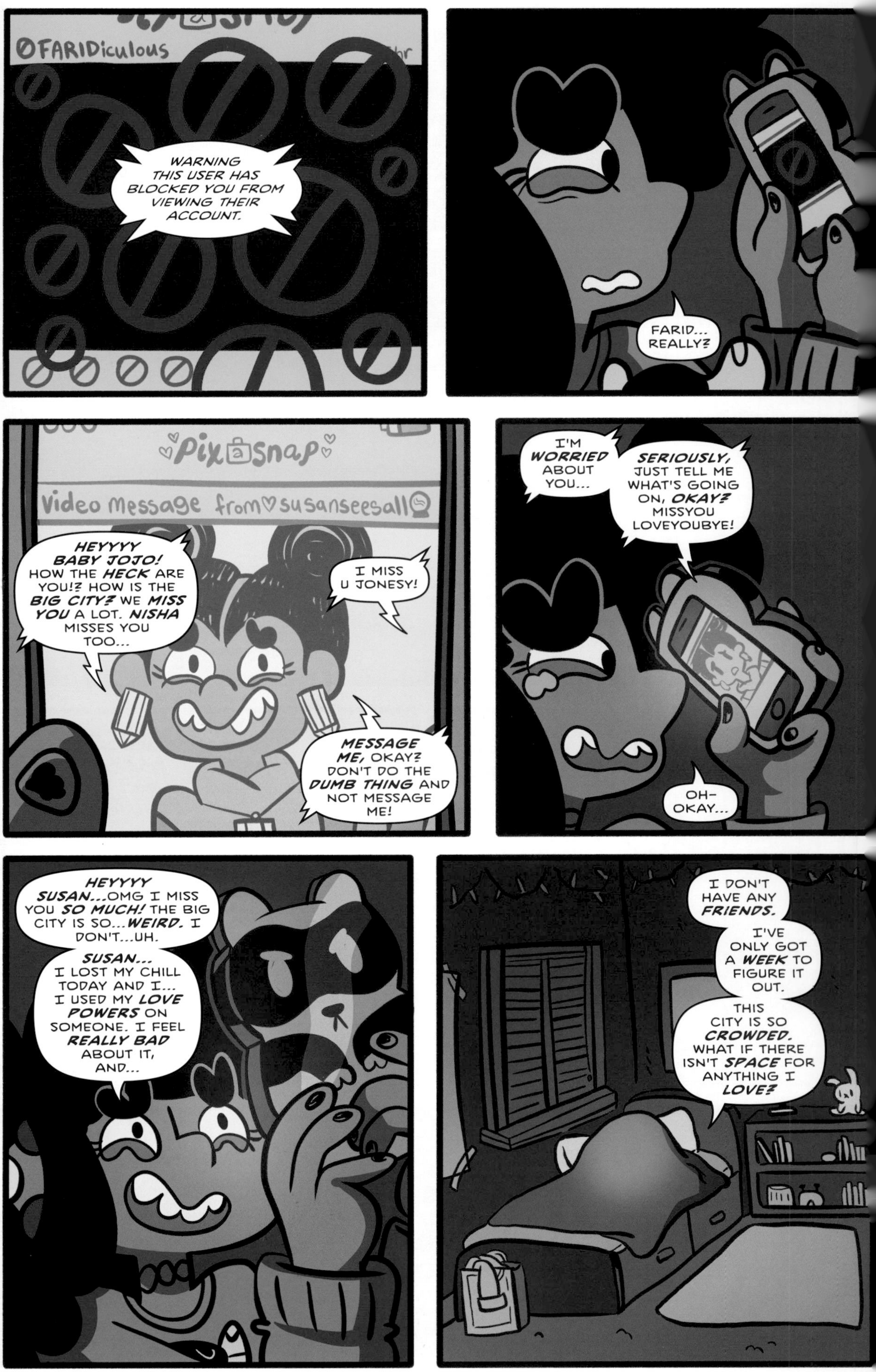
FARIDiculous
WARNING THIS USER HAS BLOCKED YOU FROM VIEWING THEIR ACCOUNT.
FARID... REALLY?
Pix@snap
Video message from susanseesall
HEYYYY BABY JOJO! HOW THE HECK ARE YOU!? HOW IS THE BIG CITY? WE MISS YOU A LOT. NISHA MISSES YOU TOO...
I MISS U JONESY!
MESSAGE ME, OKAY? DON'T DO THE DUMB THING AND NOT MESSAGE ME!
I'M WORRIED ABOUT YOU...
SERIOUSLY, JUST TELL ME WHAT'S GOING ON, OKAY? MISSYOU LOVEYOUBYE!
OH-OKAY...
HEYYYY SUSAN...OMG I MISS YOU SO MUCH! THE BIG CITY IS SO...WEIRD. I DON'T...UH.
SUSAN... I LOST MY CHILL TODAY AND I... I USED MY LOVE POWERS ON SOMEONE. I FEEL REALLY BAD ABOUT IT, AND...
I DON'T HAVE ANY FRIENDS.
I'VE ONLY GOT A WEEK TO FIGURE IT OUT.
THIS CITY IS SO CROWDED. WHAT IF THERE ISN'T SPACE FOR ANYTHING I LOVE?

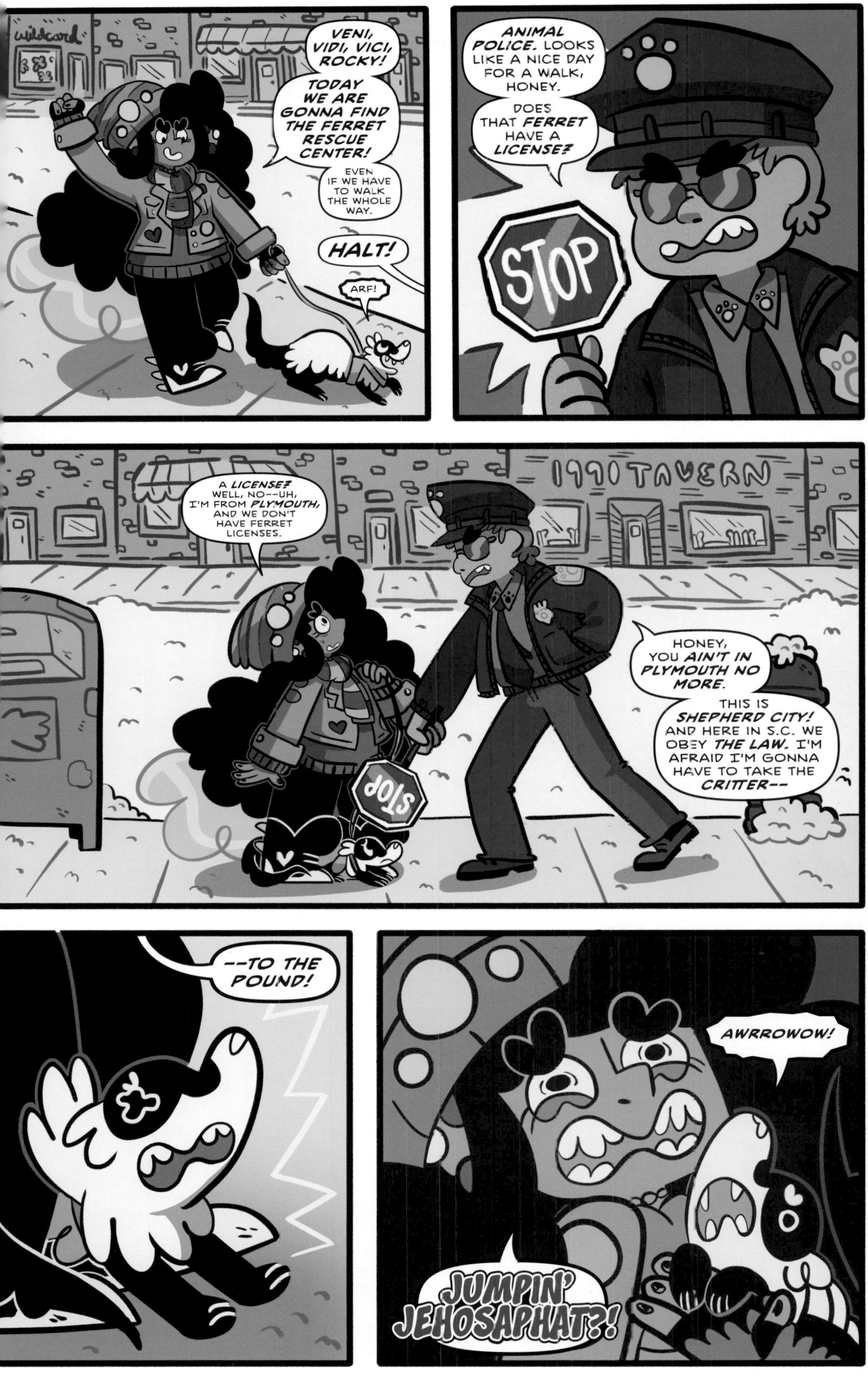

VENI, VIDI, VICI, ROCKY!
TODAY WE ARE GONNA FIND THE FERRET RESCUE CENTER!
EVEN IF WE HAVE TO WALK THE WHOLE WAY.
HALT!
ARF!
ANIMAL POLICE. LOOKS LIKE A NICE DAY FOR A WALK, HONEY.
DOES THAT FERRET HAVE A LICENSE?
STOP
A LICENSE? WELL, NO--UH, I'M FROM PLYMOUTH, AND WE DON'T HAVE FERRET LICENSES.
1991 TAVERN
HONEY, YOU AIN'T IN PLYMOUTH NO MORE.
THIS IS SHEPHERD CITY! AND HERE IN S.C. WE OBEY THE LAW. I'M AFRAID I'M GONNA HAVE TO TAKE THE CRITTER--
--TO THE POUND!
AWRROWOW!
JUMPIN' JEHOSAPHAT?!

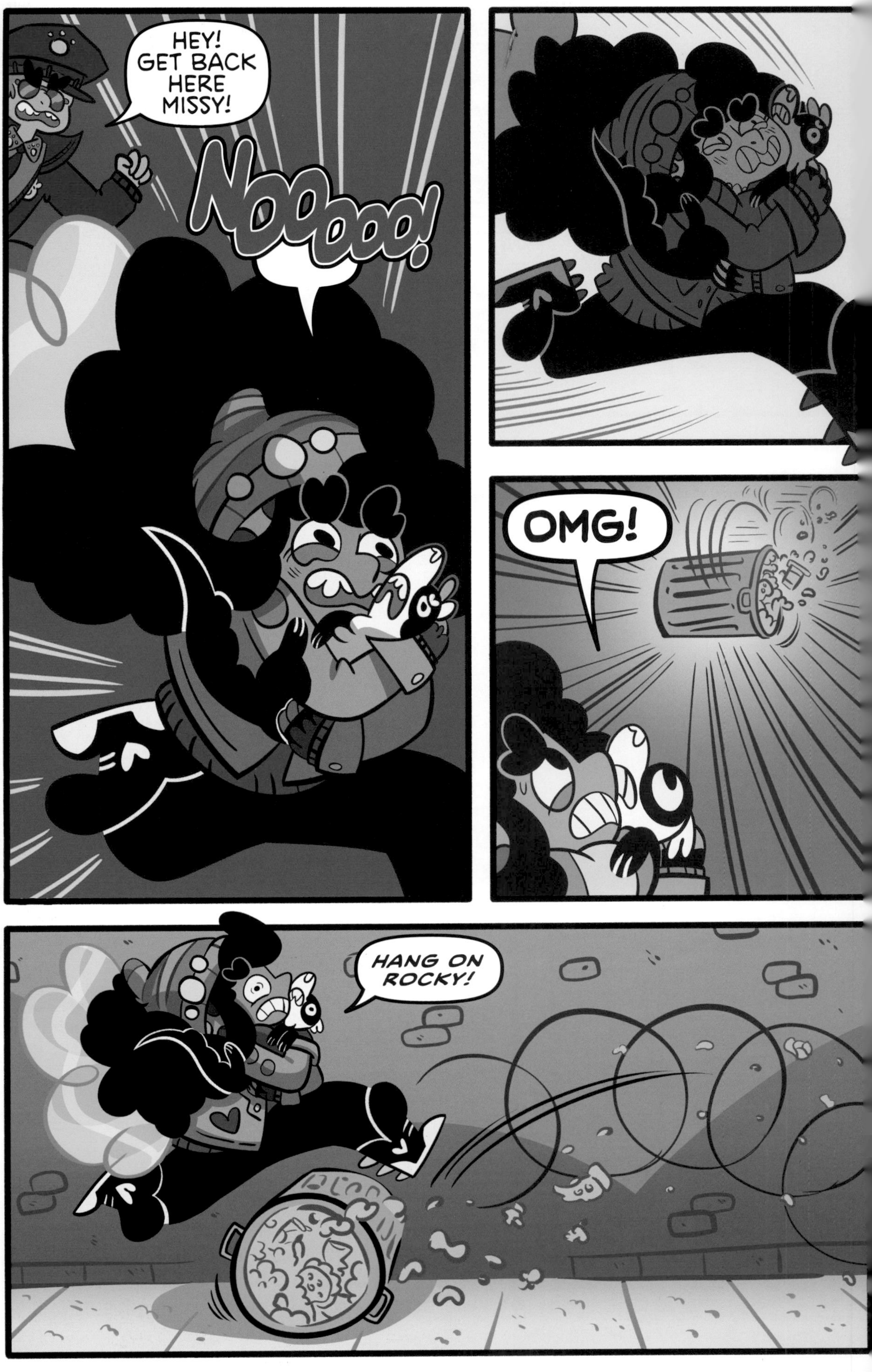
HEY! GET BACK HERE MISSY!
NOOOOOO!
OMG!
HANG ON ROCKY!

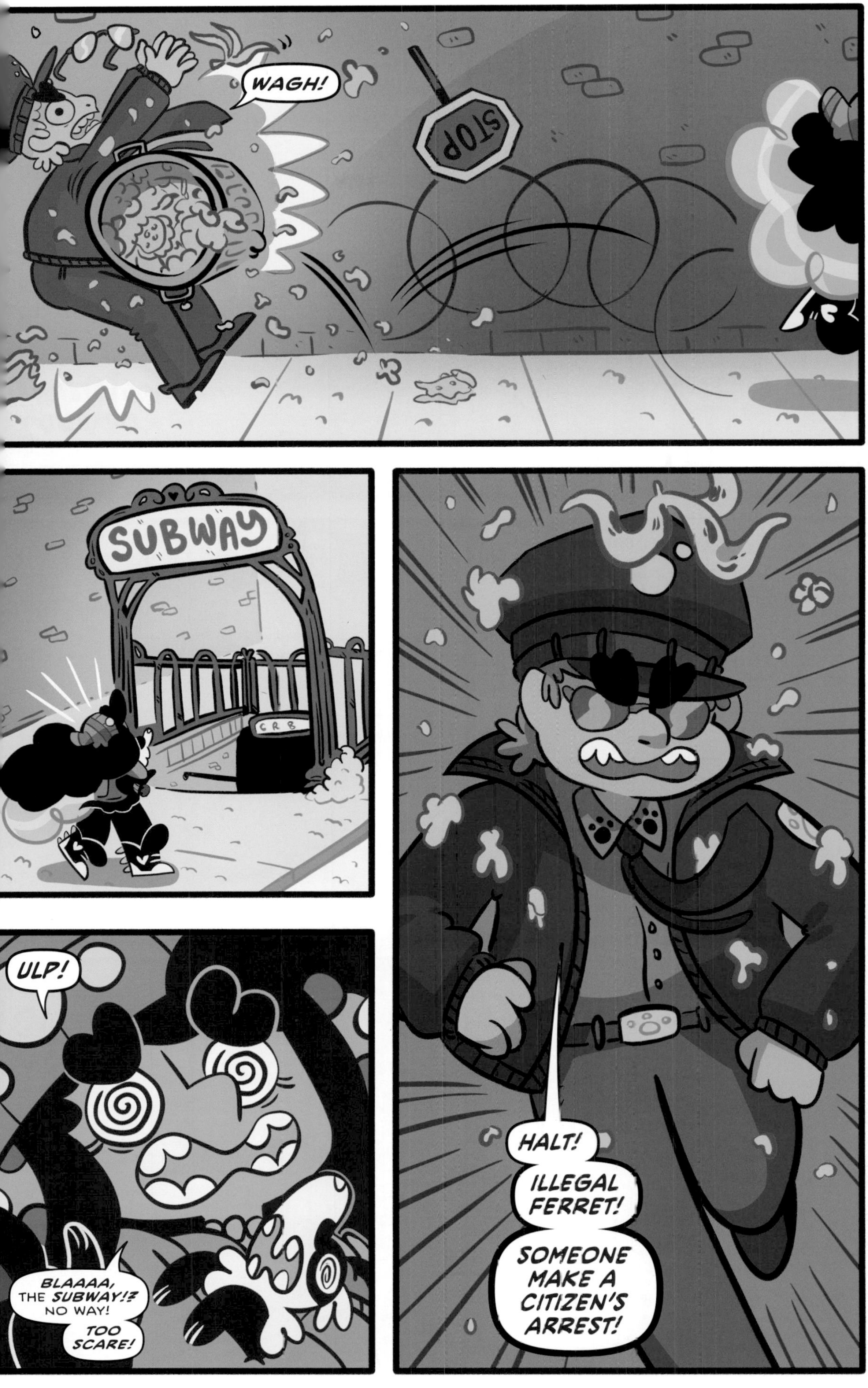
WAGH!
STOP
SUBWAY
CRB
ULP!
BLAAAA, THE SUBWAY!? NO WAY!
TOO SCARE!
HALT!
ILLEGAL FERRET!
SOMEONE MAKE A CITIZEN'S ARREST!

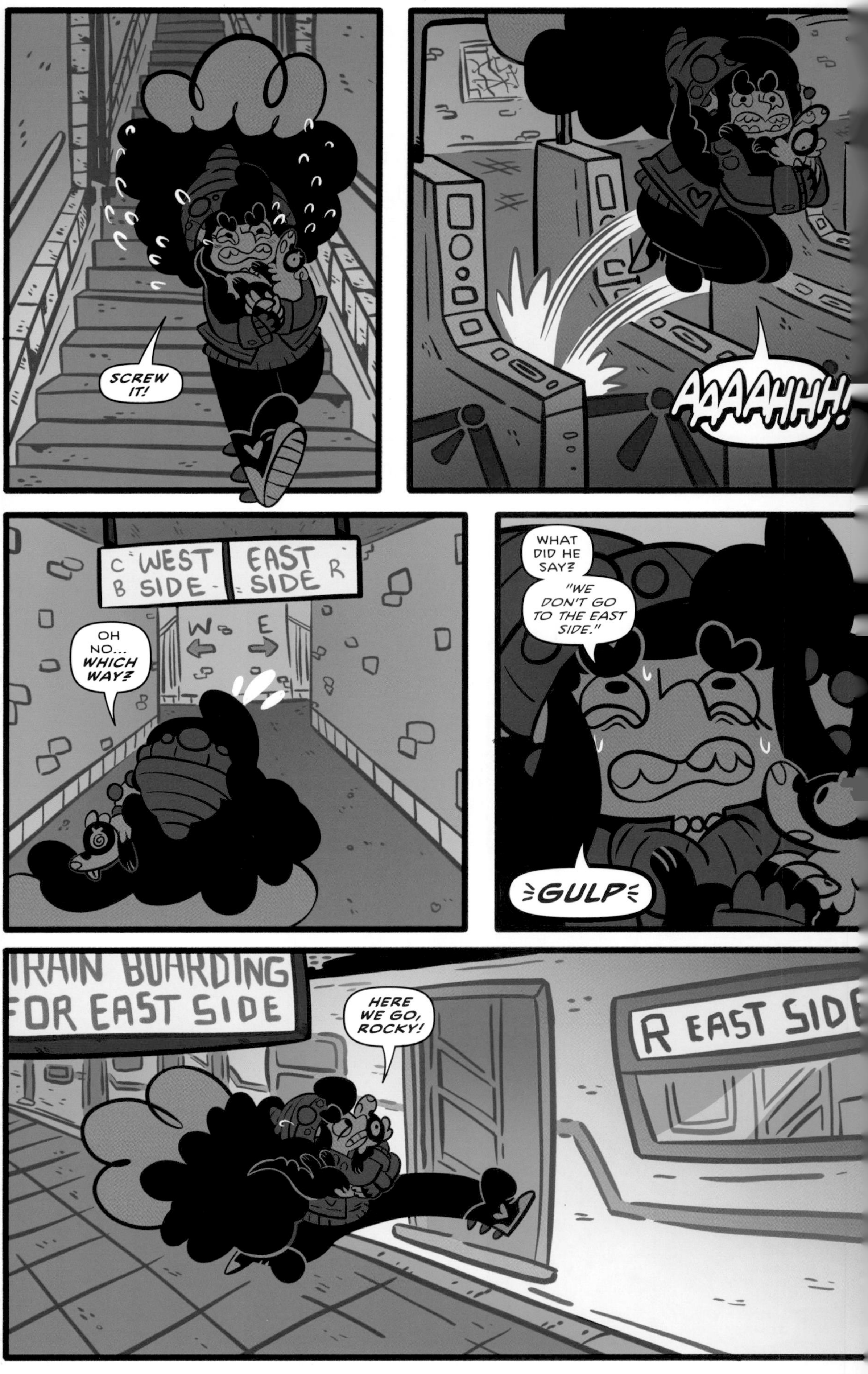
SCREW IT!
AAAAHHH!
C WEST SIDE B
EAST SIDE R
W E
OH NO... WHICH WAY?
WHAT DID HE SAY?
"WE DON'T GO TO THE EAST SIDE."
GULP
TRAIN BOARDING FOR EAST SIDE
HERE WE GO, ROCKY!
R EAST SIDE

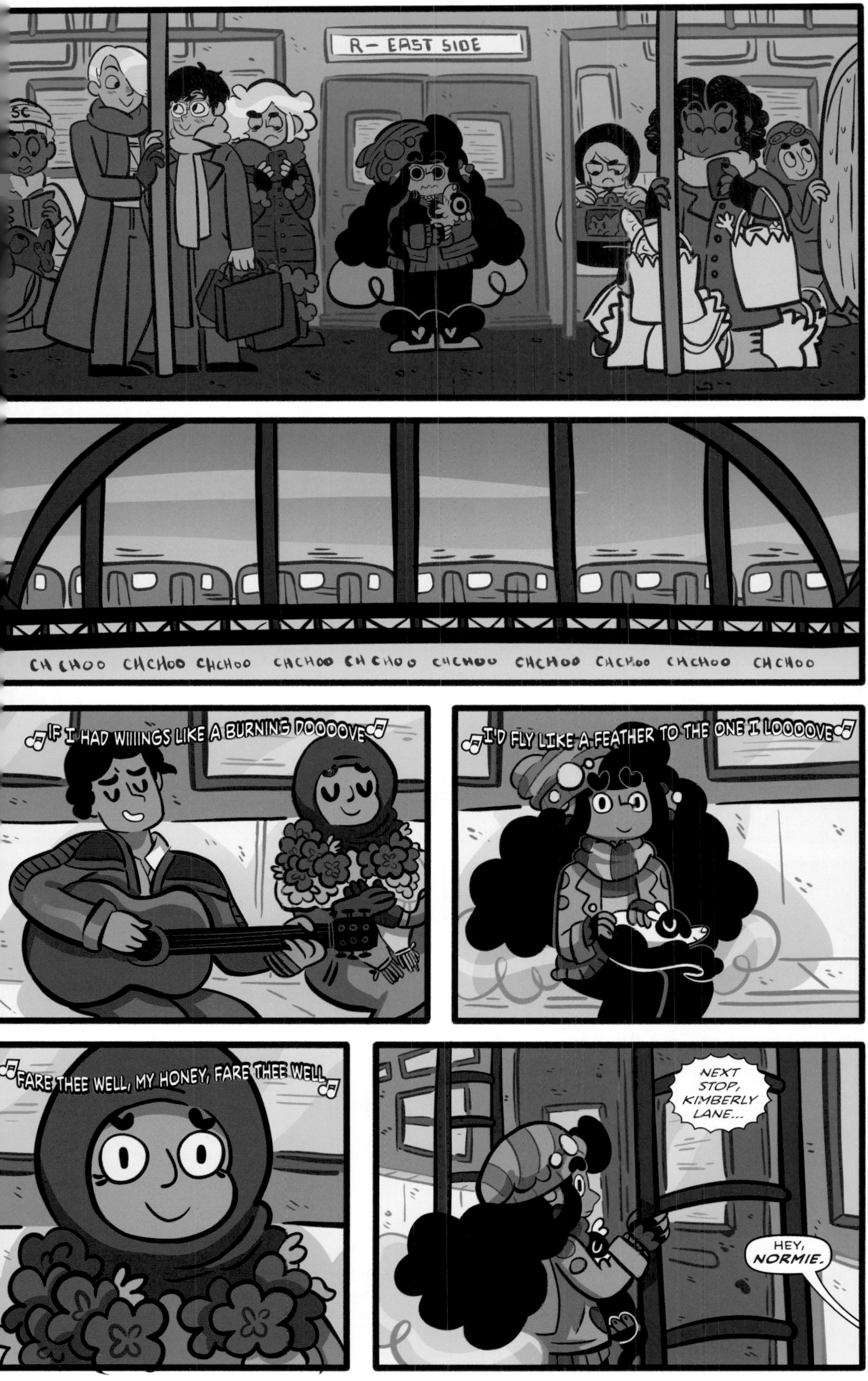
R- EAST SIDE
CH CHOO CHCHOO CHCHOO CHCHOO CH CHOO CHCHOO CHCHOO CHCHOO CHCHOO CHCHOO
IF I HAD WIIIINGS LIKE A BURNING DOOOOVE
I'D FLY LIKE A FEATHER TO THE ONE I LOOOOVE
FARE THEE WELL, MY HONEY, FARE THEE WELL
NEXT STOP, KIMBERLY LANE...
HEY, NORMIE.

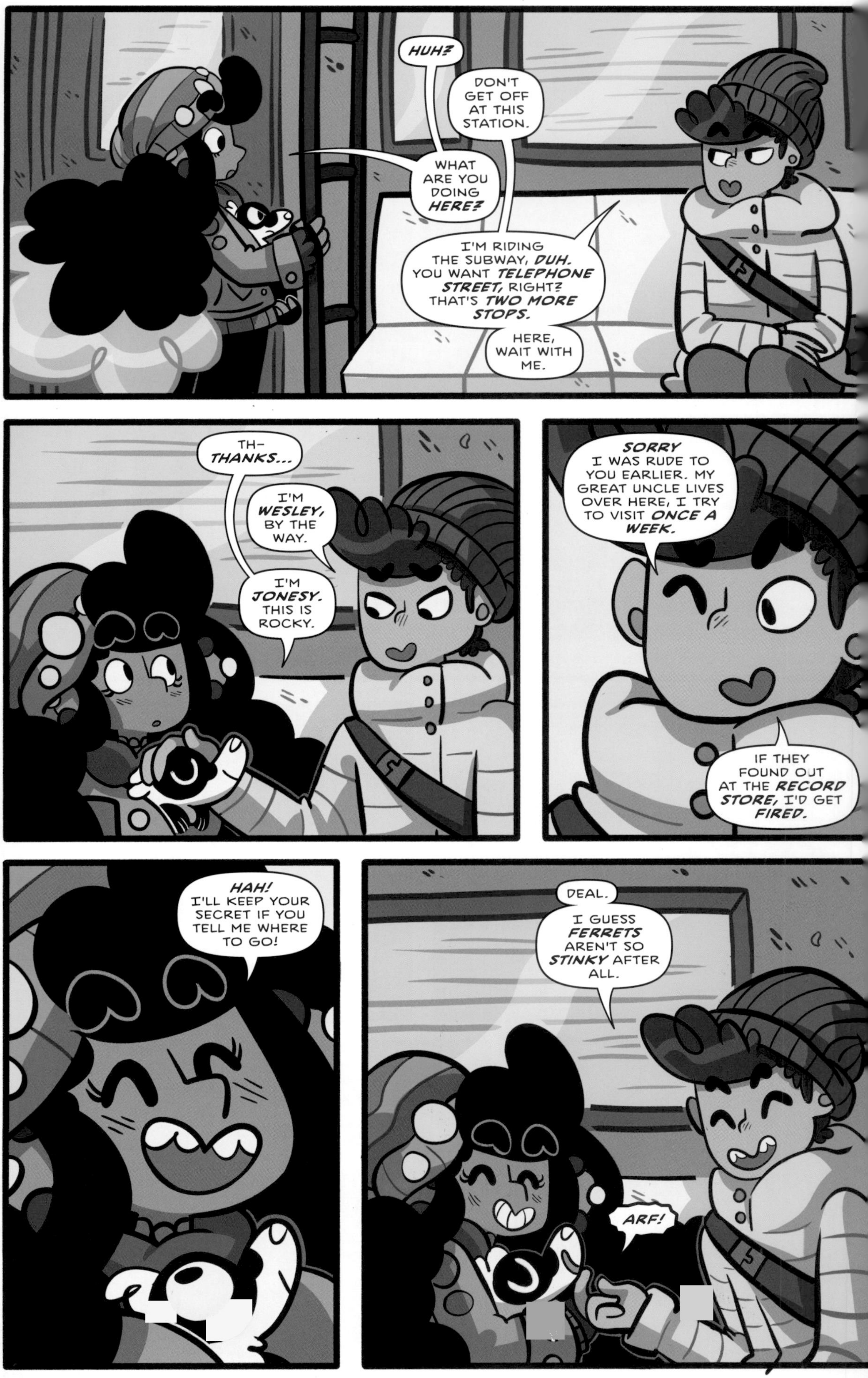
HUH?
DON'T GET OFF AT THIS STATION.
WHAT ARE YOU DOING HERE?
I'M RIDING THE SUBWAY, DUH. YOU WANT TELEPHONE STREET, RIGHT? THAT'S TWO MORE STOPS.
HERE, WAIT WITH ME.
TH- THANKS...
I'M WESLEY, BY THE WAY.
I'M JONESY. THIS IS ROCKY.
SORRY I WAS RUDE TO YOU EARLIER. MY GREAT UNCLE LIVES OVER HERE, I TRY TO VISIT ONCE A WEEK.
IF THEY FOUND OUT AT THE RECORD STORE, I'D GET FIRED.
HAH! I'LL KEEP YOUR SECRET IF YOU TELL ME WHERE TO GO!
DEAL.
I GUESS FERRETS AREN'T SO STINKY AFTER ALL.
ARF!

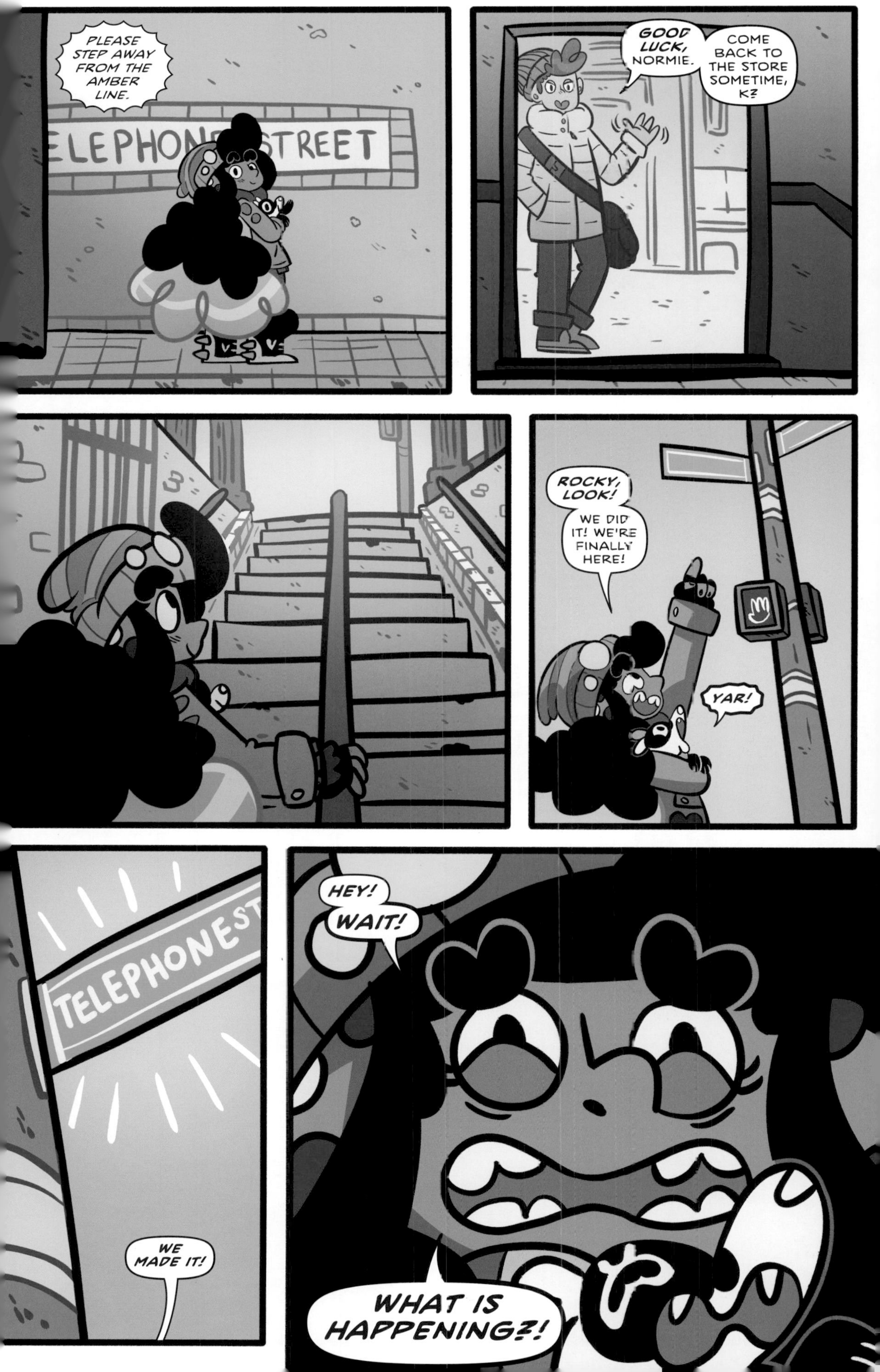
PLEASE STEP AWAY FROM THE AMBER LINE.
TELEPHONE STREET
GOOD LUCK, NORMIE.
COME BACK TO THE STORE SOMETIME, K?
ROCKY, LOOK!
WE DID IT! WE'RE FINALLY HERE!
YAR!
TELEPHONE ST
WE MADE IT!
HEY!
WAIT!
WHAT IS HAPPENING?!

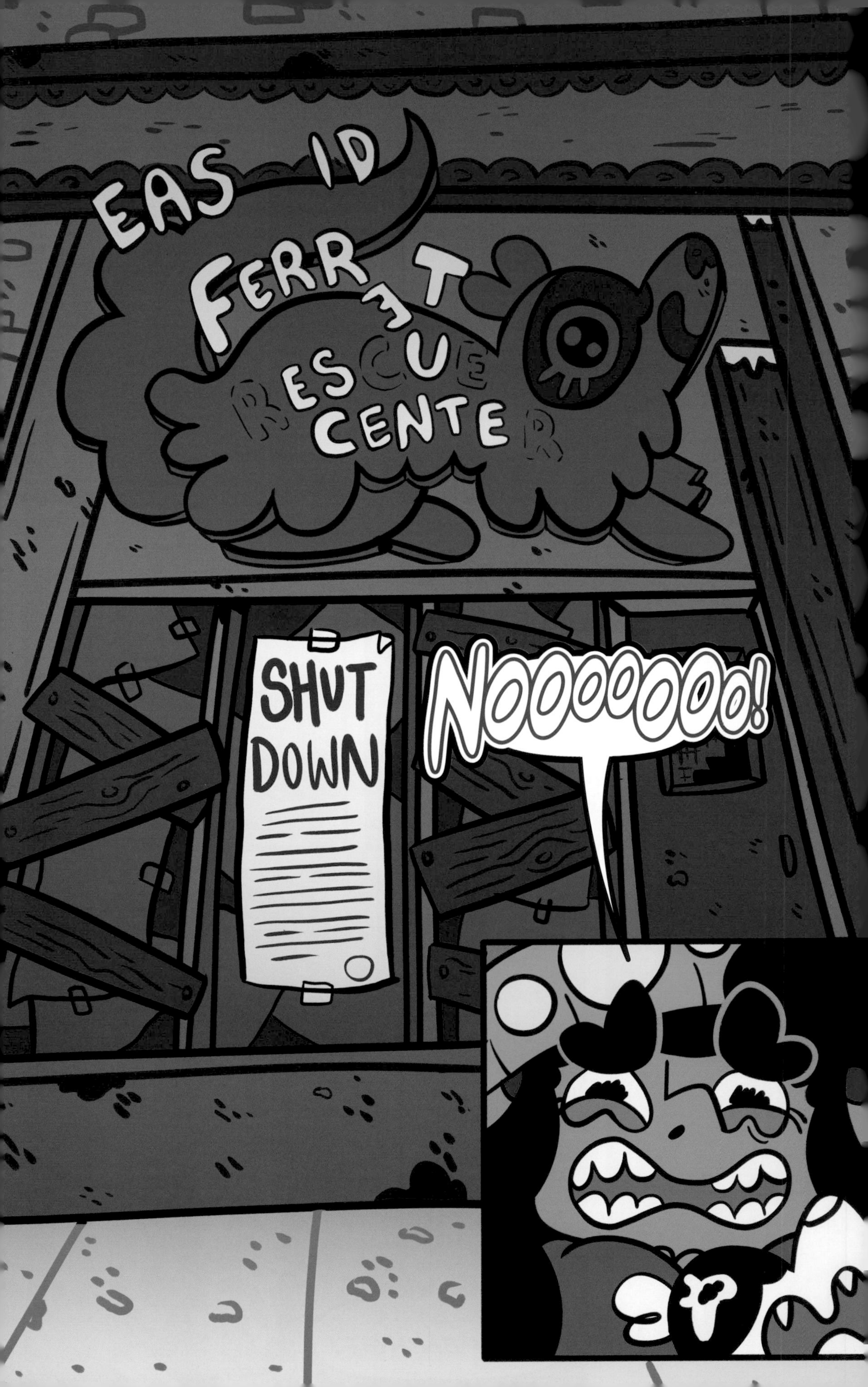
EAS ID
FERRET
RESCUE CENTER
SHUT DOWN
NOOOOOOOO!

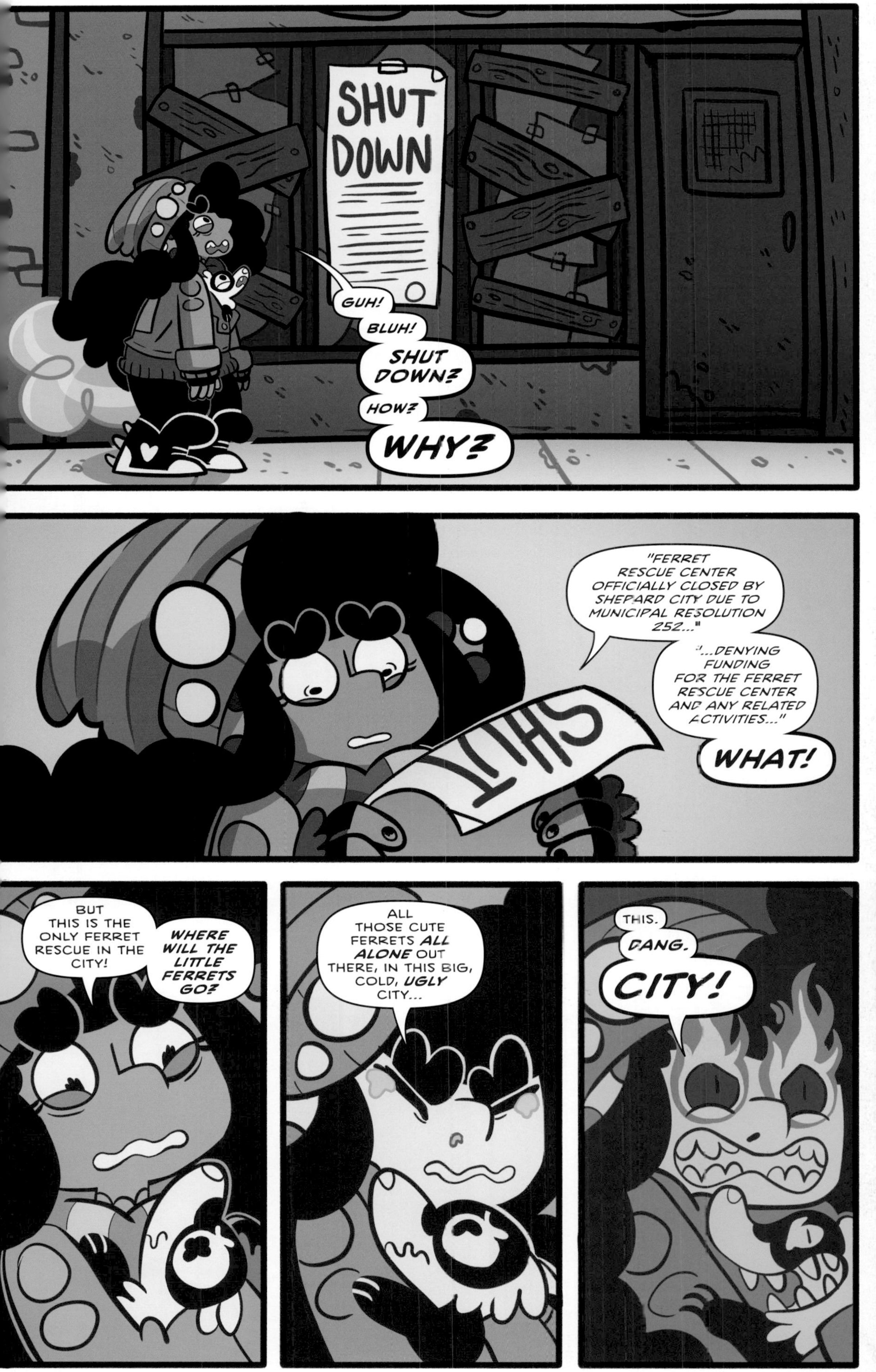
SHUT DOWN
GUH!
BLUH!
SHUT DOWN?
HOW?
WHY?
"FERRET RESCUE CENTER OFFICIALLY CLOSED BY SHEPARD CITY DUE TO MUNICIPAL RESOLUTION 252..."
"...DENYING FUNDING FOR THE FERRET RESCUE CENTER AND ANY RELATED ACTIVITIES..."
WHAT!
BUT THIS IS THE ONLY FERRET RESCUE IN THE CITY!
WHERE WILL THE LITTLE FERRETS GO?
ALL THOSE CUTE FERRETS ALL ALONE OUT THERE, IN THIS BIG, COLD, UGLY CITY...
THIS.
DANG.
CITY!

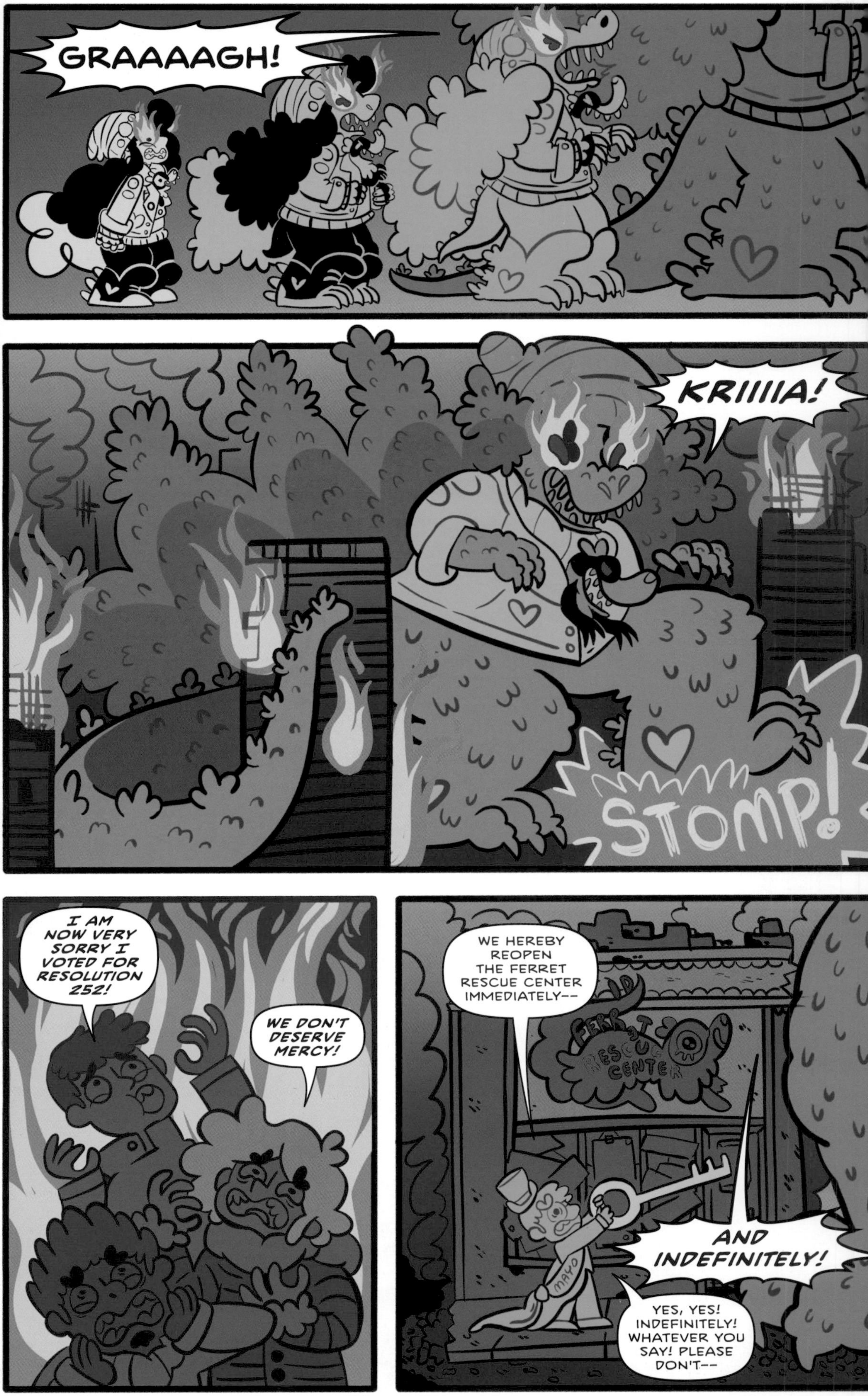
GRAAAAGH!
KRIIIIA!
STOMP!
I AM NOW VERY SORRY I VOTED FOR RESOLUTION 252!
WE DON'T DESERVE MERCY!
WE HEREBY REOPEN THE FERRET RESCUE CENTER IMMEDIATELY--
AND INDEFINITELY!
YES, YES! INDEFINITELY! WHATEVER YOU SAY! PLEASE DON'T--
FERRET RESCUE CENTER
MAYOR

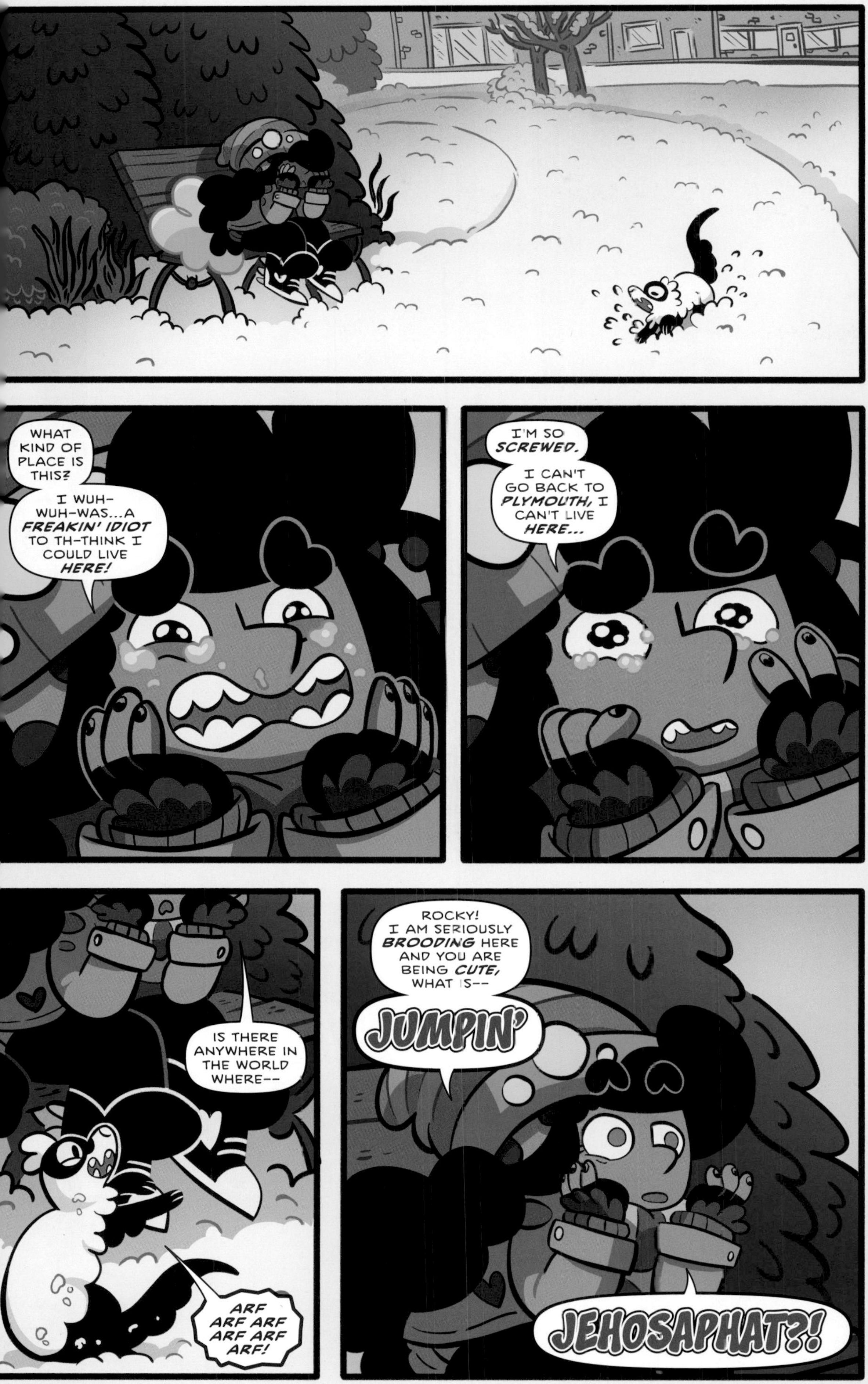
WHAT KIND OF PLACE IS THIS?
I WUH-WUH-WAS...A FREAKIN' IDIOT TO TH-THINK I COULD LIVE HERE!
I'M SO SCREWED.
I CAN'T GO BACK TO PLYMOUTH, I CAN'T LIVE HERE...
IS THERE ANYWHERE IN THE WORLD WHERE--
ARF ARF ARF ARF ARF ARF!
ROCKY! I AM SERIOUSLY BROODING HERE AND YOU ARE BEING CUTE, WHAT IS--
JUMPIN'
JEHOSAPHAT?!

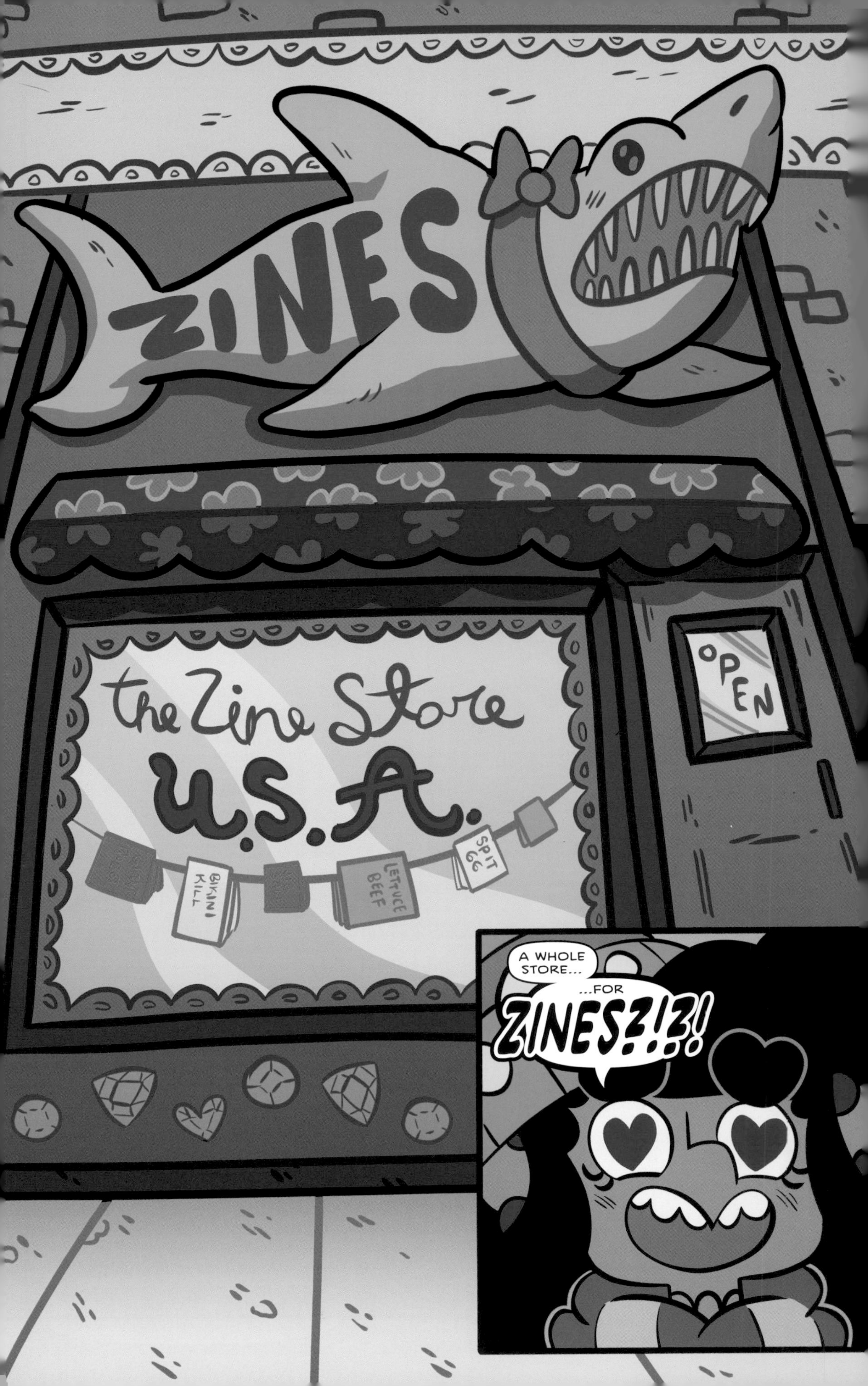
ZINES
the Zine Store
U.S.A.
OPEN
BIKINI KILL
LETTUCE BEEF
SPIT 66
A WHOLE STORE...
...FOR ZINES?!?!

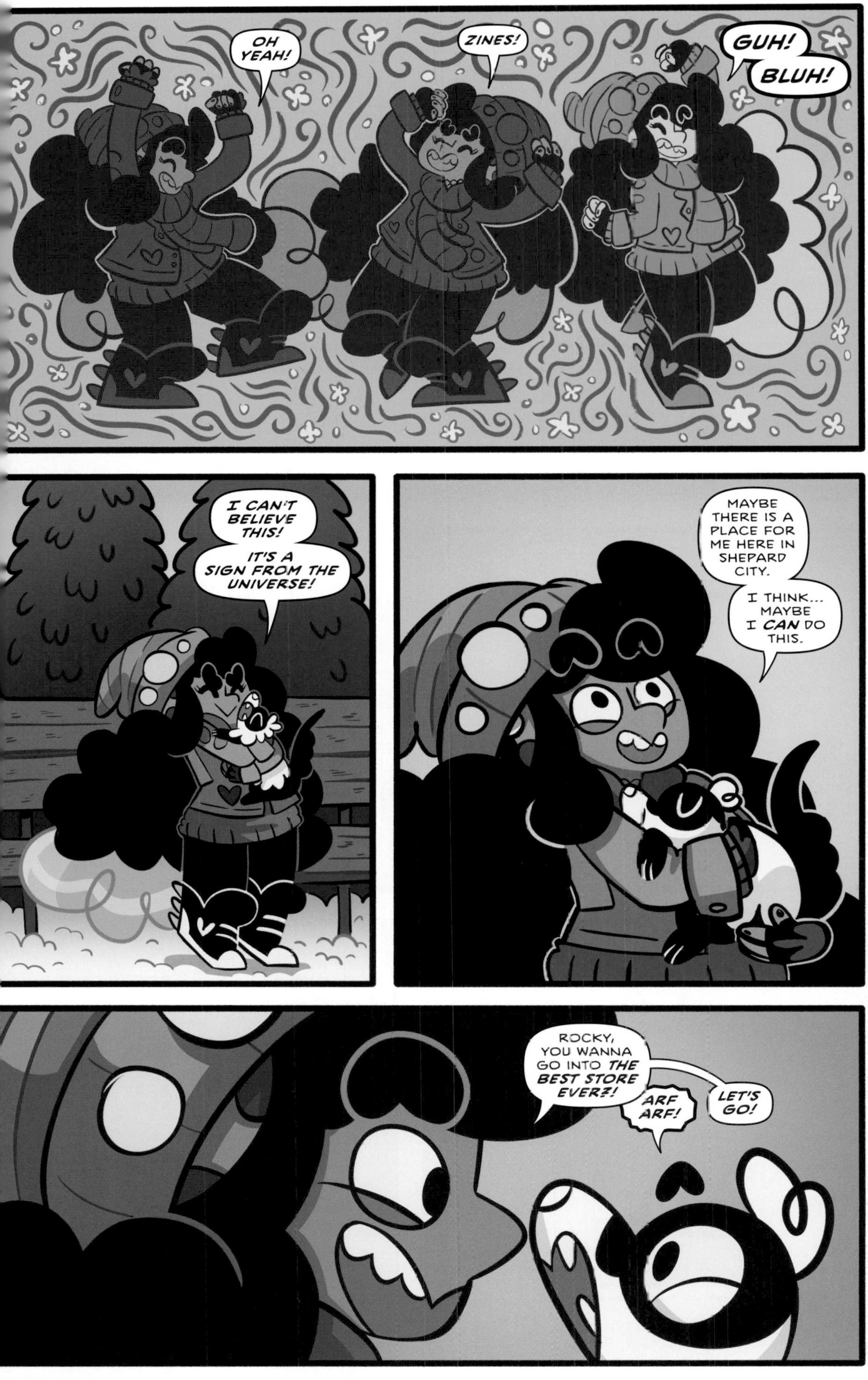
OH YEAH!
ZINES!
GUH! BLUH!
I CAN'T BELIEVE THIS!
IT'S A SIGN FROM THE UNIVERSE!
MAYBE THERE IS A PLACE FOR ME HERE IN SHEPARD CITY.
I THINK... MAYBE I CAN DO THIS.
ROCKY, YOU WANNA GO INTO THE BEST STORE EVERZ!
ARF ARF!
LET'S GO!

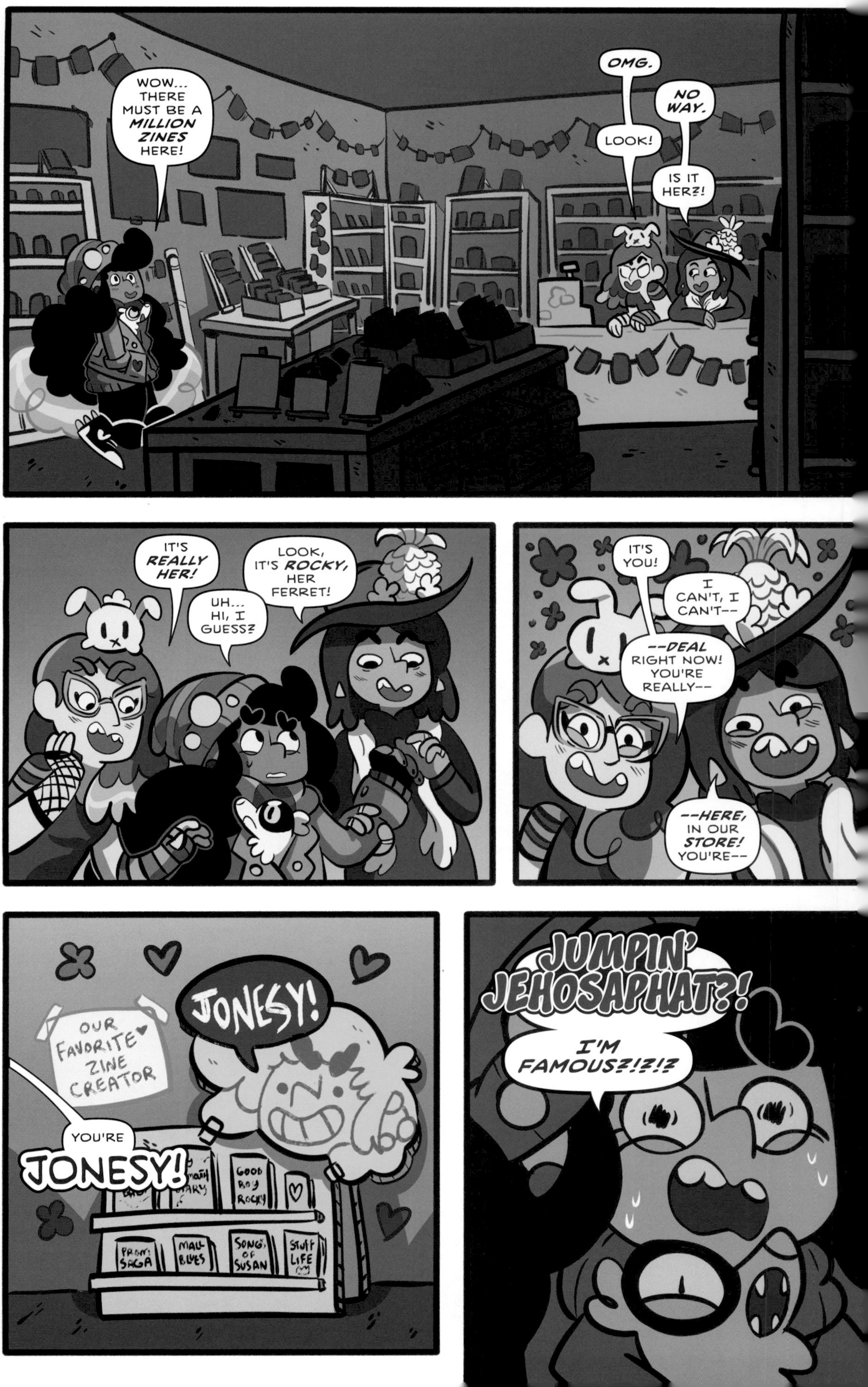
WOW... THERE MUST BE A MILLION ZINES HERE!
OMG.
LOOK!
NO WAY.
IS IT HER?!
IT'S REALLY HER!
UH... HI, I GUESS?
LOOK, IT'S ROCKY, HER FERRET!
IT'S YOU!
I CAN'T, I CAN'T--
--DEAL RIGHT NOW! YOU'RE REALLY--
--HERE, IN OUR STORE! YOU'RE--
OUR FAVORITE ZINE CREATOR
JONESY!
YOU'RE JONESY!
GOOD BOY ROCKY
PROM SAGA
MALL BLUES
SONG OF SUSAN
STUFF LIFE
JUMPIN' JEHOSAPHAT?!
I'M FAMOUS?!?!?

CHAPTER TWO

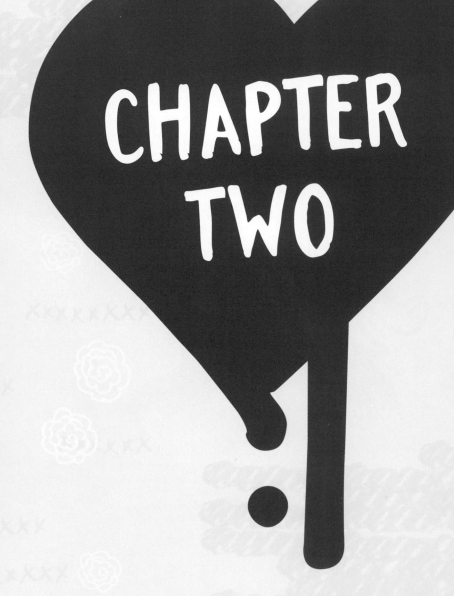

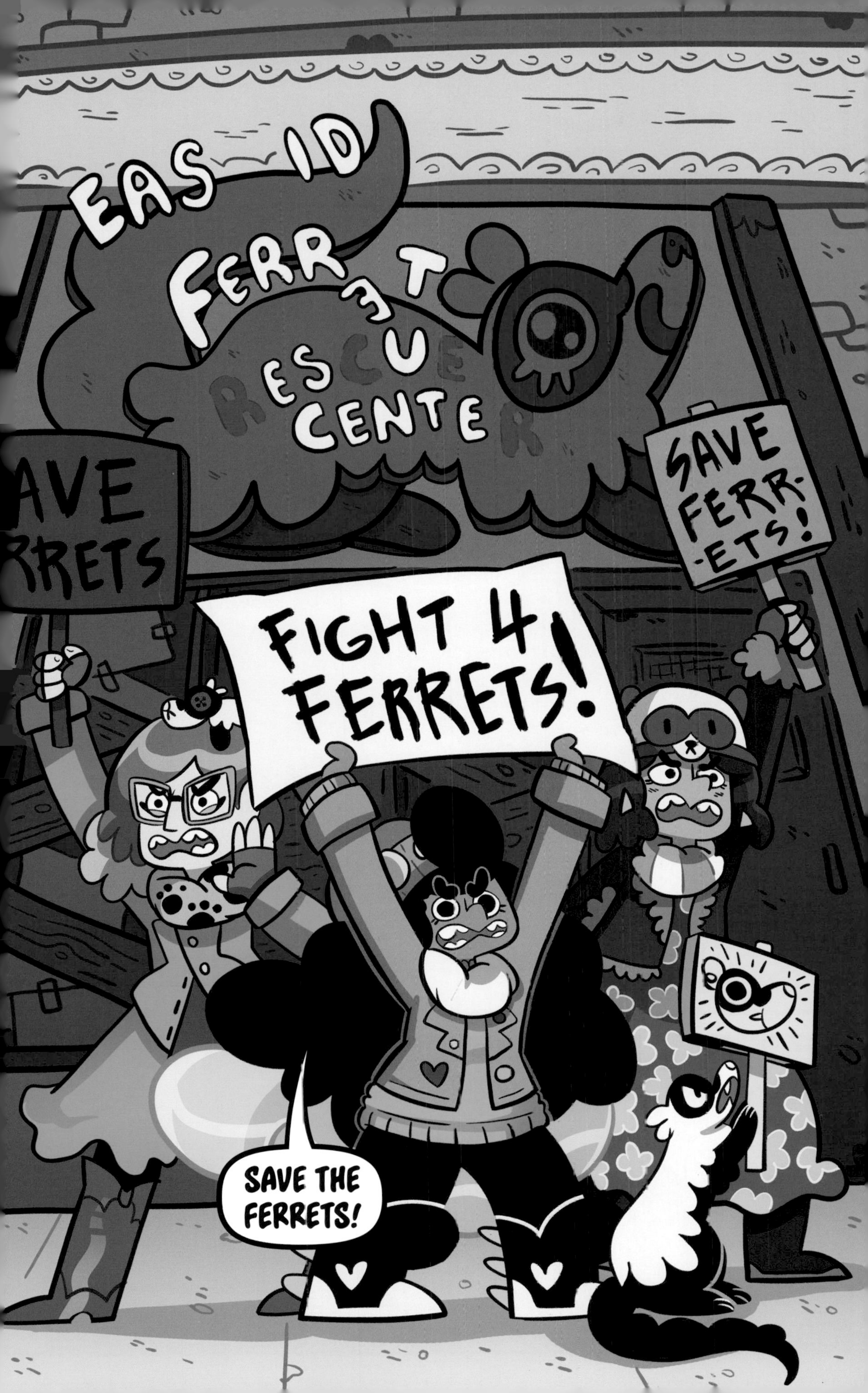
EAS ID
FERR T
RESCUE
CENTE
AVE
RRETS
SAVE
FERR
-ETS!
FIGHT 4
FERRETS!
SAVE THE
FERRETS!

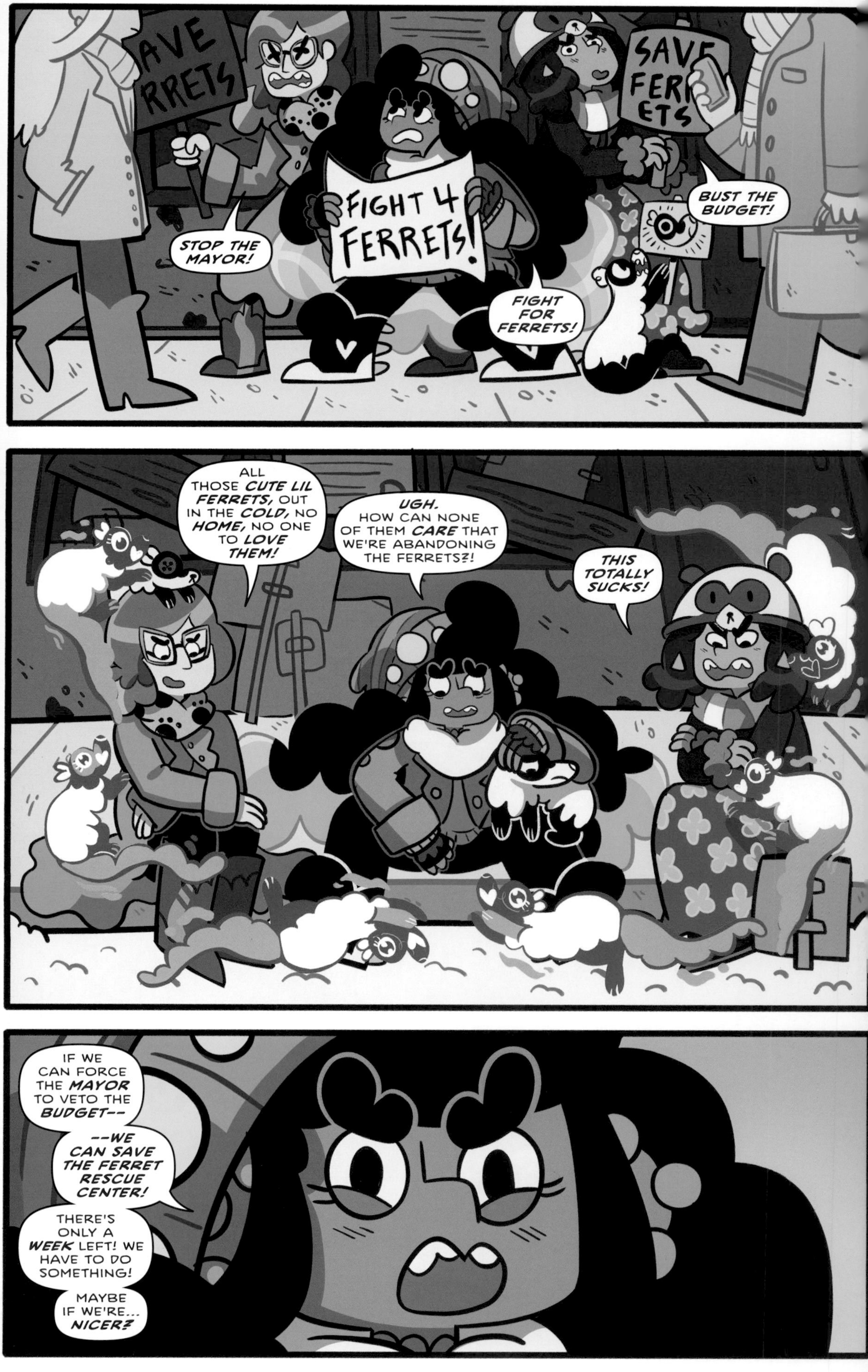
AVE RRETS
FIGHT 4 FERRETS!
SAVE FER ETS
STOP THE MAYOR!
BUST THE BUDGET!
FIGHT FOR FERRETS!
ALL THOSE CUTE LIL FERRETS, OUT IN THE COLD, NO HOME, NO ONE TO LOVE THEM!
UGH. HOW CAN NONE OF THEM CARE THAT WE'RE ABANDONING THE FERRETS?!
THIS TOTALLY SUCKS!
IF WE CAN FORCE THE MAYOR TO VETO THE BUDGET--
--WE CAN SAVE THE FERRET RESCUE CENTER!
THERE'S ONLY A WEEK LEFT! WE HAVE TO DO SOMETHING!
MAYBE IF WE'RE... NICER?

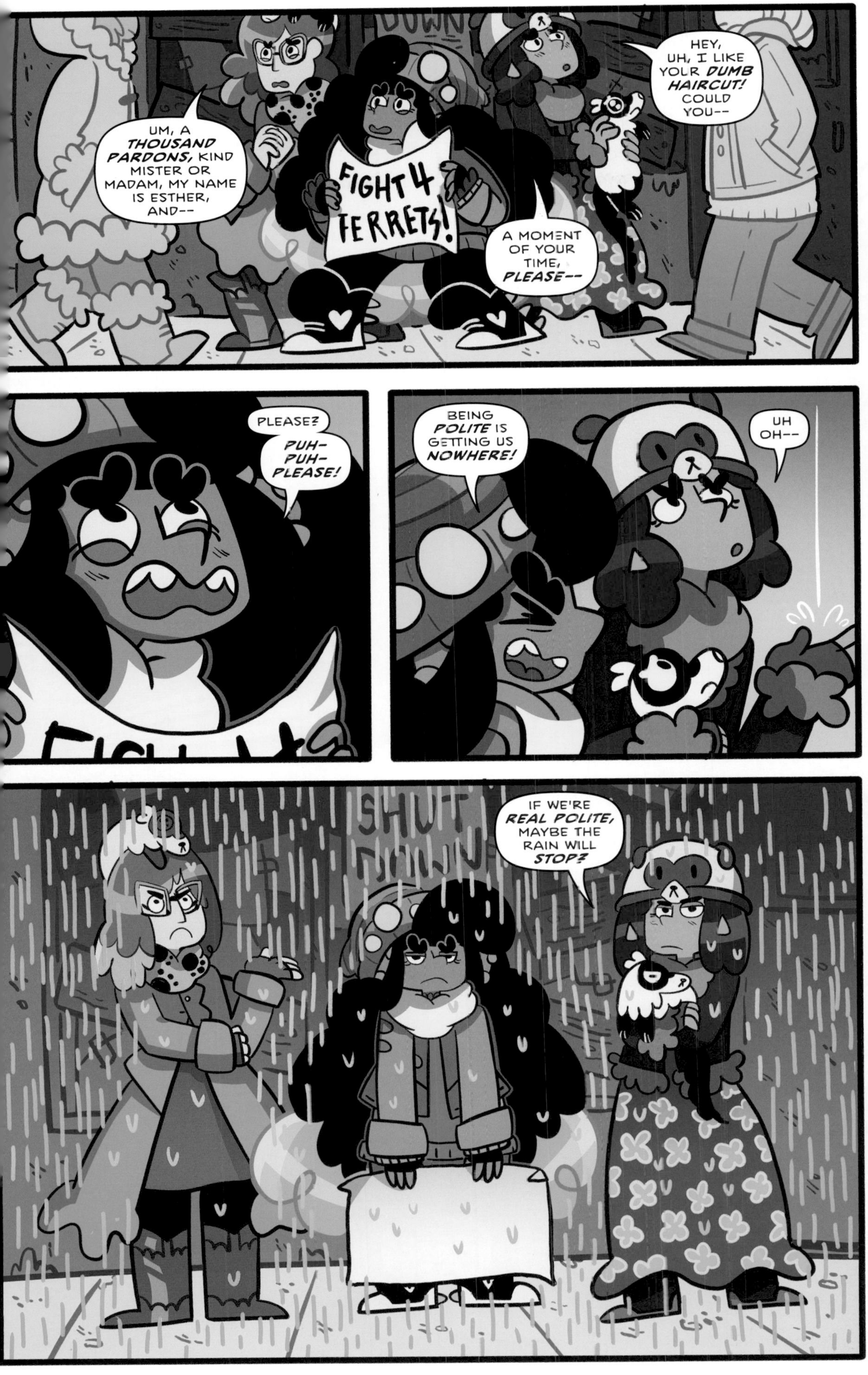
UM, A *THOUSAND PARDONS,* KIND MISTER OR MADAM, MY NAME IS ESTHER, AND--
FIGHT 4 FERRETS!
A MOMENT OF YOUR TIME, *PLEASE--*
HEY, UH, I LIKE YOUR *DUMB HAIRCUT!* COULD YOU--
PLEASE?
PUH-PUH-PLEASE!
BEING *POLITE* IS GETTING US *NOWHERE!*
UH OH--
IF WE'RE *REAL POLITE,* MAYBE THE RAIN WILL *STOP?*

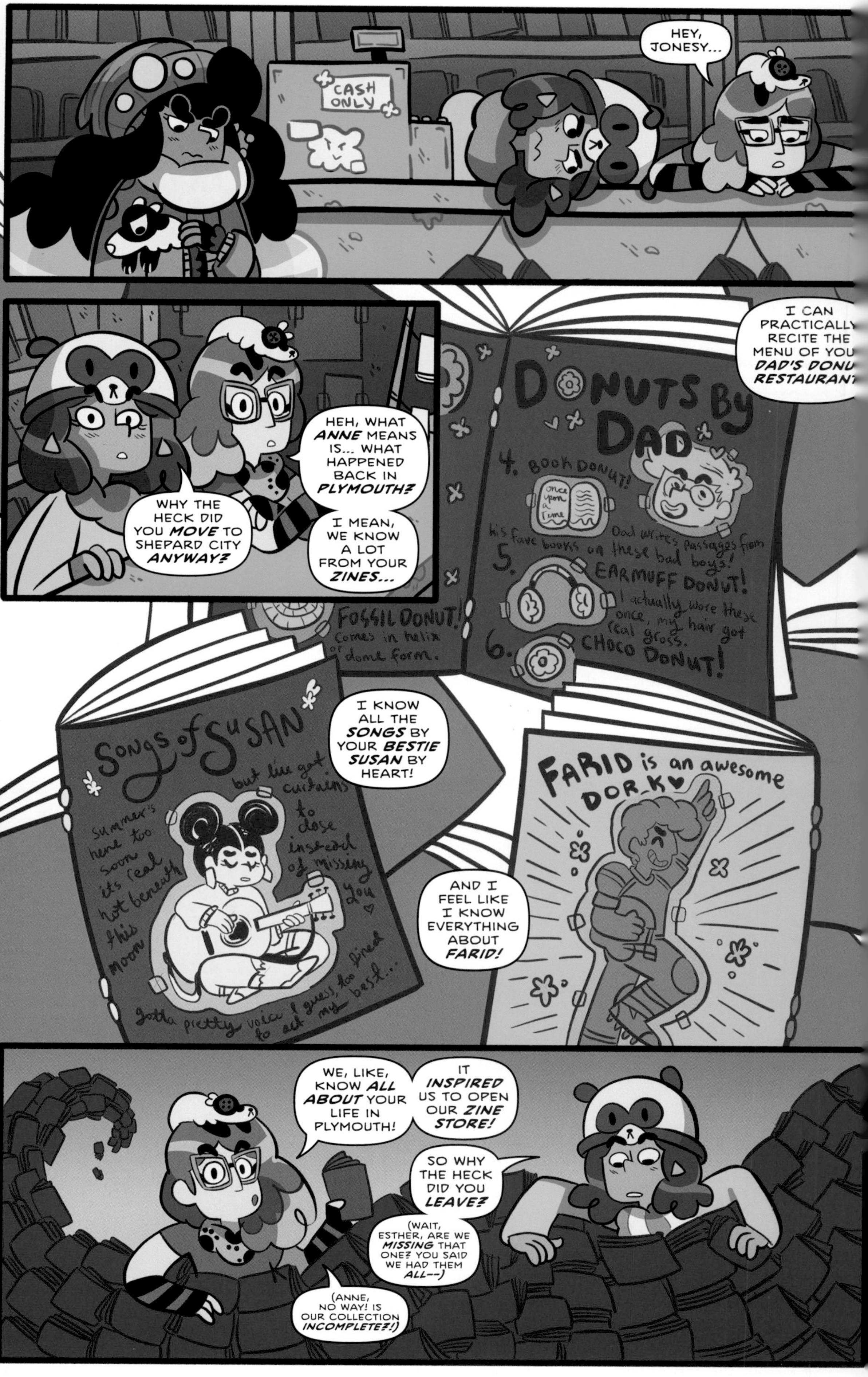

CASH ONLY
HEY, JONESY...
HEH, WHAT ANNE MEANS IS... WHAT HAPPENED BACK IN PLYMOUTH?
WHY THE HECK DID YOU MOVE TO SHEPARD CITY ANYWAY?
I MEAN, WE KNOW A LOT FROM YOUR ZINES...
I CAN PRACTICALLY RECITE THE MENU OF YOU DAD'S DONU RESTAURANT
DONUTS BY DAD
4. BOOK DONUT!
once upon a time
Dad writes passages from his fave books on these bad boys!
5. EARMUFF DONUT!
I actually wore these once, my hair got real gross.
6. CHOCO DONUT!
FOSSIL DONUT! Comes in helix or dome form.
I KNOW ALL THE SONGS BY YOUR BESTIE SUSAN BY HEART!
Songs of Susan
AND I FEEL LIKE I KNOW EVERYTHING ABOUT FARID!
FARID is an awesome DORK
WE, LIKE, KNOW ALL ABOUT YOUR LIFE IN PLYMOUTH!
IT INSPIRED US TO OPEN OUR ZINE STORE!
SO WHY THE HECK DID YOU LEAVE?
(WAIT, ESTHER, ARE WE MISSING THAT ONE? YOU SAID WE HAD THEM ALL--)
(ANNE, NO WAY! IS OUR COLLECTION INCOMPLETE?!)

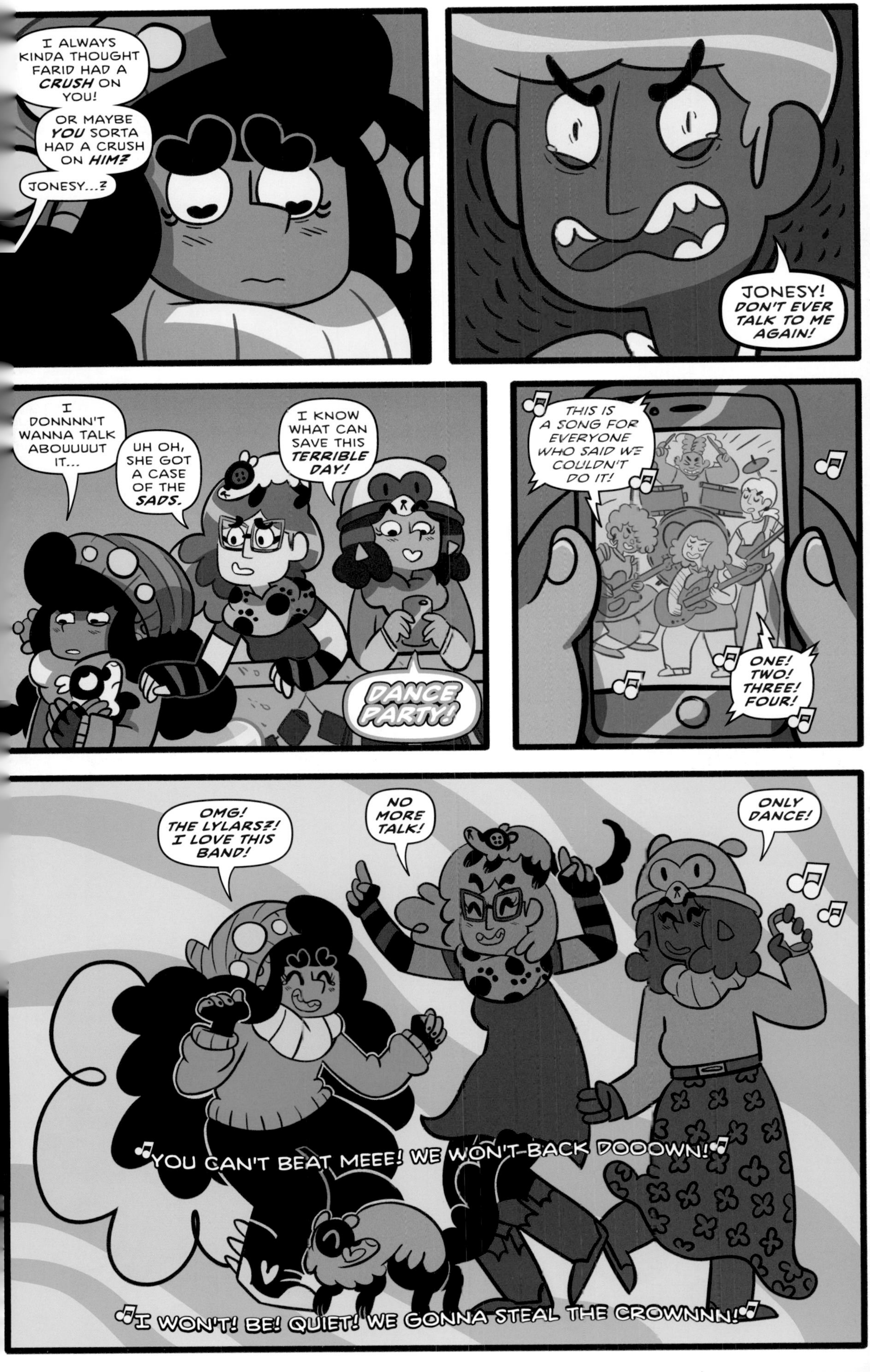
I ALWAYS KINDA THOUGHT FARID HAD A *CRUSH* ON YOU!
OR MAYBE *YOU* SORTA HAD A CRUSH ON *HIM?*
JONESY...?
JONESY! *DON'T EVER TALK TO ME AGAIN!*
I DONNNN'T WANNA TALK ABOUUUUT IT...
UH OH, SHE GOT A CASE OF THE *SADS.*
I KNOW WHAT CAN SAVE THIS *TERRIBLE DAY!*
DANCE PARTY!
THIS IS A SONG FOR EVERYONE WHO SAID WE COULDN'T DO IT!
ONE! TWO! THREE! FOUR!
OMG! THE LYLARSZ! I LOVE THIS BAND!
NO MORE TALK!
ONLY DANCE!
YOU CAN'T BEAT MEEE! WE WON'T BACK DOOOWN!
I WON'T! BE! QUIET! WE GONNA STEAL THE CROWNNNN!

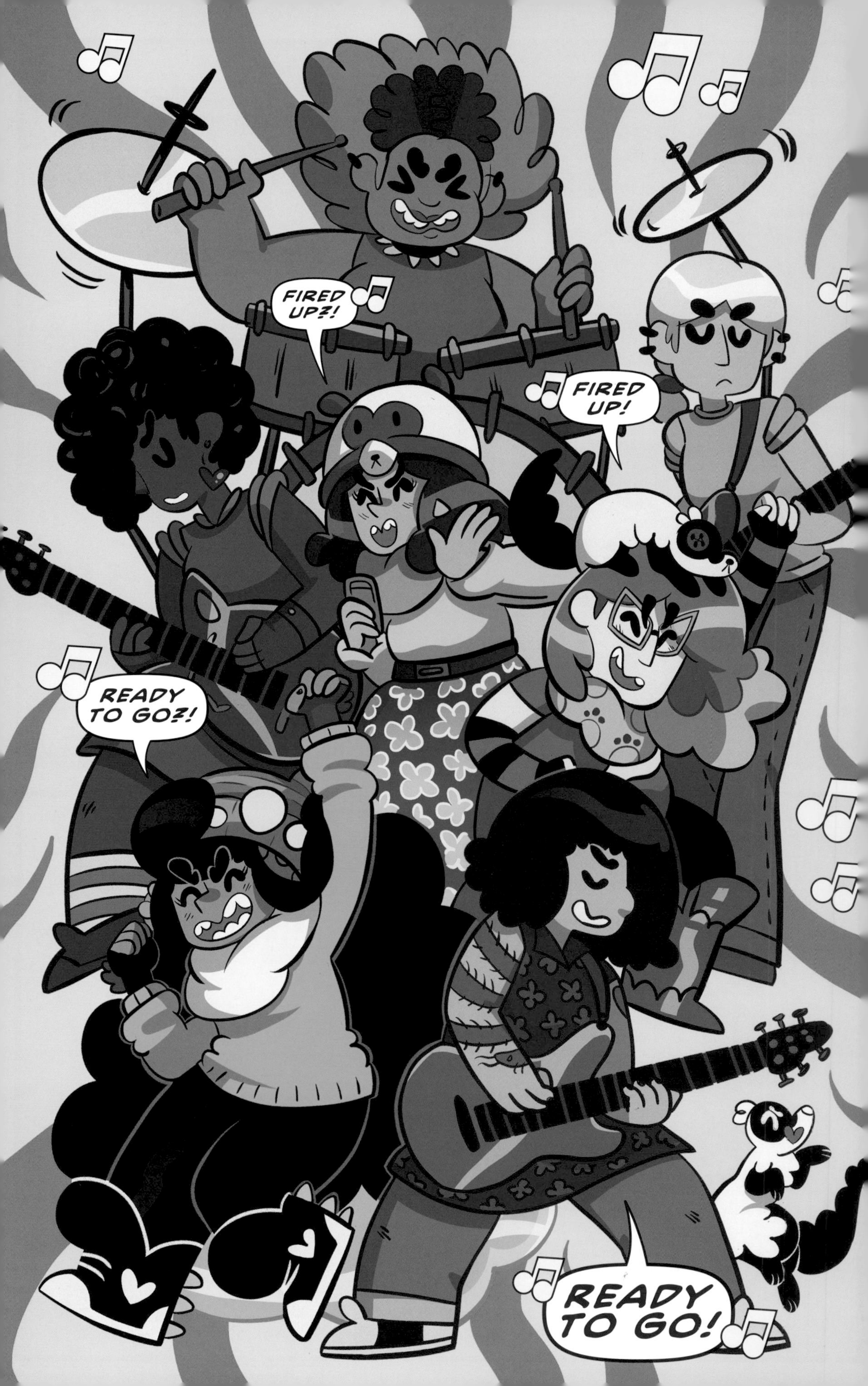
FIRED UP?!
FIRED UP!
READY TO GO?!
READY TO GO!

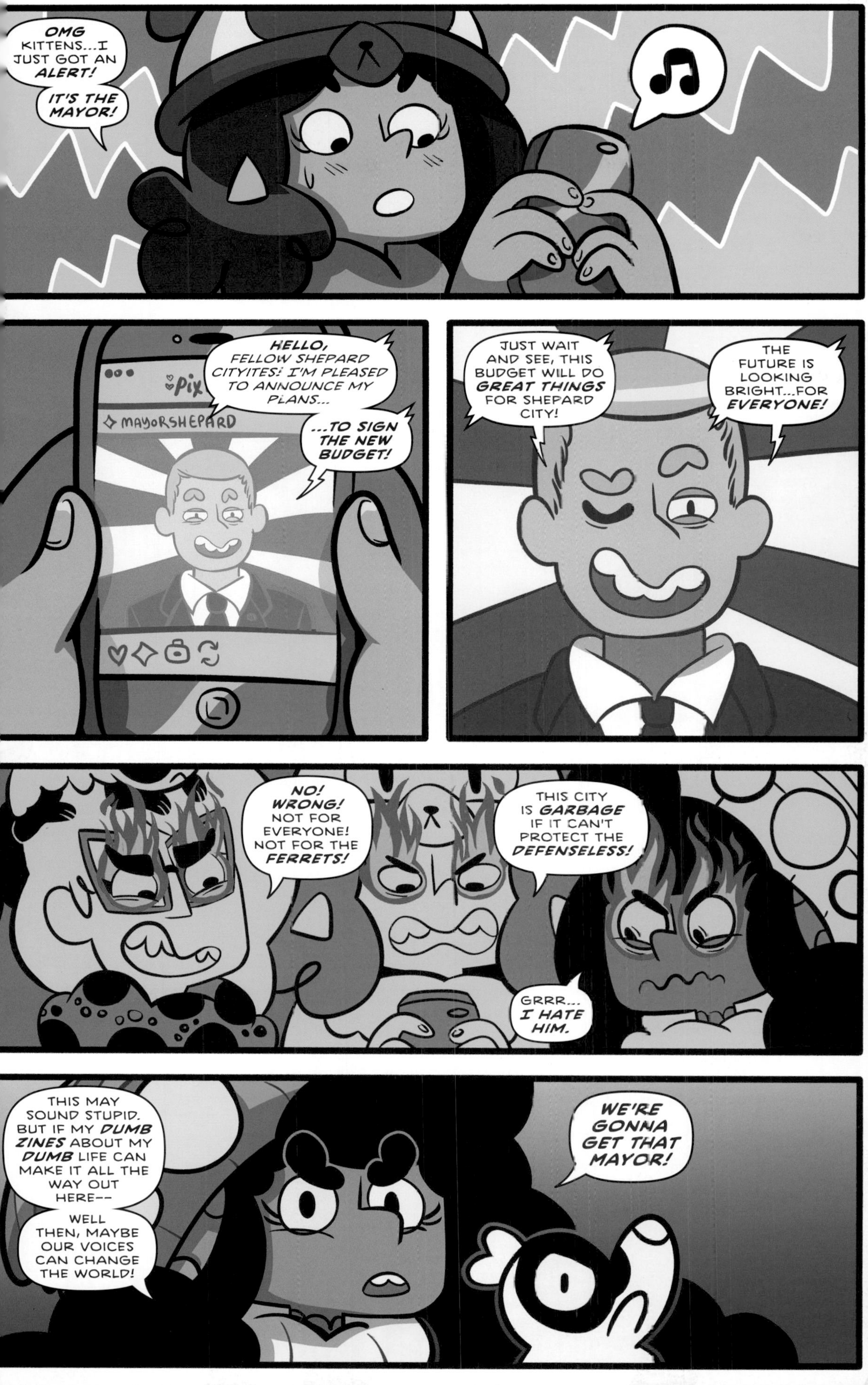
OMG KITTENS...I JUST GOT AN ALERT!
IT'S THE MAYOR!
pix
MAYORSHEPARD
HELLO, FELLOW SHEPARD CITYITES! I'M PLEASED TO ANNOUNCE MY PLANS...
...TO SIGN THE NEW BUDGET!
JUST WAIT AND SEE, THIS BUDGET WILL DO GREAT THINGS FOR SHEPARD CITY!
THE FUTURE IS LOOKING BRIGHT...FOR EVERYONE!
NO! WRONG! NOT FOR EVERYONE! NOT FOR THE FERRETS!
THIS CITY IS GARBAGE IF IT CAN'T PROTECT THE DEFENSELESS!
GRRR... I HATE HIM.
THIS MAY SOUND STUPID. BUT IF MY DUMB ZINES ABOUT MY DUMB LIFE CAN MAKE IT ALL THE WAY OUT HERE--
WELL THEN, MAYBE OUR VOICES CAN CHANGE THE WORLD!
WE'RE GONNA GET THAT MAYOR!

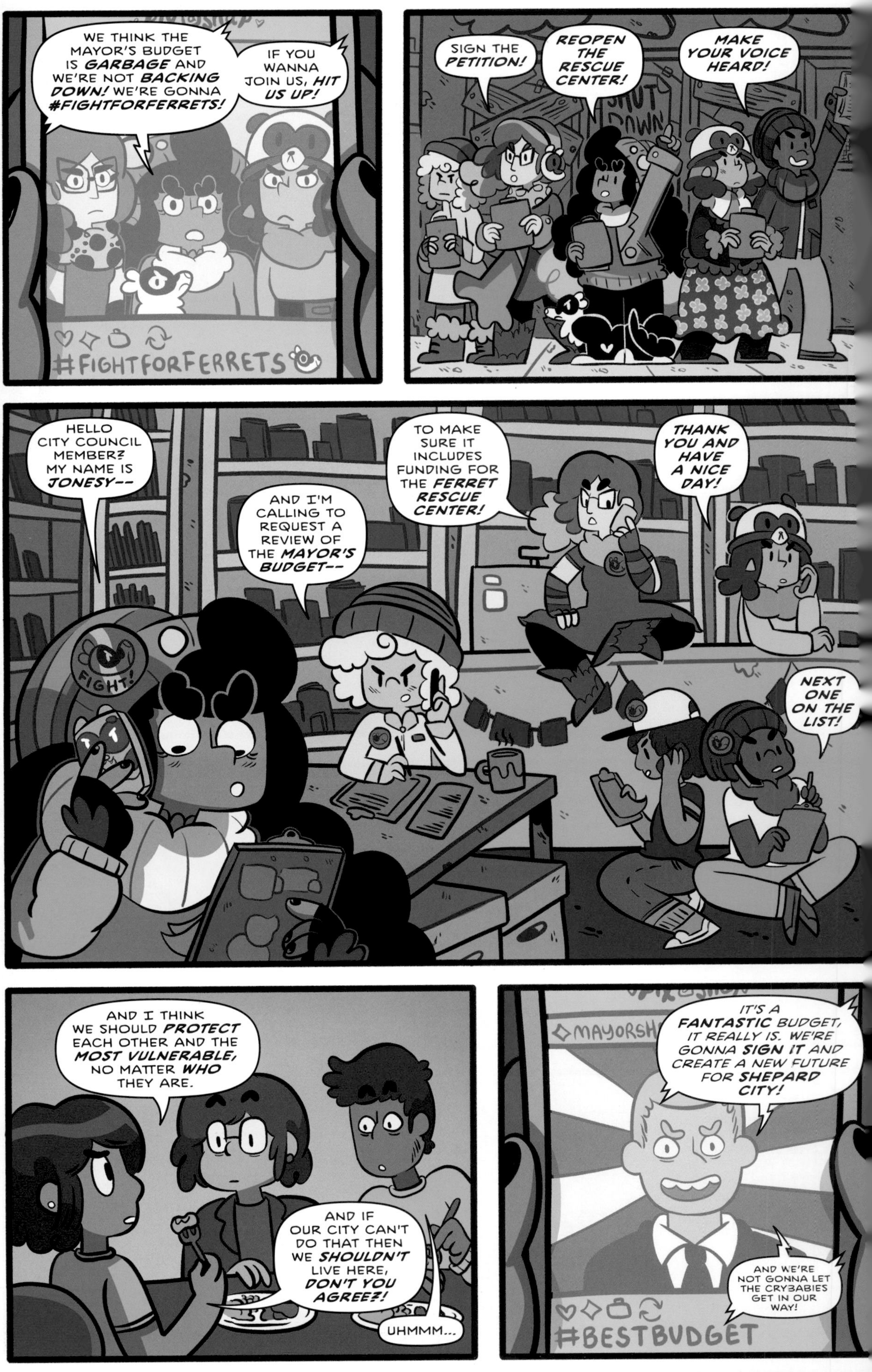
WE THINK THE MAYOR'S BUDGET IS GARBAGE AND WE'RE NOT BACKING DOWN! WE'RE GONNA #FIGHTFORFERRETS!
IF YOU WANNA JOIN US, HIT US UP!
#FIGHTFORFERRETS
SIGN THE PETITION!
REOPEN THE RESCUE CENTER!
MAKE YOUR VOICE HEARD!
HELLO CITY COUNCIL MEMBER? MY NAME IS JONESY--
AND I'M CALLING TO REQUEST A REVIEW OF THE MAYOR'S BUDGET--
TO MAKE SURE IT INCLUDES FUNDING FOR THE FERRET RESCUE CENTER!
THANK YOU AND HAVE A NICE DAY!
FIGHT!
NEXT ONE ON THE LIST!
AND I THINK WE SHOULD PROTECT EACH OTHER AND THE MOST VULNERABLE, NO MATTER WHO THEY ARE.
AND IF OUR CITY CAN'T DO THAT THEN WE SHOULDN'T LIVE HERE, DON'T YOU AGREE?!
UHMMM...
IT'S A FANTASTIC BUDGET, IT REALLY IS. WE'RE GONNA SIGN IT AND CREATE A NEW FUTURE FOR SHEPARD CITY!
AND WE'RE NOT GONNA LET THE CRYBABIES GET IN OUR WAY!
#BESTBUDGET

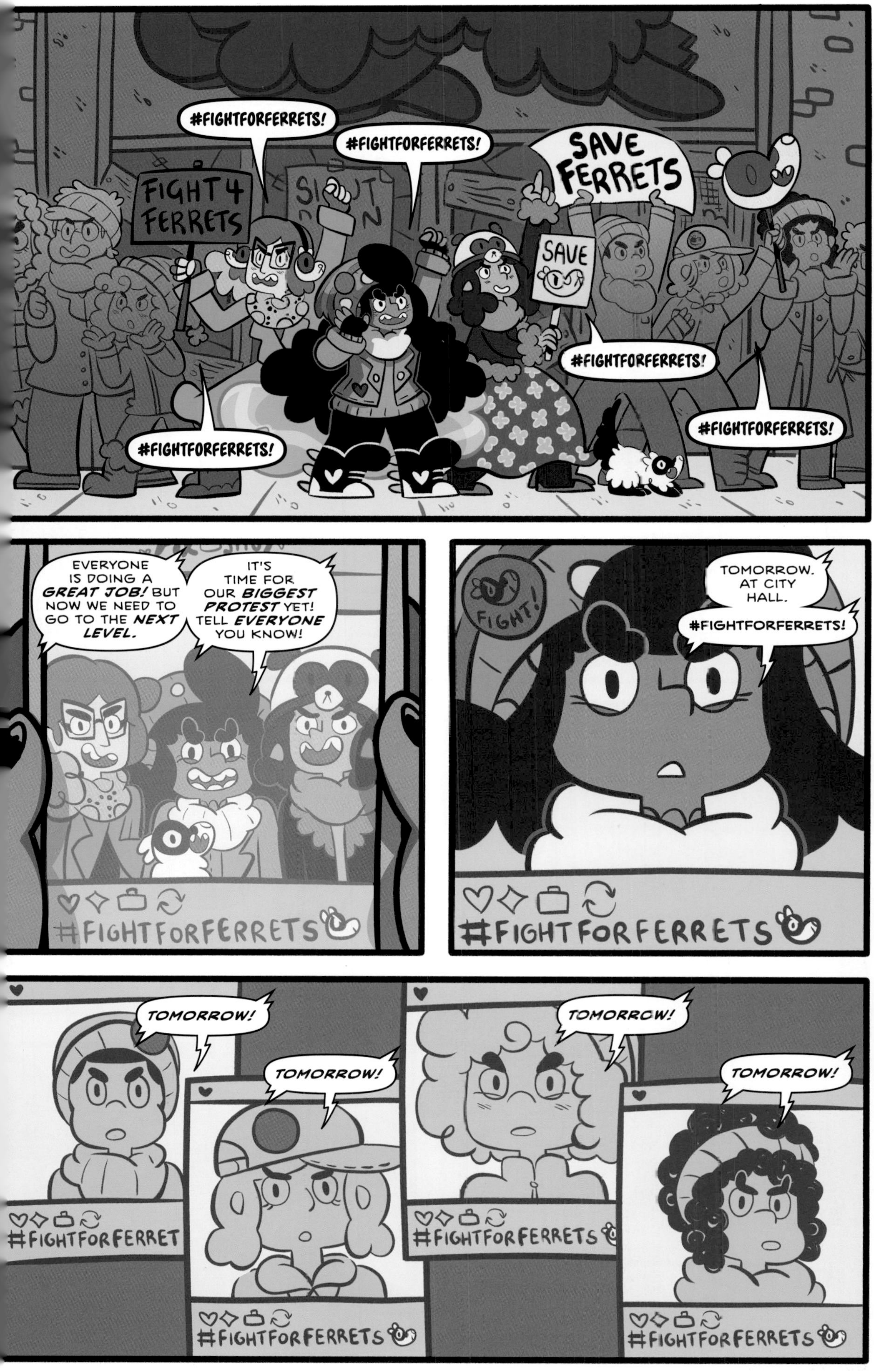

#FIGHTFORFERRETS!
#FIGHTFORFERRETS!
SAVE FERRETS
FIGHT 4 FERRETS
SAVE
#FIGHTFORFERRETS!
#FIGHTFORFERRETS!
#FIGHTFORFERRETS!
EVERYONE IS DOING A GREAT JOB! BUT NOW WE NEED TO GO TO THE NEXT LEVEL.
IT'S TIME FOR OUR BIGGEST PROTEST YET! TELL EVERYONE YOU KNOW!
#FIGHTFORFERRETS
FIGHT!
TOMORROW. AT CITY HALL.
#FIGHTFORFERRETS!
#FIGHTFORFERRETS
TOMORROW!
TOMORROW!
TOMORROW!
TOMORROW!
#FIGHTFORFERRET
#FIGHTFORFERRETS
#FIGHTFORFERRETS
#FIGHTFORFERRETS

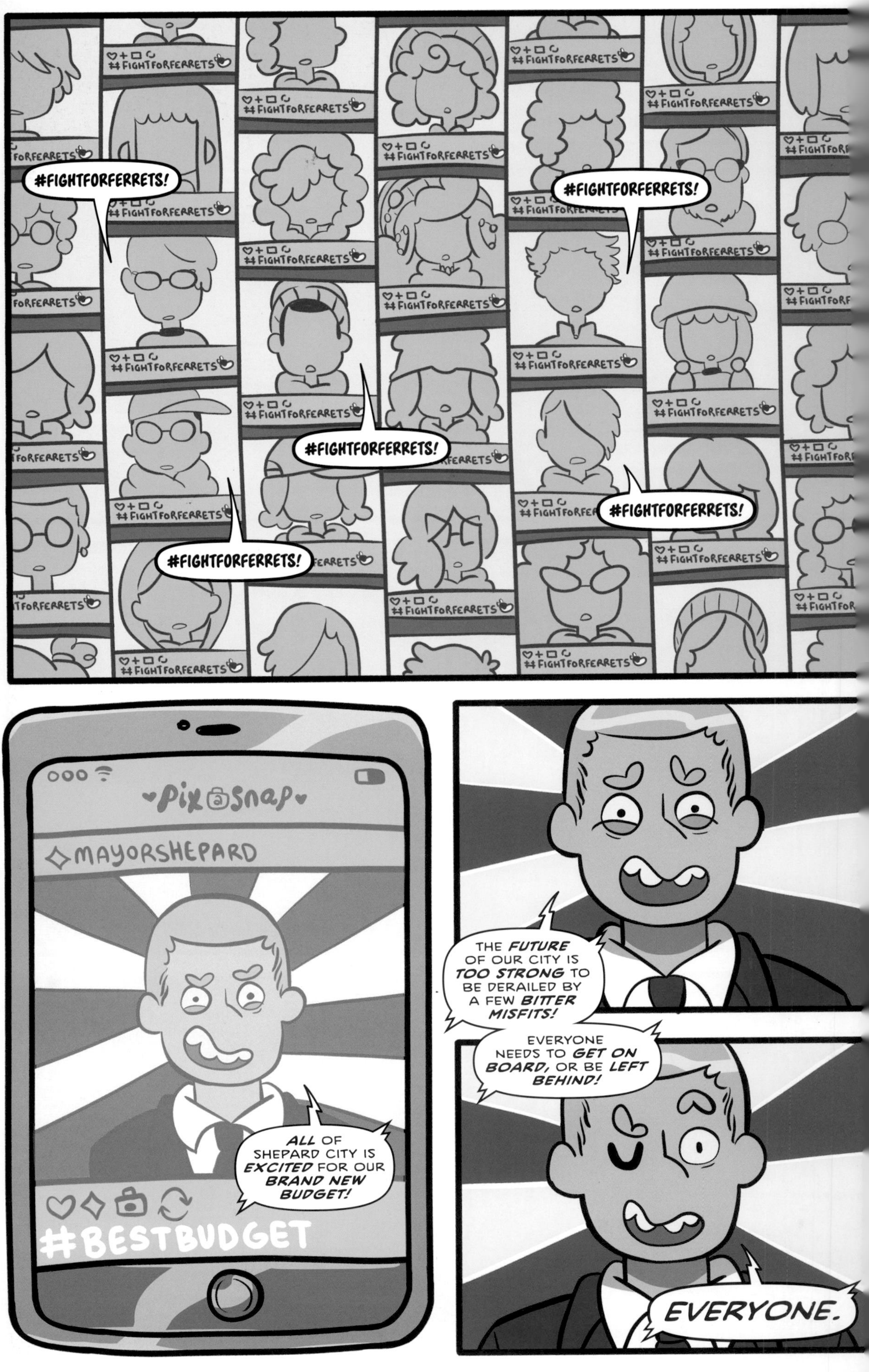
#FIGHTFORFERRETS!
#FIGHTFORFERRETS!
#FIGHTFORFERRETS!
#FIGHTFORFERRETS!
#FIGHTFORFERRETS!
Pix Snap
MAYORSHEPARD
ALL OF SHEPARD CITY IS EXCITED FOR OUR BRAND NEW BUDGET!
#BESTBUDGET
THE FUTURE OF OUR CITY IS TOO STRONG TO BE DERAILED BY A FEW BITTER MISFITS!
EVERYONE NEEDS TO GET ON BOARD, OR BE LEFT BEHIND!
EVERYONE.

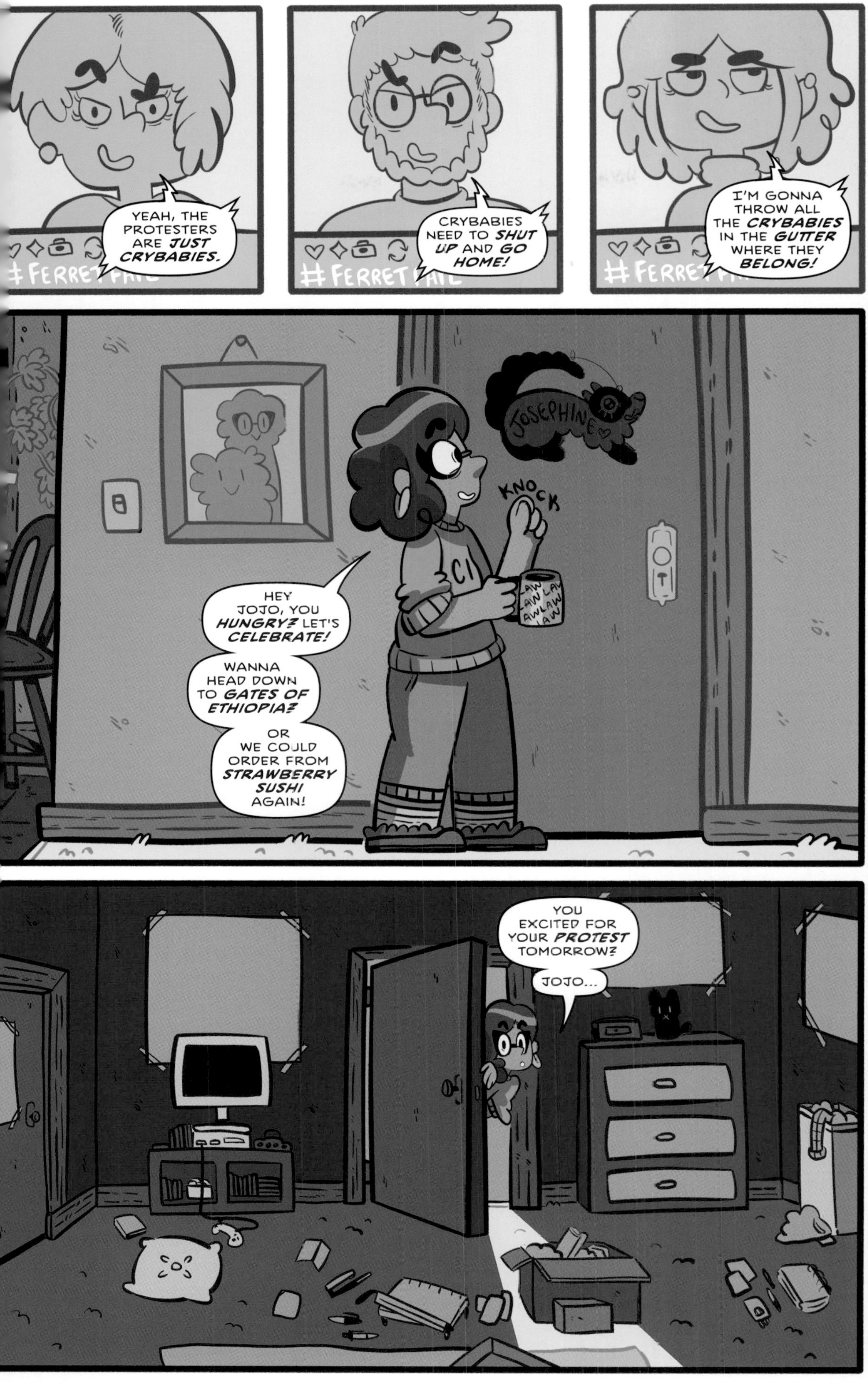
YEAH, THE PROTESTERS ARE JUST CRYBABIES.
#FERRET
CRYBABIES NEED TO SHUT UP AND GO HOME!
#FERRET
I'M GONNA THROW ALL THE CRYBABIES IN THE GUTTER WHERE THEY BELONG!
#FERRE
JOSEPHINE
KNOCK
HEY JOJO, YOU HUNGRY? LET'S CELEBRATE!
WANNA HEAD DOWN TO GATES OF ETHIOPIA?
OR WE COULD ORDER FROM STRAWBERRY SUSHI AGAIN!
YOU EXCITED FOR YOUR PROTEST TOMORROW?
JOJO...

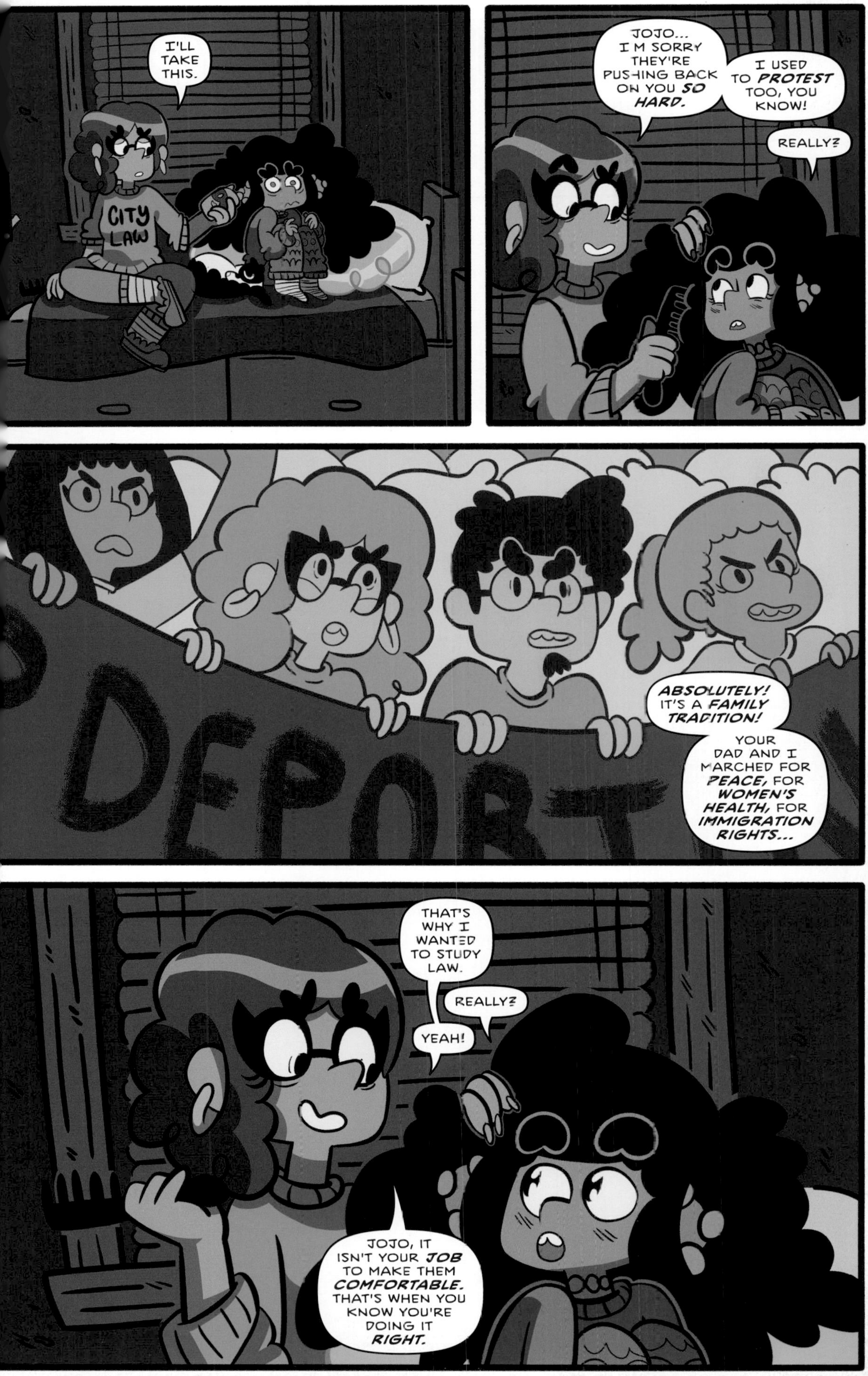
I'LL TAKE THIS.
JOJO... I'M SORRY THEY'RE PUSHING BACK ON YOU *SO HARD.*
I USED TO *PROTEST* TOO, YOU KNOW!
REALLY?
ABSOLUTELY! IT'S A ***FAMILY TRADITION!***
YOUR DAD AND I MARCHED FOR ***PEACE,*** FOR ***WOMEN'S HEALTH,*** FOR ***IMMIGRATION RIGHTS...***
DEPORT
THAT'S WHY I WANTED TO STUDY LAW.
REALLY?
YEAH!
JOJO, IT ISN'T YOUR ***JOB*** TO MAKE THEM ***COMFORTABLE.*** THAT'S WHEN YOU KNOW YOU'RE DOING IT ***RIGHT.***

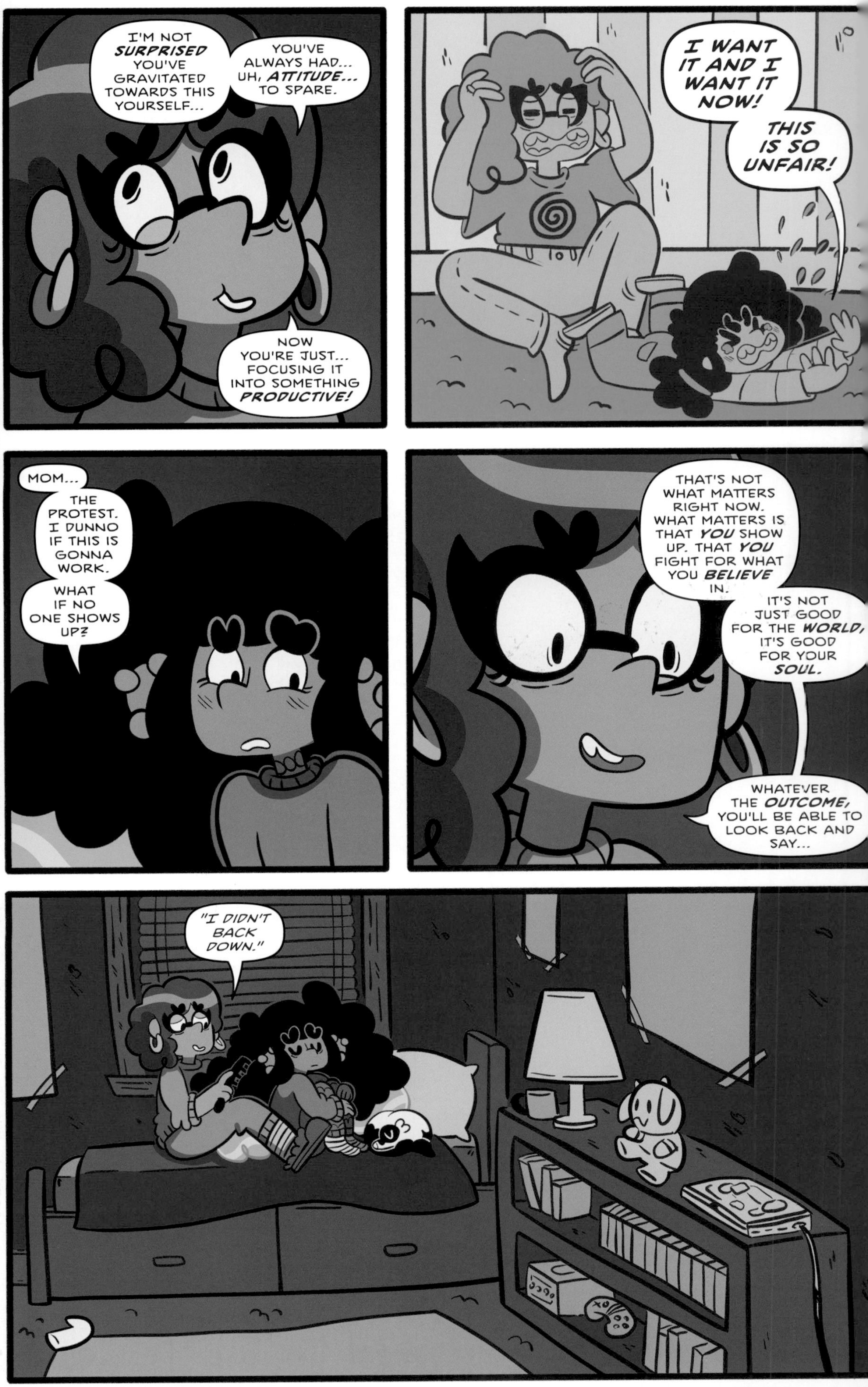
I'M NOT SURPRISED YOU'VE GRAVITATED TOWARDS THIS YOURSELF...
YOU'VE ALWAYS HAD... UH, ATTITUDE... TO SPARE.
NOW YOU'RE JUST... FOCUSING IT INTO SOMETHING PRODUCTIVE!
I WANT IT AND I WANT IT NOW!
THIS IS SO UNFAIR!
MOM...
THE PROTEST. I DUNNO IF THIS IS GONNA WORK.
WHAT IF NO ONE SHOWS UP?
THAT'S NOT WHAT MATTERS RIGHT NOW. WHAT MATTERS IS THAT YOU SHOW UP. THAT YOU FIGHT FOR WHAT YOU BELIEVE IN.
IT'S NOT JUST GOOD FOR THE WORLD, IT'S GOOD FOR YOUR SOUL.
WHATEVER THE OUTCOME, YOU'LL BE ABLE TO LOOK BACK AND SAY...
"I DIDN'T BACK DOWN."

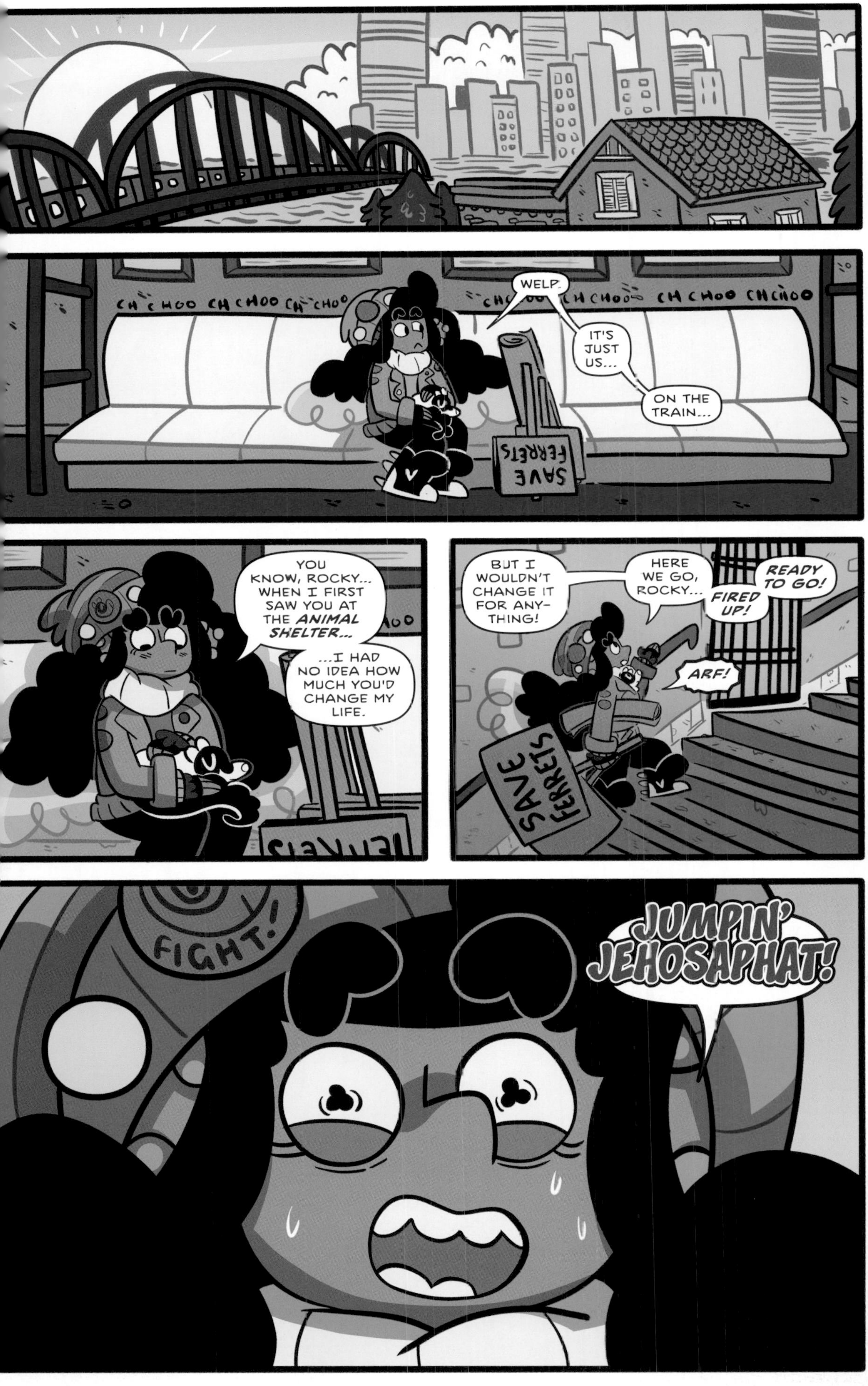
CH CHOO CH CHOO CH CHOO
CH CHOO CH CHOO CH CHOO CH CHOO
WELP.
IT'S JUST US...
ON THE TRAIN...
SAVE FERRETS
YOU KNOW, ROCKY... WHEN I FIRST SAW YOU AT THE ANIMAL SHELTER...
...I HAD NO IDEA HOW MUCH YOU'D CHANGE MY LIFE.
BUT I WOULDN'T CHANGE IT FOR ANY-THING!
HERE WE GO, ROCKY...
READY TO GO!
FIRED UP!
ARF!
SAVE FERRETS
FIGHT!
JUMPIN' JEHOSAPHAT!

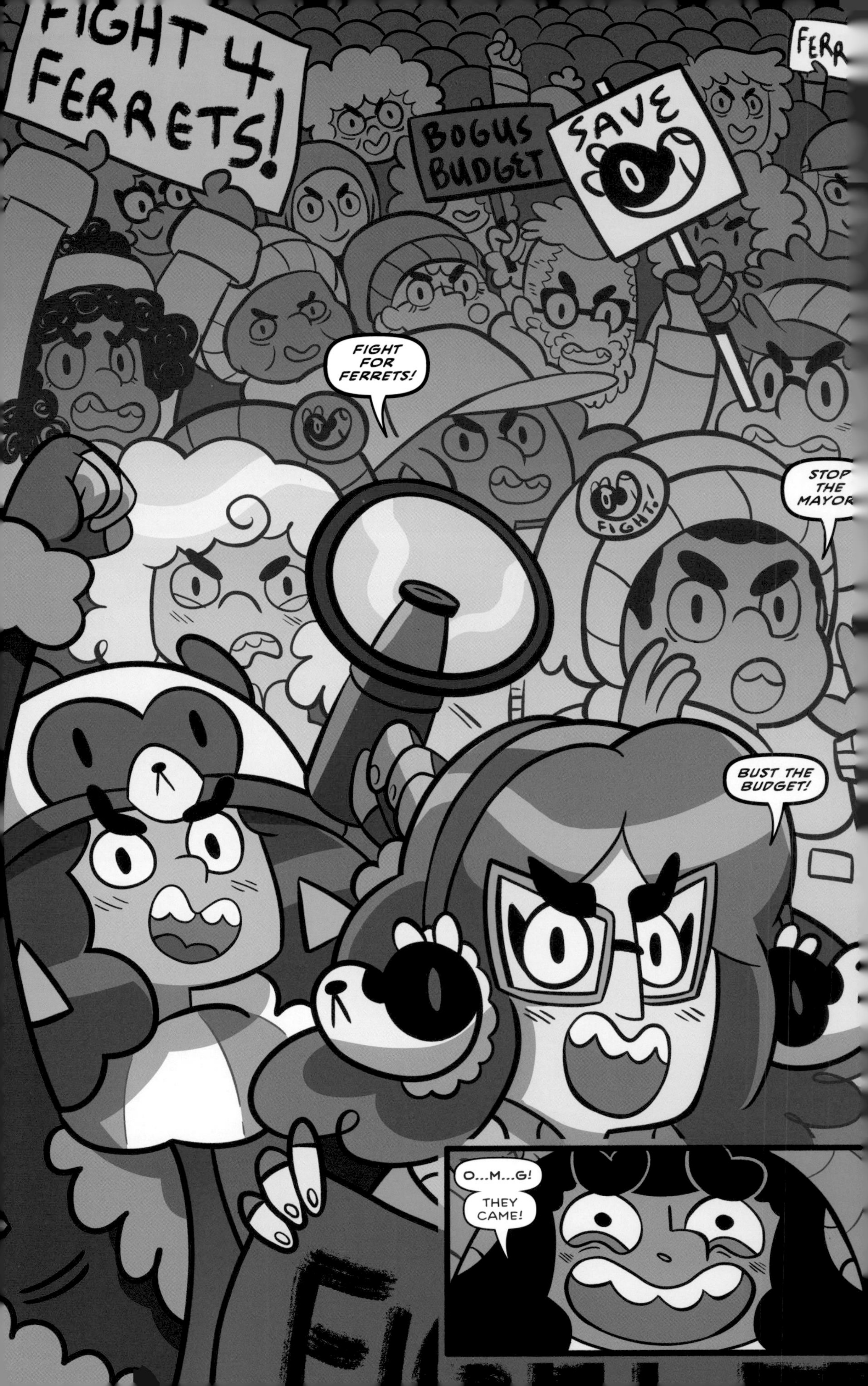
FIGHT 4 FERRETS!
BOGUS BUDGET
SAVE
FERR
FIGHT FOR FERRETS!
FIGHT!
STOP THE MAYOR
BUST THE BUDGET!
O...M...G!
THEY CAME!

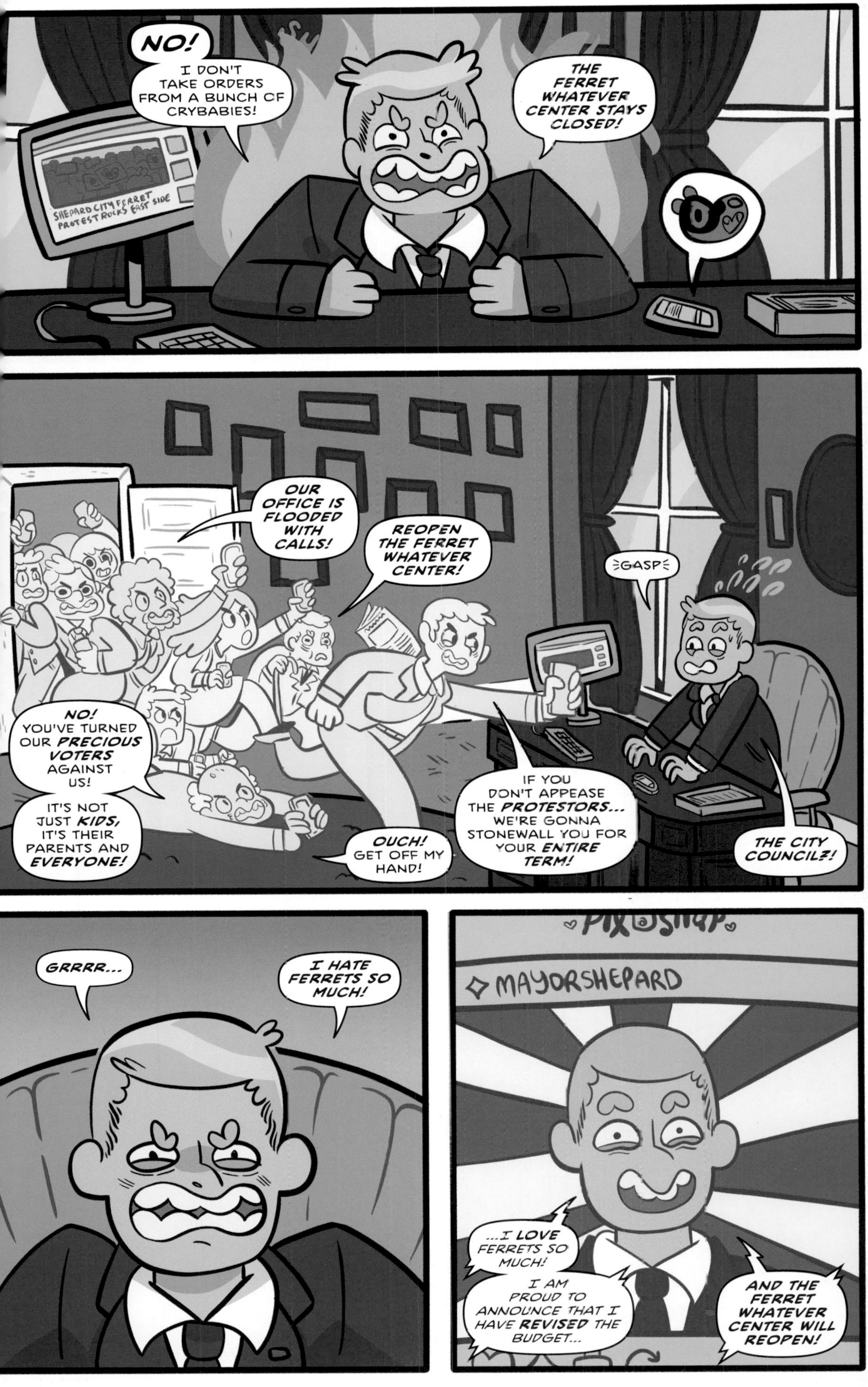
NO! I DON'T TAKE ORDERS FROM A BUNCH OF CRYBABIES!
SHEPARD CITY FERRET PROTEST ROCKS EAST SIDE
THE FERRET WHATEVER CENTER STAYS CLOSED!
OUR OFFICE IS FLOODED WITH CALLS!
REOPEN THE FERRET WHATEVER CENTER!
GASP
NO! YOU'VE TURNED OUR PRECIOUS VOTERS AGAINST US!
IT'S NOT JUST KIDS, IT'S THEIR PARENTS AND EVERYONE!
OUCH! GET OFF MY HAND!
IF YOU DON'T APPEASE THE PROTESTORS... WE'RE GONNA STONEWALL YOU FOR YOUR ENTIRE TERM!
THE CITY COUNCIL?!
GRRRR...
I HATE FERRETS SO MUCH!
MAYORSHEPARD
...I LOVE FERRETS SO MUCH!
I AM PROUD TO ANNOUNCE THAT I HAVE REVISED THE BUDGET...
AND THE FERRET WHATEVER CENTER WILL REOPEN!

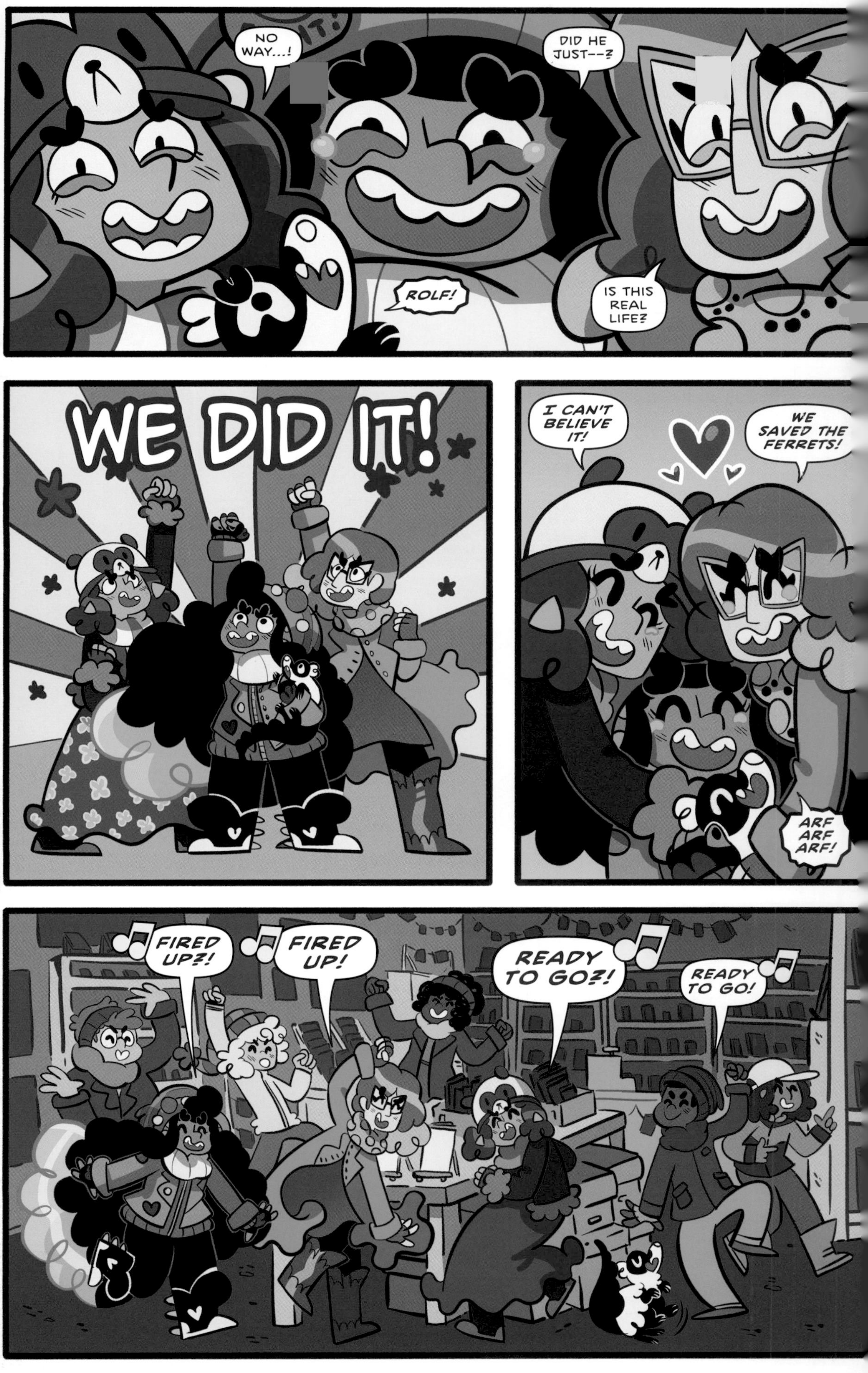

NO WAY...!
DID HE JUST--?
ROLF!
IS THIS REAL LIFE?
WE DID IT!
I CAN'T BELIEVE IT!
WE SAVED THE FERRETS!
ARF ARF ARF!
FIRED UP?!
FIRED UP!
READY TO GO?!
READY TO GO!

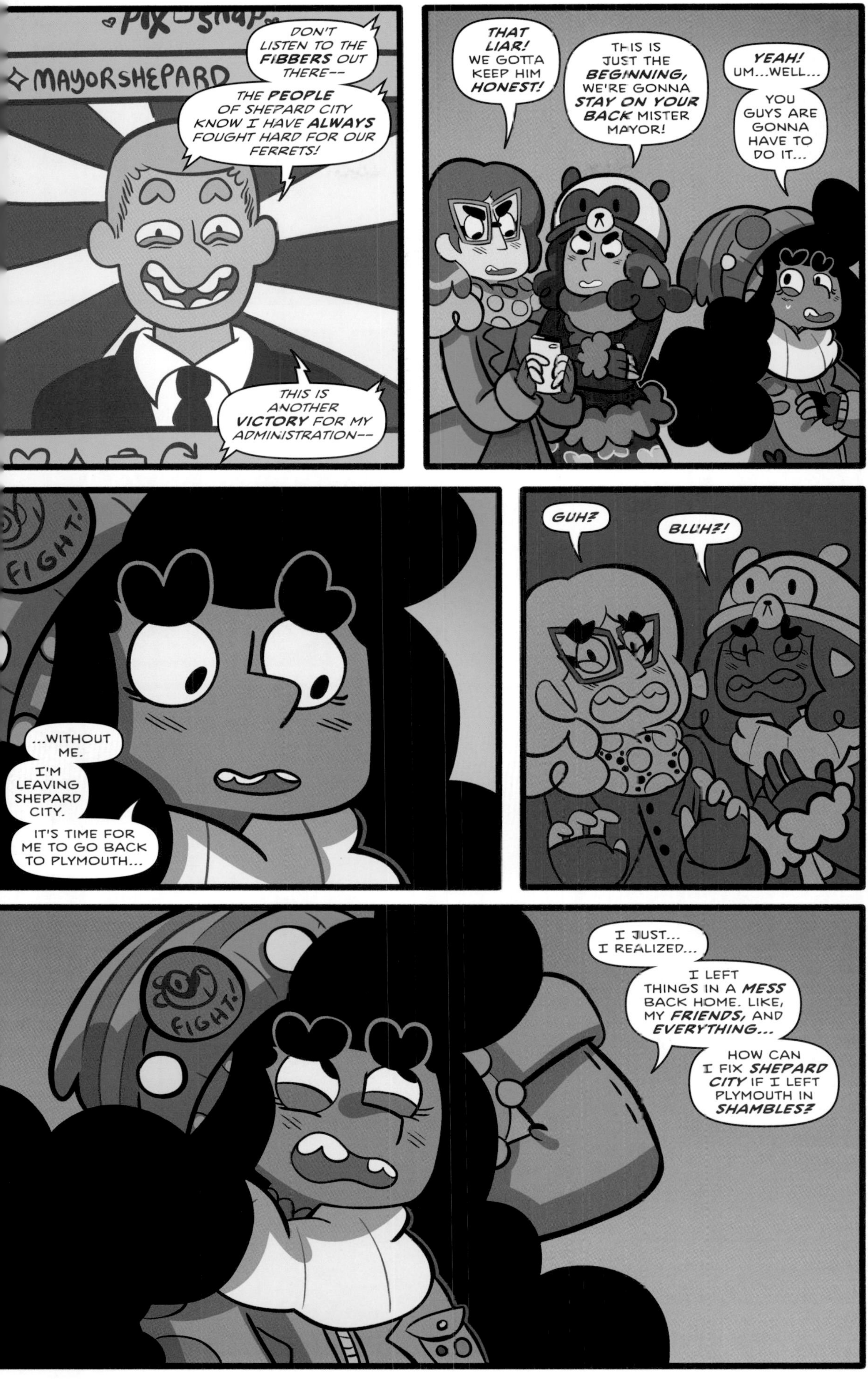
PIX SNAP
MAYORSHEPARD
DON'T LISTEN TO THE FIBBERS OUT THERE--
THE PEOPLE OF SHEPARD CITY KNOW I HAVE ALWAYS FOUGHT HARD FOR OUR FERRETS!
THIS IS ANOTHER VICTORY FOR MY ADMINISTRATION--
THAT LIAR! WE GOTTA KEEP HIM HONEST!
THIS IS JUST THE BEGINNING, WE'RE GONNA STAY ON YOUR BACK MISTER MAYOR!
YEAH! UM...WELL...
YOU GUYS ARE GONNA HAVE TO DO IT...
FIGHT!
...WITHOUT ME.
I'M LEAVING SHEPARD CITY.
IT'S TIME FOR ME TO GO BACK TO PLYMOUTH...
GUH?
BLUH?!
FIGHT!
I JUST... I REALIZED...
I LEFT THINGS IN A MESS BACK HOME. LIKE, MY FRIENDS, AND EVERYTHING...
HOW CAN I FIX SHEPARD CITY IF I LEFT PLYMOUTH IN SHAMBLES?

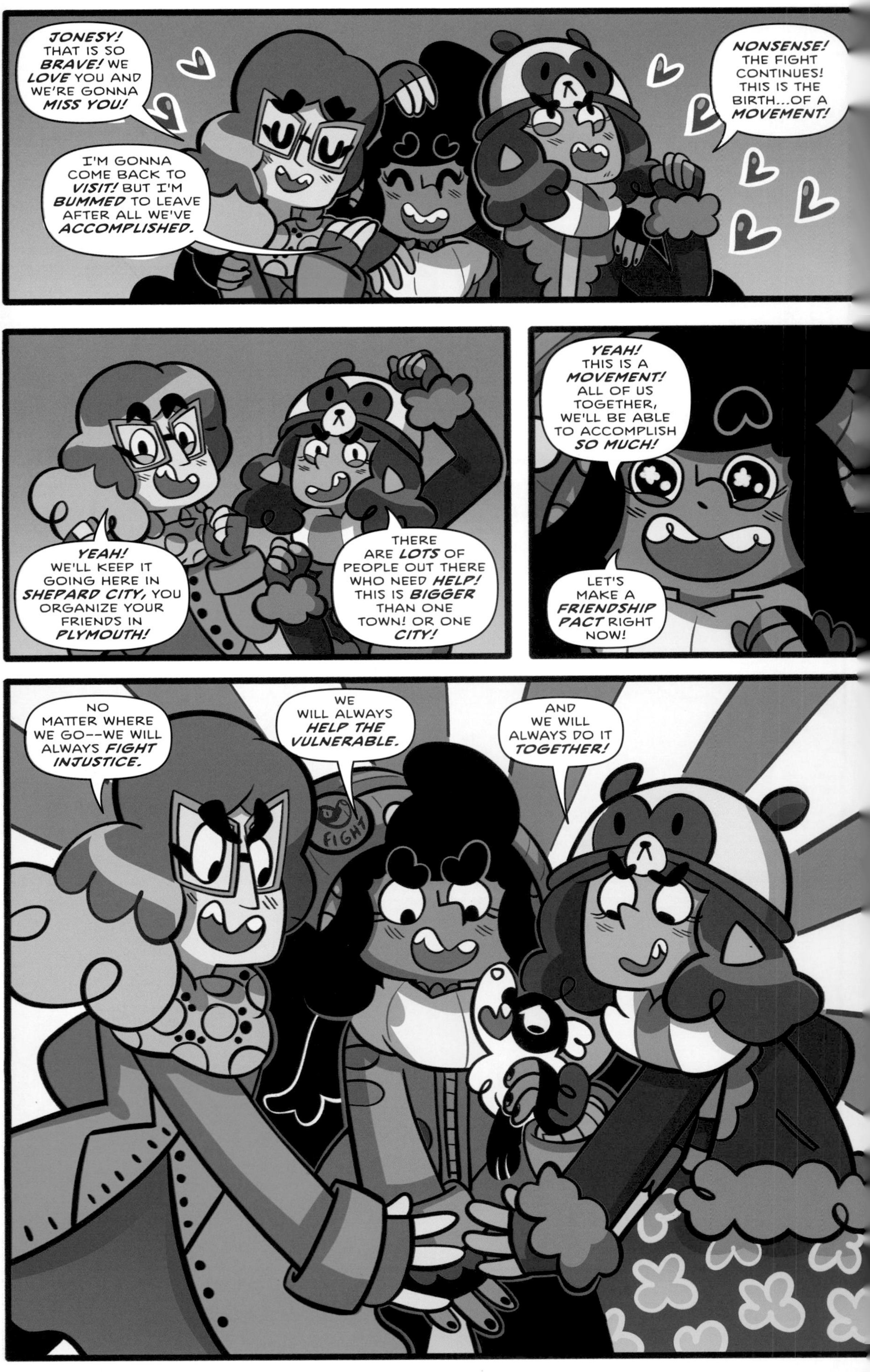
JONESY! THAT IS SO BRAVE! WE LOVE YOU AND WE'RE GONNA MISS YOU!
I'M GONNA COME BACK TO VISIT! BUT I'M BUMMED TO LEAVE AFTER ALL WE'VE ACCOMPLISHED.
NONSENSE! THE FIGHT CONTINUES! THIS IS THE BIRTH...OF A MOVEMENT!
YEAH! WE'LL KEEP IT GOING HERE IN SHEPARD CITY, YOU ORGANIZE YOUR FRIENDS IN PLYMOUTH!
THERE ARE LOTS OF PEOPLE OUT THERE WHO NEED HELP! THIS IS BIGGER THAN ONE TOWN! OR ONE CITY!
YEAH! THIS IS A MOVEMENT! ALL OF US TOGETHER, WE'LL BE ABLE TO ACCOMPLISH SO MUCH!
LET'S MAKE A FRIENDSHIP PACT RIGHT NOW!
NO MATTER WHERE WE GO--WE WILL ALWAYS FIGHT INJUSTICE.
WE WILL ALWAYS HELP THE VULNERABLE.
AND WE WILL ALWAYS DO IT TOGETHER!
FIGHT

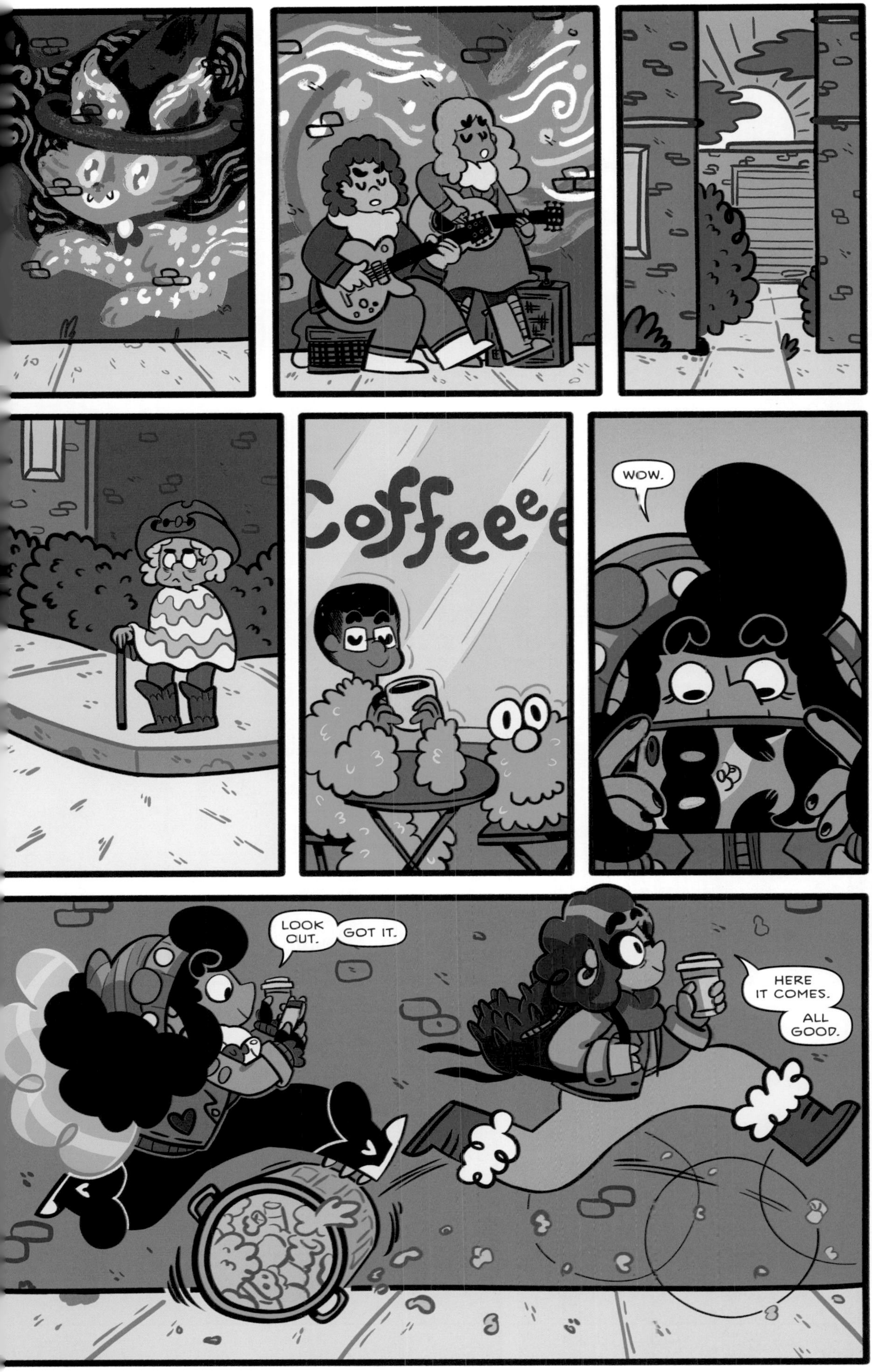
Coffeee
WOW.
LOOK OUT.
GOT IT.
HERE IT COMES.
ALL GOOD.

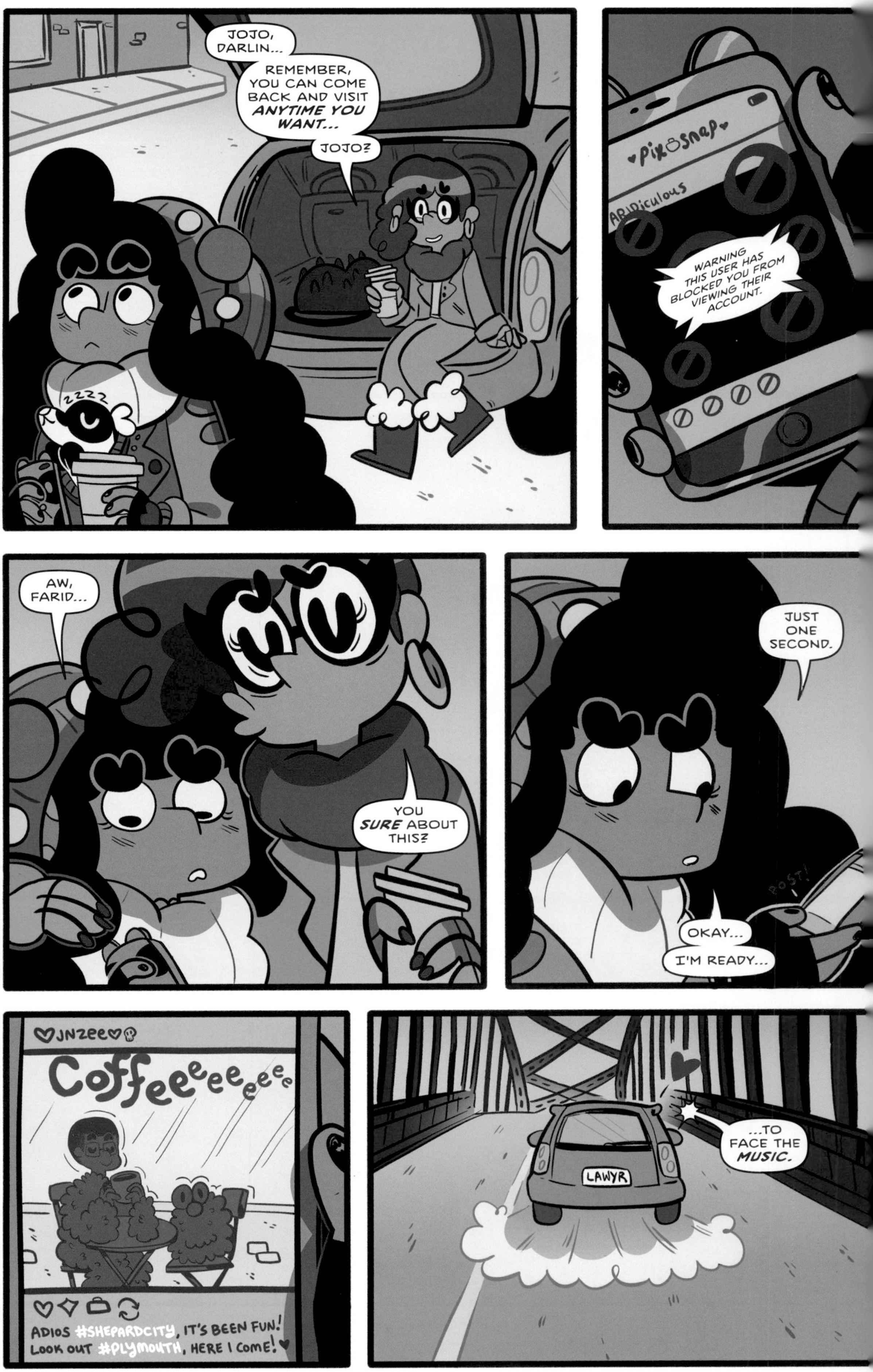
JOJO, DARLIN...
REMEMBER, YOU CAN COME BACK AND VISIT *ANYTIME YOU WANT...*
JOJO?
pix snap
ARIDiculous
WARNING THIS USER HAS BLOCKED YOU FROM VIEWING THEIR ACCOUNT.
AW, FARID...
YOU *SURE* ABOUT THIS?
JUST ONE SECOND.
POST!
OKAY...
I'M READY...
JNZEE
Coffeeeeeeee
ADIOS #SHEPARDCITY, IT'S BEEN FUN! Look out #PLYMOUTH, HERE I COME!
LAWYR
...TO FACE THE *MUSIC.*

CHAPTER THREE

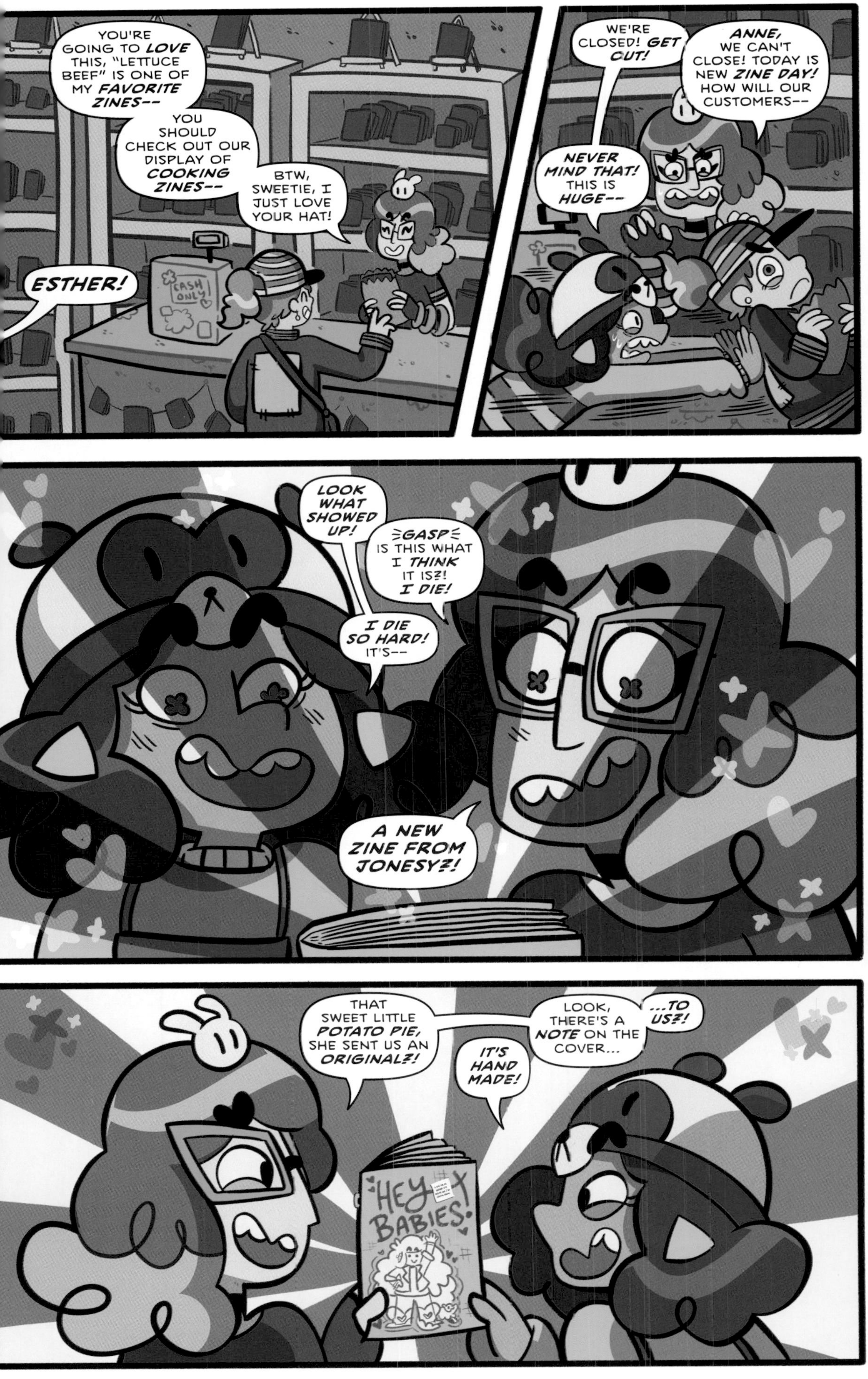
YOU'RE GOING TO LOVE THIS, "LETTUCE BEEF" IS ONE OF MY FAVORITE ZINES--
YOU SHOULD CHECK OUT OUR DISPLAY OF COOKING ZINES--
BTW, SWEETIE, I JUST LOVE YOUR HAT!
ESTHER!
CASH ONLY
WE'RE CLOSED! GET OUT!
ANNE, WE CAN'T CLOSE! TODAY IS NEW ZINE DAY! HOW WILL OUR CUSTOMERS--
NEVER MIND THAT! THIS IS HUGE--
LOOK WHAT SHOWED UP!
GASP IS THIS WHAT I THINK IT IS?! I DIE!
I DIE SO HARD! IT'S--
A NEW ZINE FROM JONESY?!
THAT SWEET LITTLE POTATO PIE, SHE SENT US AN ORIGINAL?!
IT'S HAND MADE!
LOOK, THERE'S A NOTE ON THE COVER...
...TO US?!
HEY BABIES!

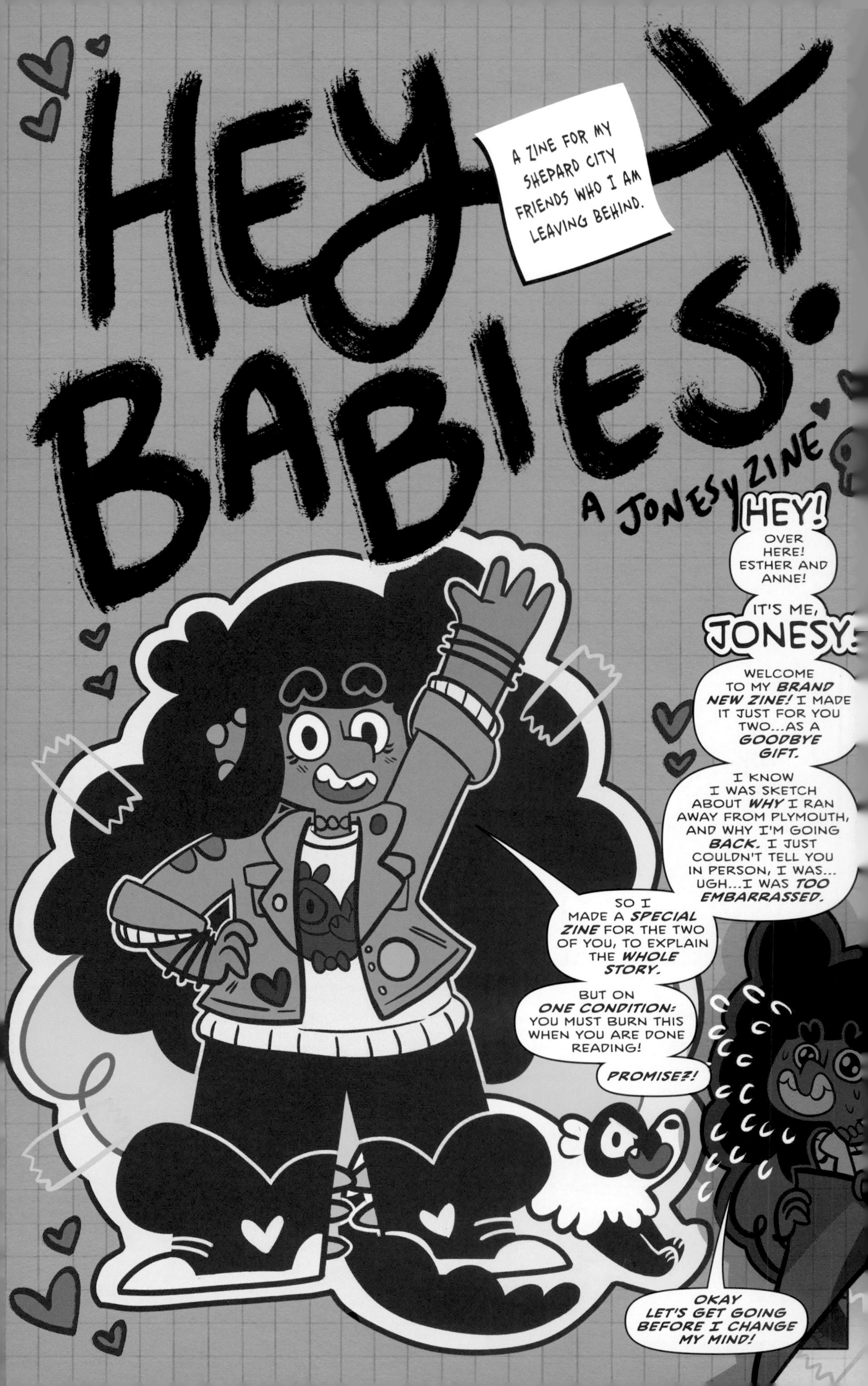
HEY BABIES!
A ZINE FOR MY SHEPARD CITY FRIENDS WHO I AM LEAVING BEHIND.
A JONESY ZINE
HEY!
OVER HERE! ESTHER AND ANNE!
IT'S ME, JONESY!
WELCOME TO MY BRAND NEW ZINE! I MADE IT JUST FOR YOU TWO...AS A GOODBYE GIFT.
I KNOW I WAS SKETCH ABOUT WHY I RAN AWAY FROM PLYMOUTH, AND WHY I'M GOING BACK. I JUST COULDN'T TELL YOU IN PERSON, I WAS... UGH...I WAS TOO EMBARRASSED.
SO I MADE A SPECIAL ZINE FOR THE TWO OF YOU, TO EXPLAIN THE WHOLE STORY.
BUT ON ONE CONDITION: YOU MUST BURN THIS WHEN YOU ARE DONE READING!
PROMISE?!
OKAY LET'S GET GOING BEFORE I CHANGE MY MIND!

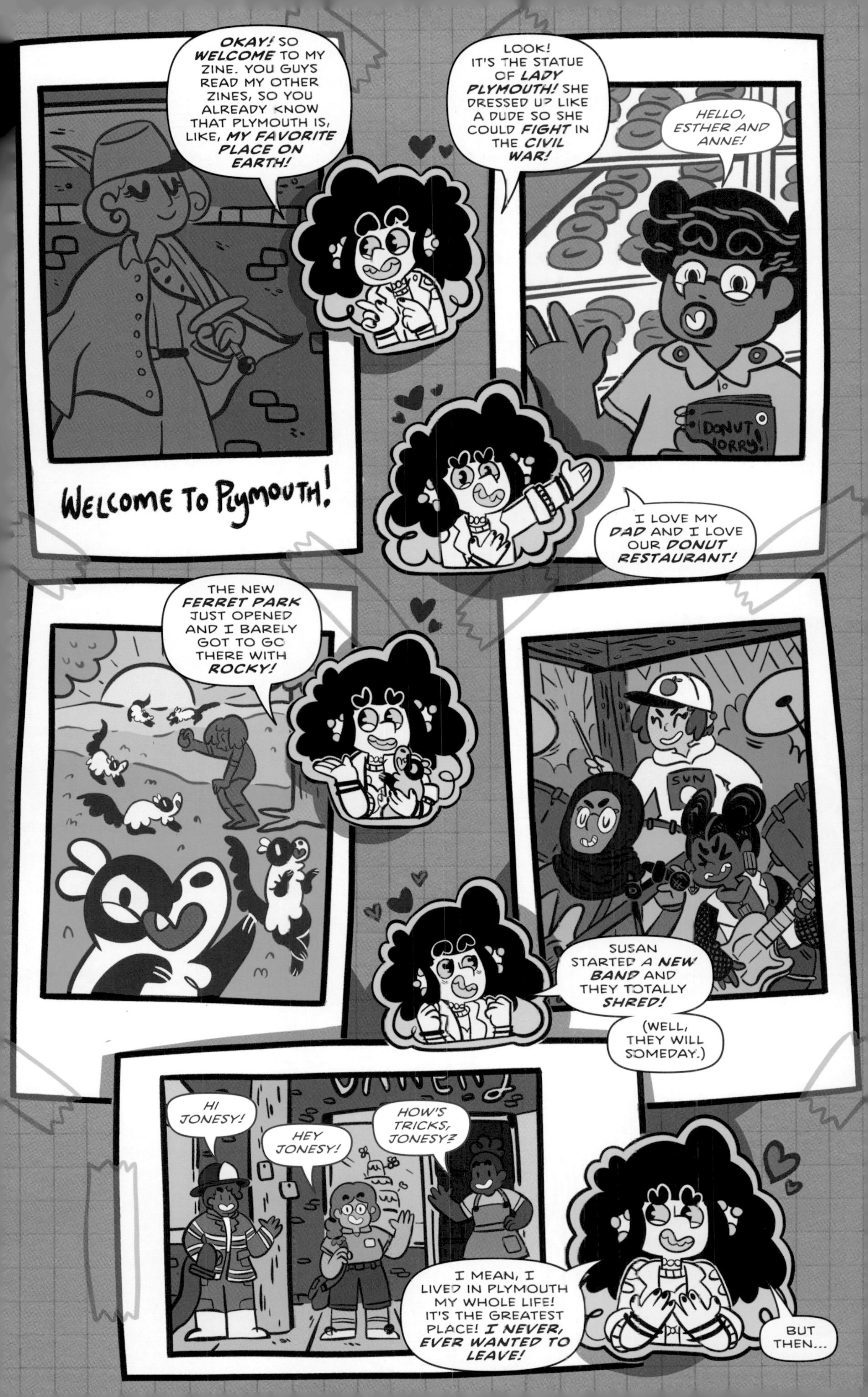
OKAY! SO WELCOME TO MY ZINE. YOU GUYS READ MY OTHER ZINES, SO YOU ALREADY KNOW THAT PLYMOUTH IS, LIKE, MY FAVORITE PLACE ON EARTH!
WELCOME TO PLYMOUTH!
LOOK! IT'S THE STATUE OF LADY PLYMOUTH! SHE DRESSED UP LIKE A DUDE SO SHE COULD FIGHT IN THE CIVIL WAR!
HELLO, ESTHER AND ANNE!
DONUT WORRY!
I LOVE MY DAD AND I LOVE OUR DONUT RESTAURANT!
THE NEW FERRET PARK JUST OPENED AND I BARELY GOT TO GO THERE WITH ROCKY!
SUN
SUSAN STARTED A NEW BAND AND THEY TOTALLY SHRED!
(WELL, THEY WILL SOMEDAY.)
HI JONESY!
HEY JONESY!
HOW'S TRICKS, JONESY?
I MEAN, I LIVED IN PLYMOUTH MY WHOLE LIFE! IT'S THE GREATEST PLACE! I NEVER, EVER WANTED TO LEAVE!
BUT THEN...

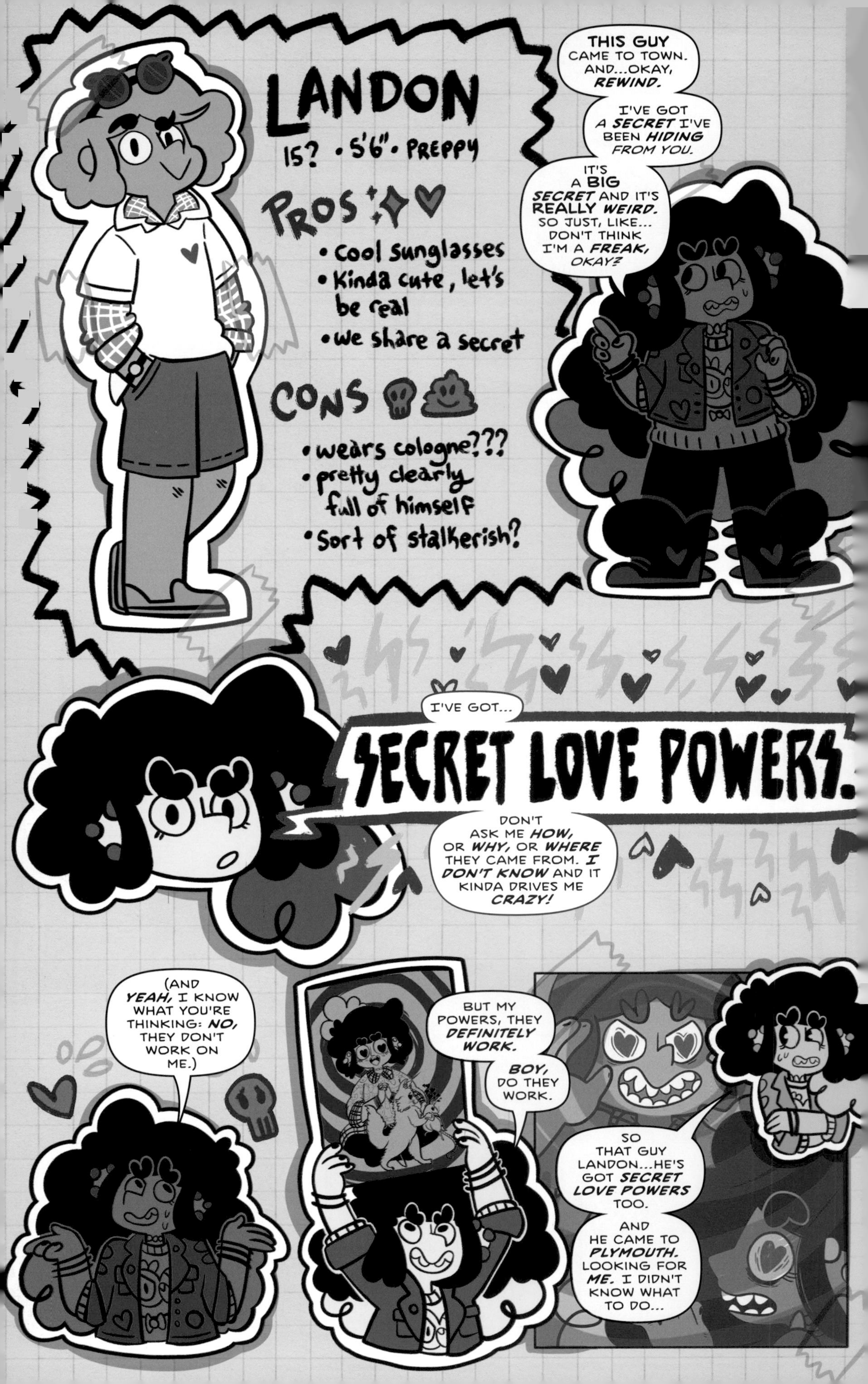
LANDON
15? • 5'6" • PREPPY
PROS
• Cool sunglasses
• Kinda cute, let's be real
• we share a secret
CONS
• wears cologne???
• pretty clearly full of himself
• Sort of stalkerish?
THIS GUY CAME TO TOWN. AND...OKAY, REWIND.
I'VE GOT A SECRET I'VE BEEN HIDING FROM YOU.
IT'S A BIG SECRET AND IT'S REALLY WEIRD. SO JUST, LIKE... DON'T THINK I'M A FREAK, OKAY?
I'VE GOT...
SECRET LOVE POWERS.
DON'T ASK ME HOW, OR WHY, OR WHERE THEY CAME FROM. I DON'T KNOW AND IT KINDA DRIVES ME CRAZY!
(AND YEAH, I KNOW WHAT YOU'RE THINKING: NO, THEY DON'T WORK ON ME.)
BUT MY POWERS, THEY DEFINITELY WORK.
BOY, DO THEY WORK.
SO THAT GUY LANDON...HE'S GOT SECRET LOVE POWERS TOO.
AND HE CAME TO PLYMOUTH. LOOKING FOR ME. I DIDN'T KNOW WHAT TO DO...

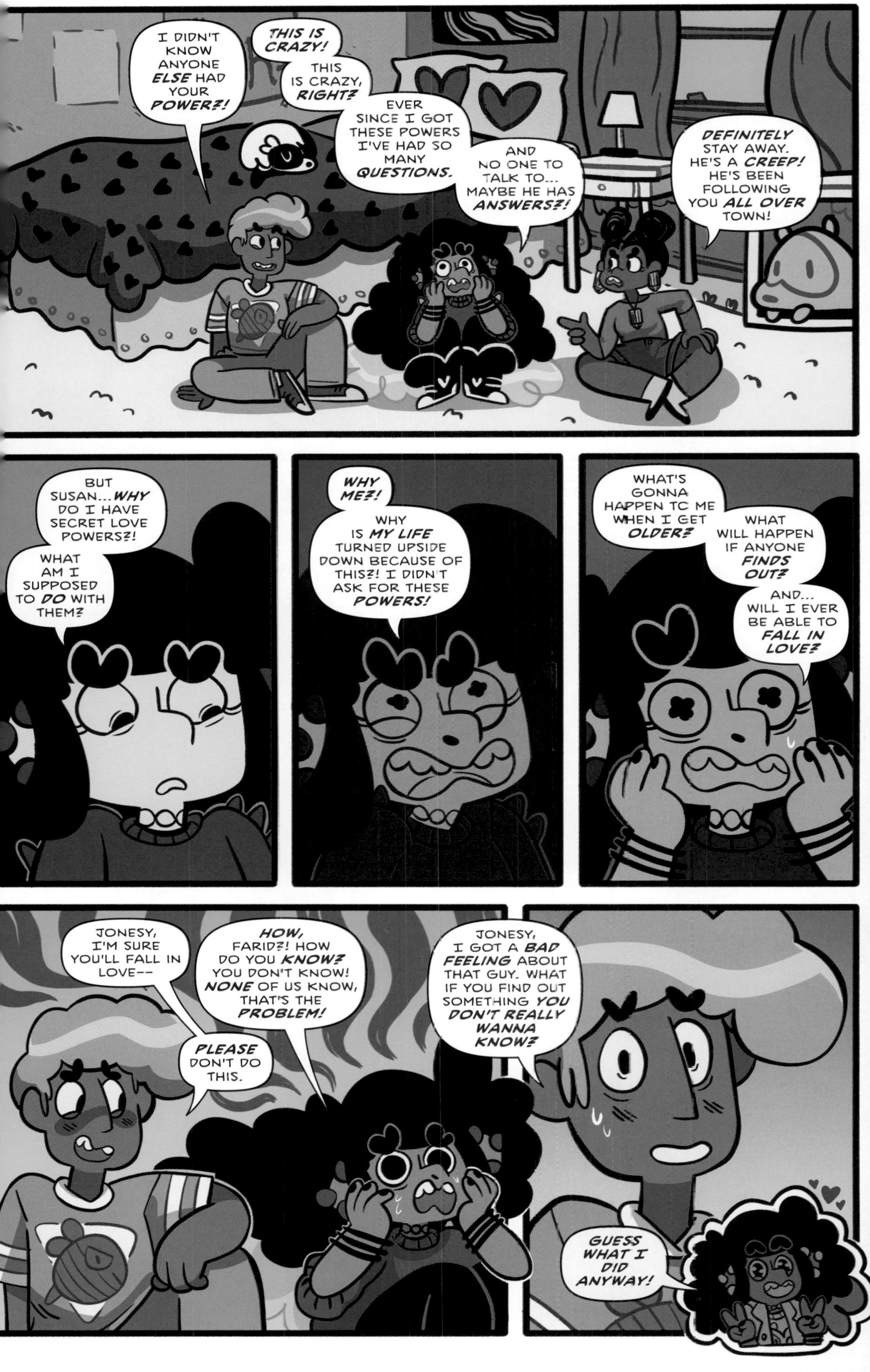
I DIDN'T KNOW ANYONE ELSE HAD YOUR POWER?!
THIS IS CRAZY!
THIS IS CRAZY, RIGHT?
EVER SINCE I GOT THESE POWERS I'VE HAD SO MANY QUESTIONS.
AND NO ONE TO TALK TO... MAYBE HE HAS ANSWERS?!
DEFINITELY STAY AWAY. HE'S A CREEP! HE'S BEEN FOLLOWING YOU ALL OVER TOWN!
BUT SUSAN...WHY DO I HAVE SECRET LOVE POWERS?!
WHAT AM I SUPPOSED TO DO WITH THEM?
WHY ME?!
WHY IS MY LIFE TURNED UPSIDE DOWN BECAUSE OF THIS?! I DIDN'T ASK FOR THESE POWERS!
WHAT'S GONNA HAPPEN TO ME WHEN I GET OLDER?
WHAT WILL HAPPEN IF ANYONE FINDS OUT?
AND... WILL I EVER BE ABLE TO FALL IN LOVE?
JONESY, I'M SURE YOU'LL FALL IN LOVE--
HOW, FARID?! HOW DO YOU KNOW? YOU DON'T KNOW! NONE OF US KNOW, THAT'S THE PROBLEM!
PLEASE DON'T DO THIS.
JONESY, I GOT A BAD FEELING ABOUT THAT GUY. WHAT IF YOU FIND OUT SOMETHING YOU DON'T REALLY WANNA KNOW?
GUESS WHAT I DID ANYWAY!

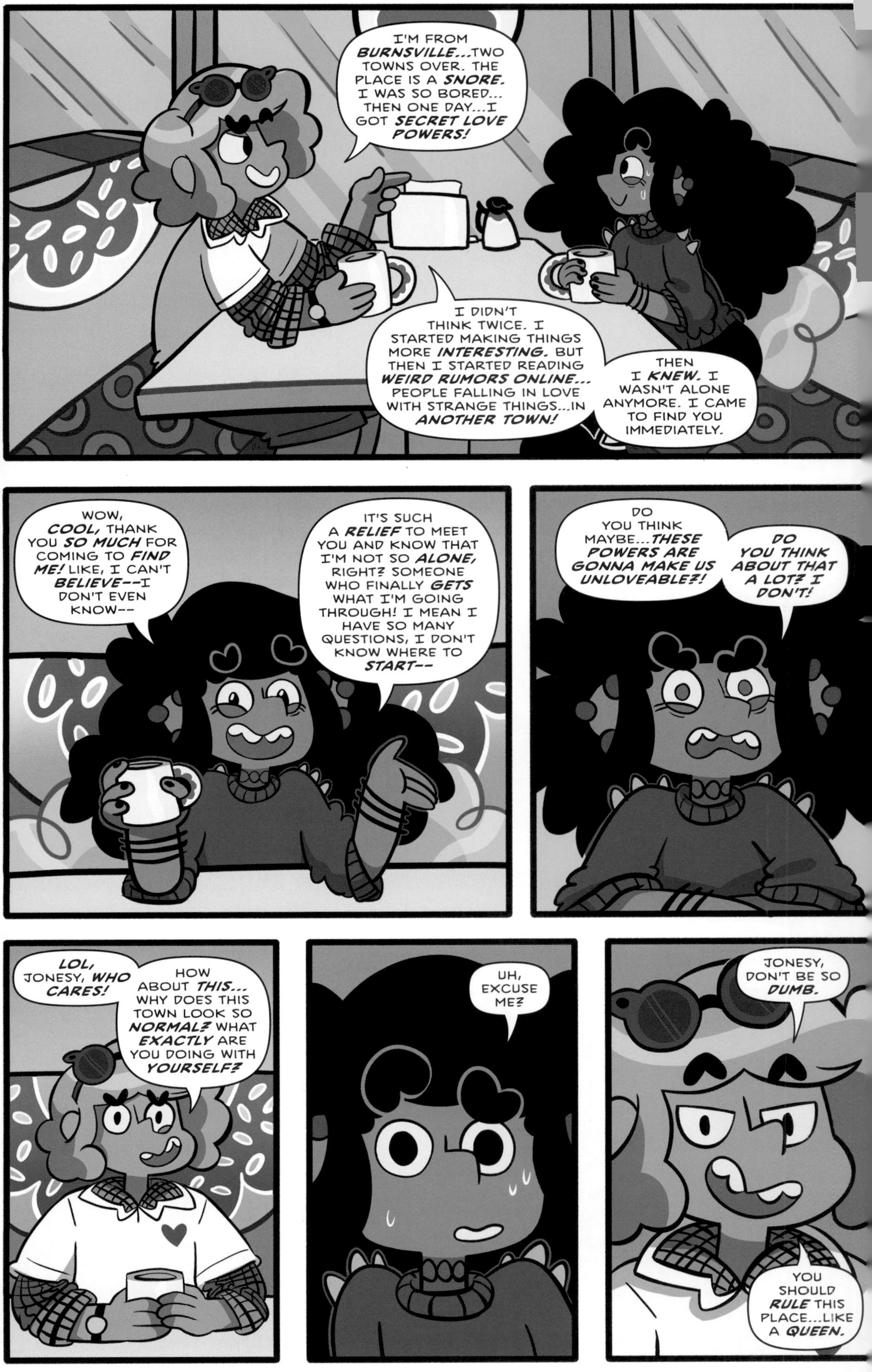
I'M FROM BURNSVILLE...TWO TOWNS OVER. THE PLACE IS A SNORE. I WAS SO BORED... THEN ONE DAY...I GOT SECRET LOVE POWERS!
I DIDN'T THINK TWICE. I STARTED MAKING THINGS MORE INTERESTING. BUT THEN I STARTED READING WEIRD RUMORS ONLINE... PEOPLE FALLING IN LOVE WITH STRANGE THINGS...IN ANOTHER TOWN!
THEN I KNEW. I WASN'T ALONE ANYMORE. I CAME TO FIND YOU IMMEDIATELY.
WOW, COOL, THANK YOU SO MUCH FOR COMING TO FIND ME! LIKE, I CAN'T BELIEVE--I DON'T EVEN KNOW--
IT'S SUCH A RELIEF TO MEET YOU AND KNOW THAT I'M NOT SO ALONE, RIGHT? SOMEONE WHO FINALLY GETS WHAT I'M GOING THROUGH! I MEAN I HAVE SO MANY QUESTIONS, I DON'T KNOW WHERE TO START--
DO YOU THINK MAYBE...THESE POWERS ARE GONNA MAKE US UNLOVEABLE?!
DO YOU THINK ABOUT THAT A LOT? I DON'T!
LOL, JONESY, WHO CARES!
HOW ABOUT THIS... WHY DOES THIS TOWN LOOK SO NORMAL? WHAT EXACTLY ARE YOU DOING WITH YOURSELF?
UH, EXCUSE ME?
JONESY, DON'T BE SO DUMB.
YOU SHOULD RULE THIS PLACE...LIKE A QUEEN.

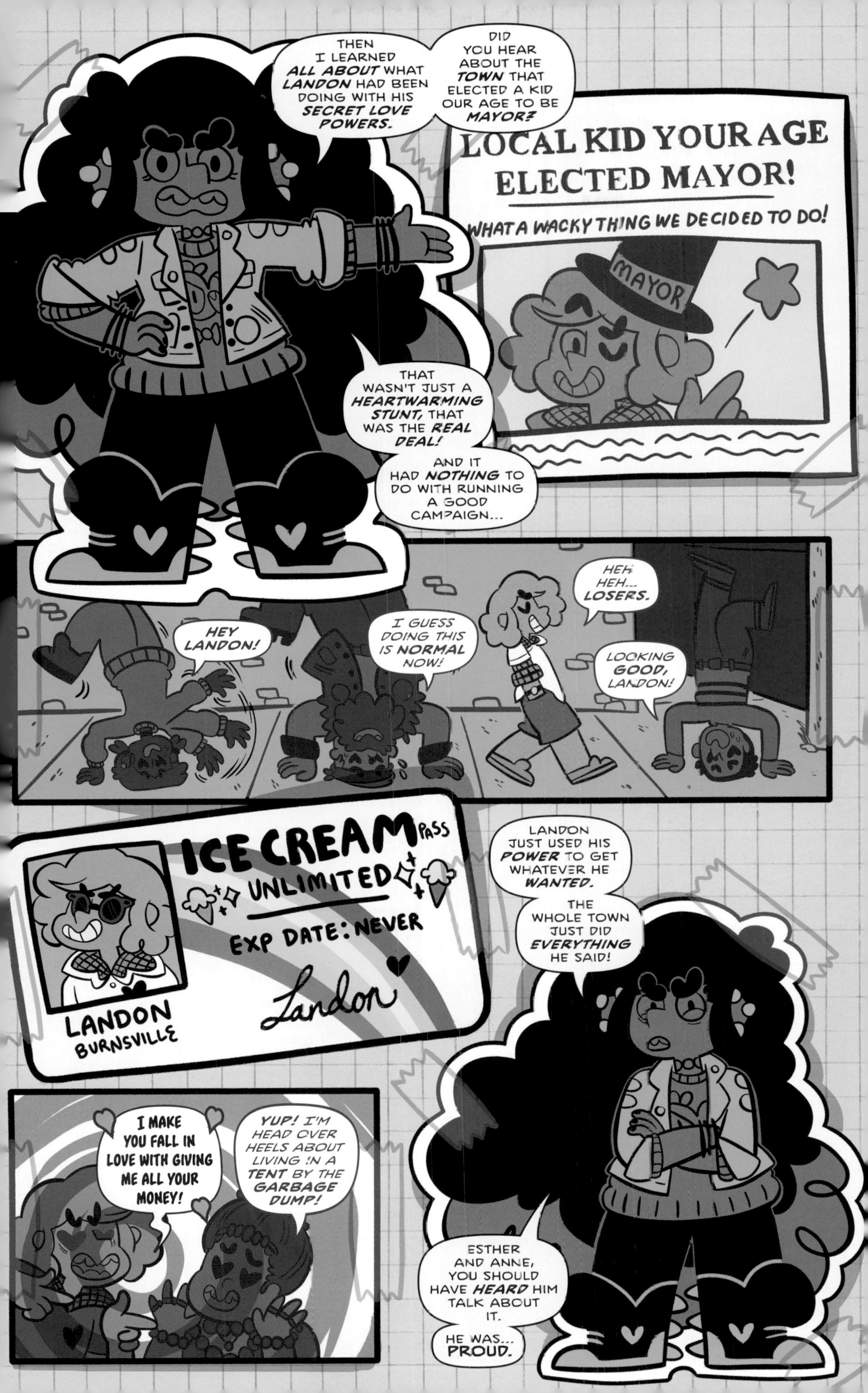

THEN I LEARNED ALL ABOUT WHAT LANDON HAD BEEN DOING WITH HIS SECRET LOVE POWERS.
DID YOU HEAR ABOUT THE TOWN THAT ELECTED A KID OUR AGE TO BE MAYOR?
LOCAL KID YOUR AGE ELECTED MAYOR!
WHAT A WACKY THING WE DECIDED TO DO!
MAYOR
THAT WASN'T JUST A HEARTWARMING STUNT, THAT WAS THE REAL DEAL!
AND IT HAD NOTHING TO DO WITH RUNNING A GOOD CAMPAIGN...
HEY LANDON!
I GUESS DOING THIS IS NORMAL NOW!
HEH HEH... LOSERS.
LOOKING GOOD, LANDON!
ICE CREAM PASS
UNLIMITED
EXP DATE: NEVER
Landon
LANDON BURNSVILLE
LANDON JUST USED HIS POWER TO GET WHATEVER HE WANTED.
THE WHOLE TOWN JUST DID EVERYTHING HE SAID!
I MAKE YOU FALL IN LOVE WITH GIVING ME ALL YOUR MONEY!
YUP! I'M HEAD OVER HEELS ABOUT LIVING IN A TENT BY THE GARBAGE DUMP!
ESTHER AND ANNE, YOU SHOULD HAVE HEARD HIM TALK ABOUT IT.
HE WAS... PROUD.

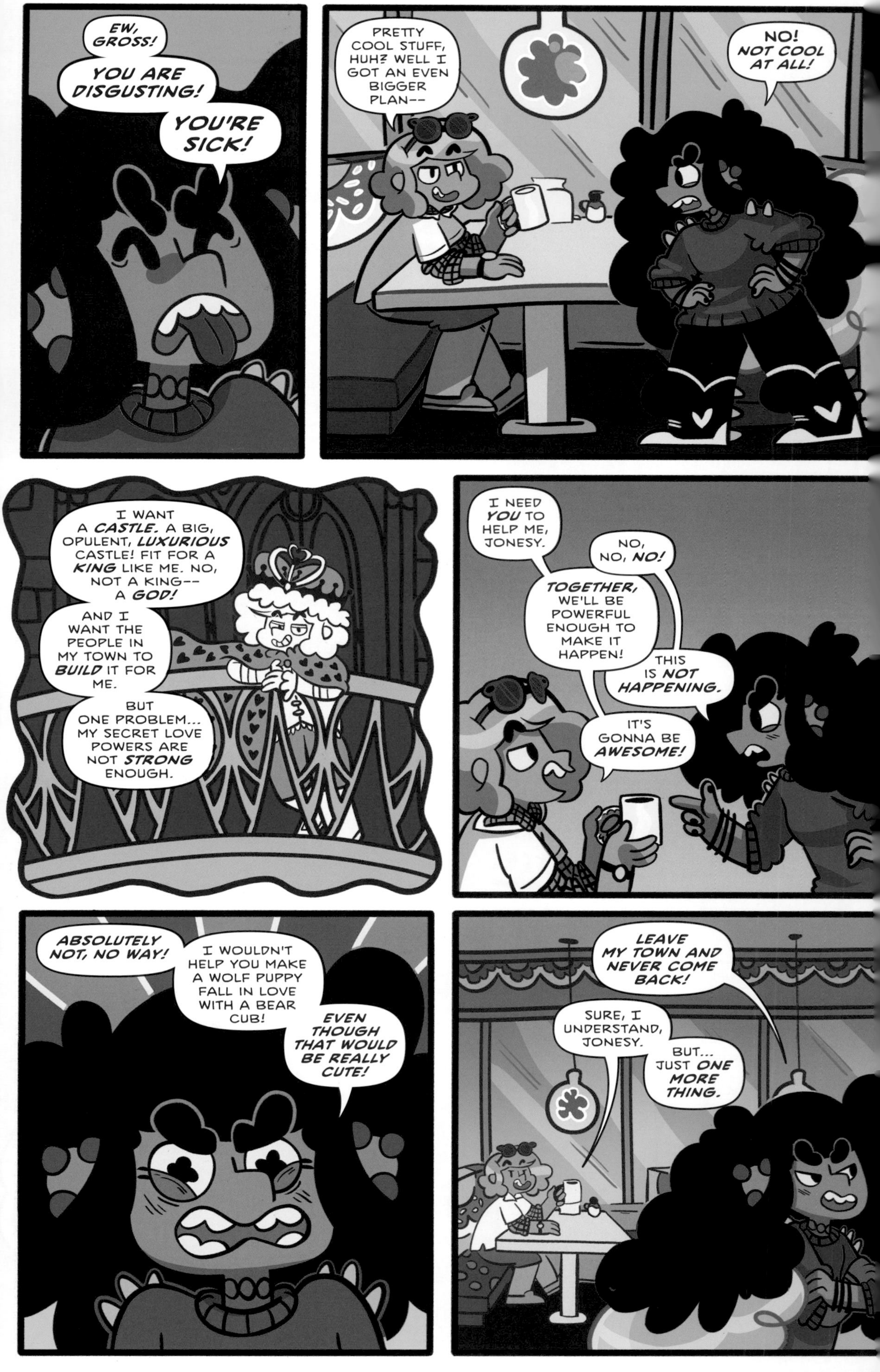
EW, GROSS!
YOU ARE DISGUSTING!
YOU'RE SICK!
PRETTY COOL STUFF, HUH? WELL I GOT AN EVEN BIGGER PLAN--
NO! NOT COOL AT ALL!
I WANT A CASTLE. A BIG, OPULENT, LUXURIOUS CASTLE! FIT FOR A KING LIKE ME. NO, NOT A KING-- A GOD!
AND I WANT THE PEOPLE IN MY TOWN TO BUILD IT FOR ME.
BUT ONE PROBLEM... MY SECRET LOVE POWERS ARE NOT STRONG ENOUGH.
I NEED YOU TO HELP ME, JONESY.
NO, NO, NO!
TOGETHER, WE'LL BE POWERFUL ENOUGH TO MAKE IT HAPPEN!
THIS IS NOT HAPPENING.
IT'S GONNA BE AWESOME!
ABSOLUTELY NOT, NO WAY!
I WOULDN'T HELP YOU MAKE A WOLF PUPPY FALL IN LOVE WITH A BEAR CUB!
EVEN THOUGH THAT WOULD BE REALLY CUTE!
LEAVE MY TOWN AND NEVER COME BACK!
SURE, I UNDERSTAND, JONESY.
BUT... JUST ONE MORE THING.

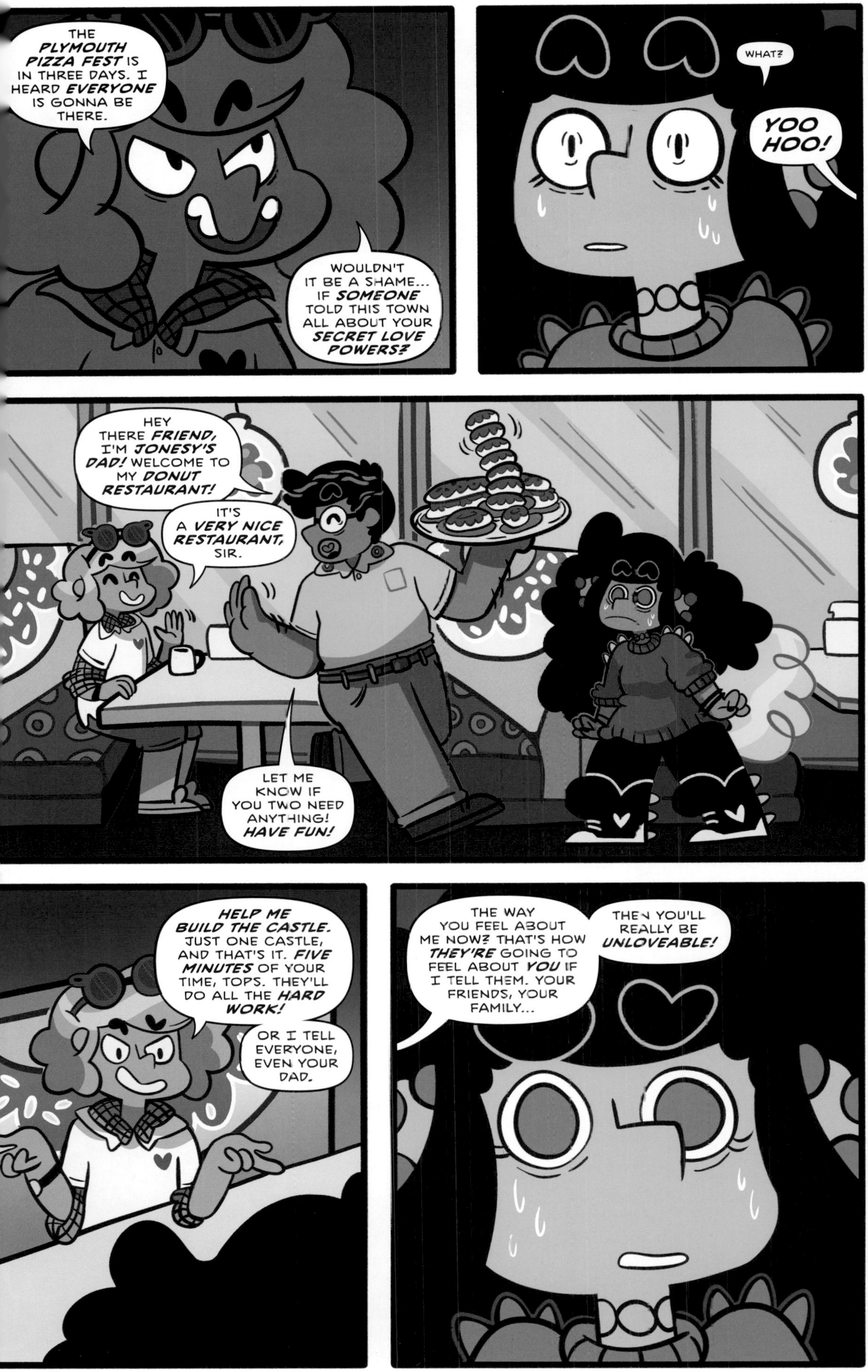
THE PLYMOUTH PIZZA FEST IS IN THREE DAYS. I HEARD EVERYONE IS GONNA BE THERE.
WOULDN'T IT BE A SHAME... IF SOMEONE TOLD THIS TOWN ALL ABOUT YOUR SECRET LOVE POWERS?
WHAT?
YOO HOO!
HEY THERE FRIEND, I'M JONESY'S DAD! WELCOME TO MY DONUT RESTAURANT!
IT'S A VERY NICE RESTAURANT, SIR.
LET ME KNOW IF YOU TWO NEED ANYTHING! HAVE FUN!
HELP ME BUILD THE CASTLE. JUST ONE CASTLE, AND THAT'S IT. FIVE MINUTES OF YOUR TIME, TOPS. THEY'LL DO ALL THE HARD WORK!
OR I TELL EVERYONE, EVEN YOUR DAD.
THE WAY YOU FEEL ABOUT ME NOW? THAT'S HOW THEY'RE GOING TO FEEL ABOUT YOU IF I TELL THEM. YOUR FRIENDS, YOUR FAMILY...
THEN YOU'LL REALLY BE UNLOVEABLE!

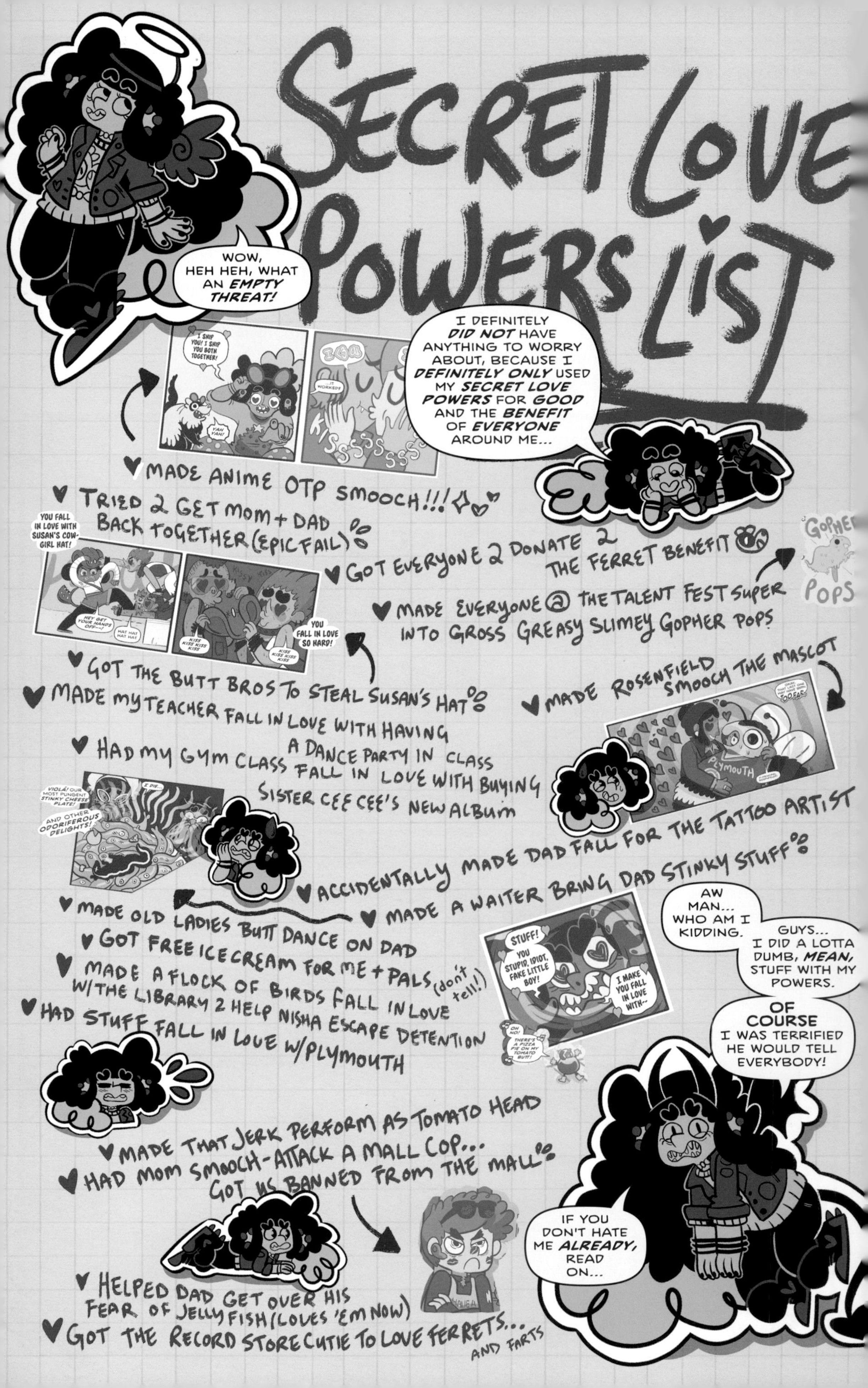
SECRET LOVE POWERS LIST
WOW, HEH HEH, WHAT AN *EMPTY THREAT!*
I DEFINITELY *DID NOT* HAVE ANYTHING TO WORRY ABOUT, BECAUSE I *DEFINITELY ONLY* USED MY *SECRET LOVE POWERS* FOR *GOOD* AND THE *BENEFIT* OF *EVERYONE* AROUND ME...
I SHIP YOU! I SHIP YOU BOTH TOGETHER!
YAH YAH!
...IT WORKED!
KISSSSSSSSSS
♥ MADE ANIME OTP SMOOCH!!!
♥ TRIED 2 GET MOM + DAD BACK TOGETHER (EPIC FAIL)
YOU FALL IN LOVE WITH SUSAN'S COW-GIRL HAT!
HEY GET YOUR HANDS OFF--!
HAT HAT HAT HAT
KISS KISS KISS KISS
KISS KISS KISS KISS
YOU FALL IN LOVE SO HARD!
♥ GOT EVERYONE 2 DONATE 2 THE FERRET BENEFIT
GOPHER POPS
♥ MADE EVERYONE @ THE TALENT FEST SUPER INTO GROSS GREASY SLIMEY GOPHER POPS
♥ GOT THE BUTT BROS TO STEAL SUSAN'S HAT
♥ MADE MY TEACHER FALL IN LOVE WITH HAVING A DANCE PARTY IN CLASS
♥ HAD MY GYM CLASS FALL IN LOVE WITH BUYING SISTER CEE CEE'S NEW ALBUM
♥ MADE ROSENFIELD SMOOCH THE MASCOT
PLYMOUTH
VIOLÀ! OUR MOST PUNGENT STINKY CHEESE PLATE!
AND OTHER ODORIFEROUS DELIGHTS!
I DID...
♥ ACCIDENTALLY MADE DAD FALL FOR THE TATTOO ARTIST
♥ MADE A WAITER BRING DAD STINKY STUFF
♥ MADE OLD LADIES BUTT DANCE ON DAD
♥ GOT FREE ICE CREAM FOR ME + PALS (don't tell!)
♥ MADE A FLOCK OF BIRDS FALL IN LOVE W/THE LIBRARY 2 HELP NISHA ESCAPE DETENTION
♥ HAD STUFF FALL IN LOVE W/PLYMOUTH
STUFF!
YOU STUPID, IDIOT, FAKE LITTLE BOY!
I MAKE YOU FALL IN LOVE WITH--
OH NO! THERE'S A PIZZA PIE ON MY TOMATO BUTT!
AW MAN... WHO AM I KIDDING.
GUYS... I DID A LOTTA DUMB, *MEAN,* STUFF WITH MY POWERS.
OF COURSE I WAS TERRIFIED HE WOULD TELL EVERYBODY!
♥ MADE THAT JERK PERFORM AS TOMATO HEAD
♥ MADE THAT JERK SMOOCH-ATTACK A MALL COP...
♥ HAD MOM SMOOCH-ATTACK A MALL COP... GOT US BANNED FROM THE MALL
IF YOU DON'T HATE ME *ALREADY,* READ ON...
♥ HELPED DAD GET OVER HIS FEAR OF JELLYFISH (LOVES 'EM NOW)
♥ GOT THE RECORD STORE CUTIE TO LOVE FERRETS... AND FARTS

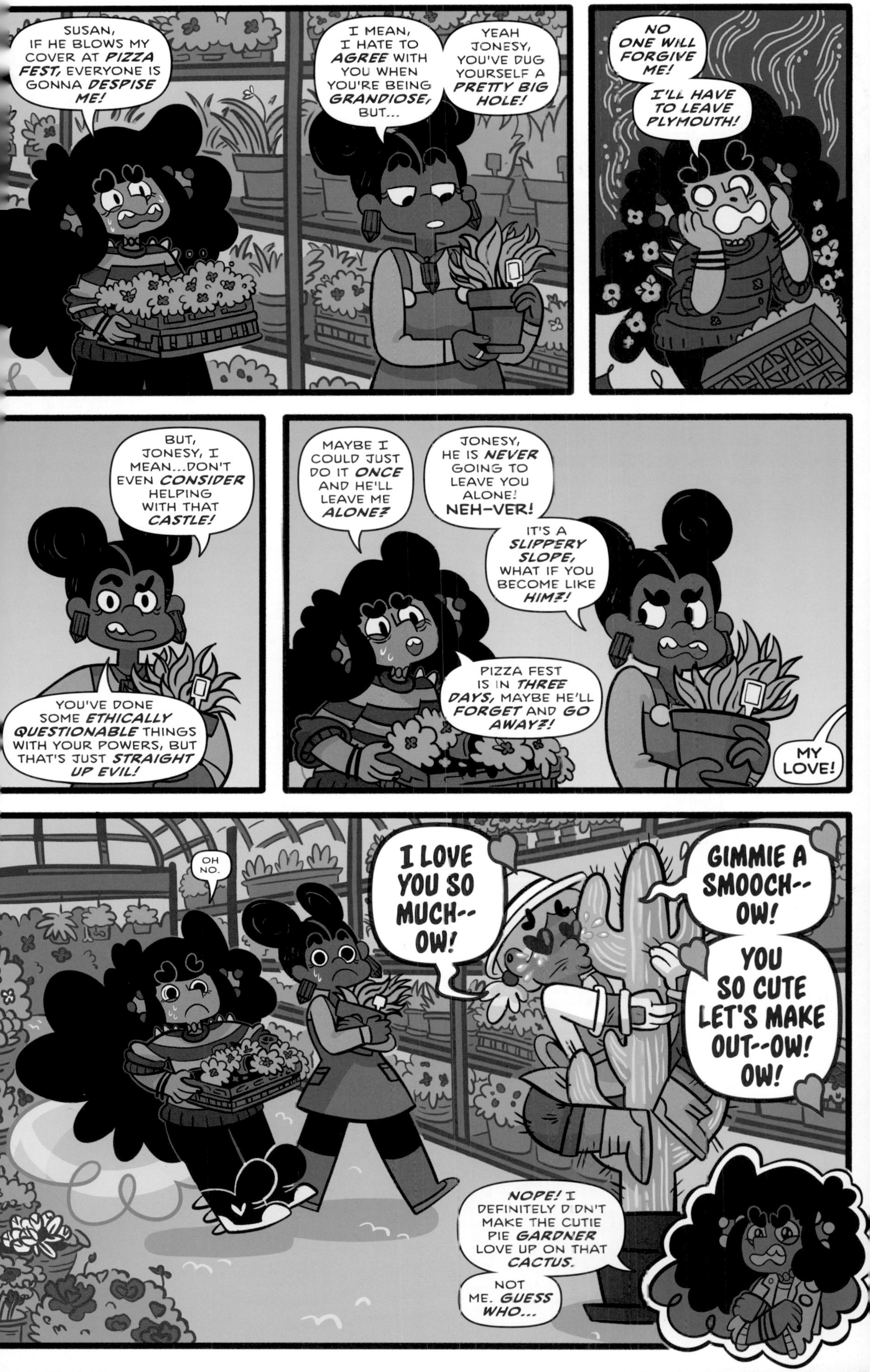
SUSAN, IF HE BLOWS MY COVER AT PIZZA FEST, EVERYONE IS GONNA DESPISE ME!
I MEAN, I HATE TO AGREE WITH YOU WHEN YOU'RE BEING GRANDIOSE, BUT...
YEAH JONESY, YOU'VE DUG YOURSELF A PRETTY BIG HOLE!
NO ONE WILL FORGIVE ME!
I'LL HAVE TO LEAVE PLYMOUTH!
BUT, JONESY, I MEAN...DON'T EVEN CONSIDER HELPING WITH THAT CASTLE!
YOU'VE DONE SOME ETHICALLY QUESTIONABLE THINGS WITH YOUR POWERS, BUT THAT'S JUST STRAIGHT UP EVIL!
MAYBE I COULD JUST DO IT ONCE AND HE'LL LEAVE ME ALONE?
JONESY, HE IS NEVER GOING TO LEAVE YOU ALONE! NEH-VER!
IT'S A SLIPPERY SLOPE, WHAT IF YOU BECOME LIKE HIM?!
PIZZA FEST IS IN THREE DAYS, MAYBE HE'LL FORGET AND GO AWAY?!
MY LOVE!
OH NO.
I LOVE YOU SO MUCH--OW!
GIMMIE A SMOOCH--OW!
YOU SO CUTE LET'S MAKE OUT--OW! OW!
NOPE! I DEFINITELY DIDN'T MAKE THE CUTIE PIE GARDNER LOVE UP ON THAT CACTUS.
NOT ME. GUESS WHO...

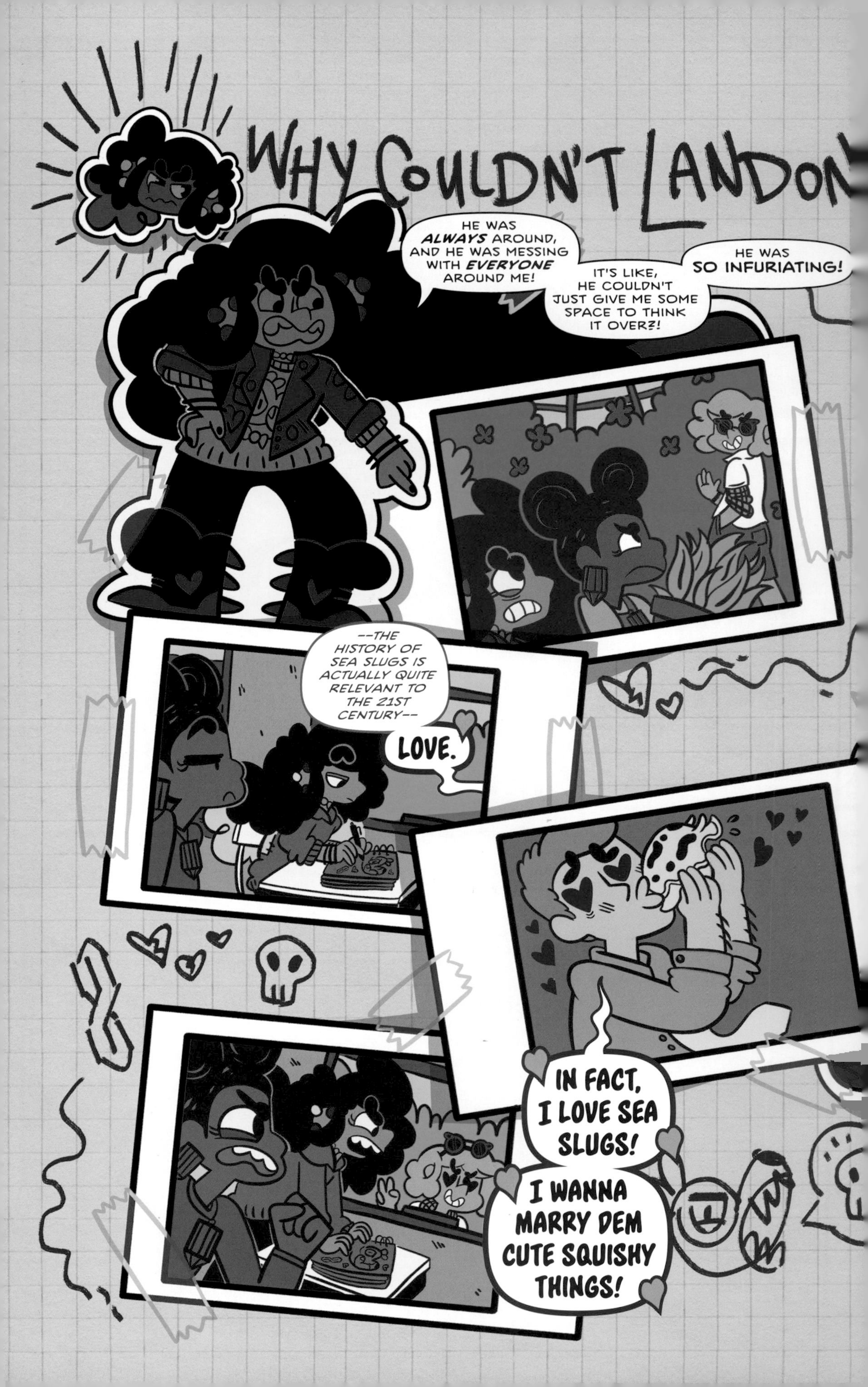
WHY COULDN'T LANDON
HE WAS ALWAYS AROUND, AND HE WAS MESSING WITH EVERYONE AROUND ME!
IT'S LIKE, HE COULDN'T JUST GIVE ME SOME SPACE TO THINK IT OVER?!
HE WAS SO INFURIATING!
--THE HISTORY OF SEA SLUGS IS ACTUALLY QUITE RELEVANT TO THE 21ST CENTURY--
LOVE.
IN FACT, I LOVE SEA SLUGS!
I WANNA MARRY DEM CUTE SQUISHY THINGS!

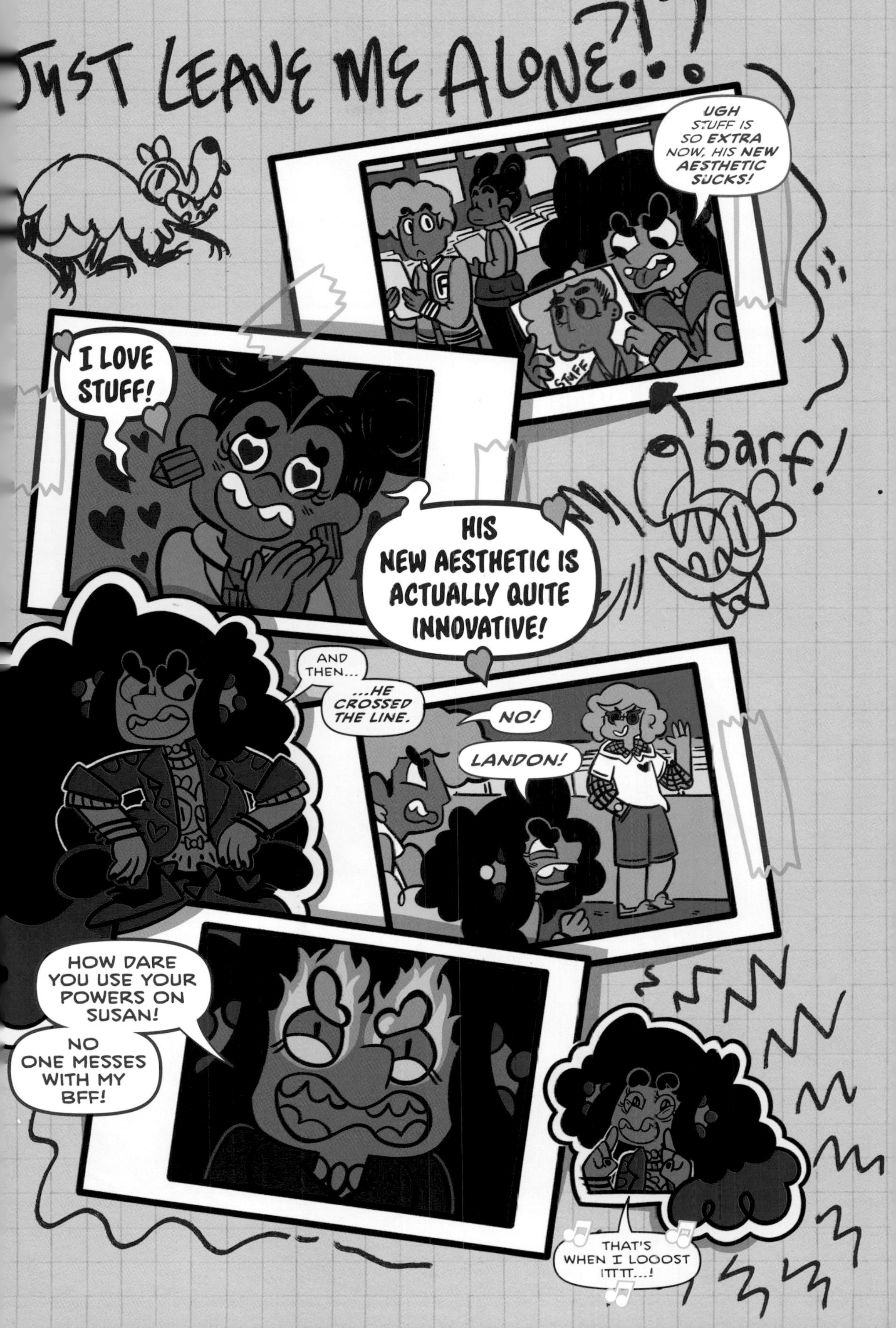

JUST LEAVE ME ALONE?!?
UGH STUFF IS SO EXTRA NOW, HIS NEW AESTHETIC SUCKS!
STUFF
barf!
I LOVE STUFF!
HIS NEW AESTHETIC IS ACTUALLY QUITE INNOVATIVE!
AND THEN...
...HE CROSSED THE LINE.
NO!
LANDON!
HOW DARE YOU USE YOUR POWERS ON SUSAN!
NO ONE MESSES WITH MY BFF!
THAT'S WHEN I LOOOST ITTTT...!

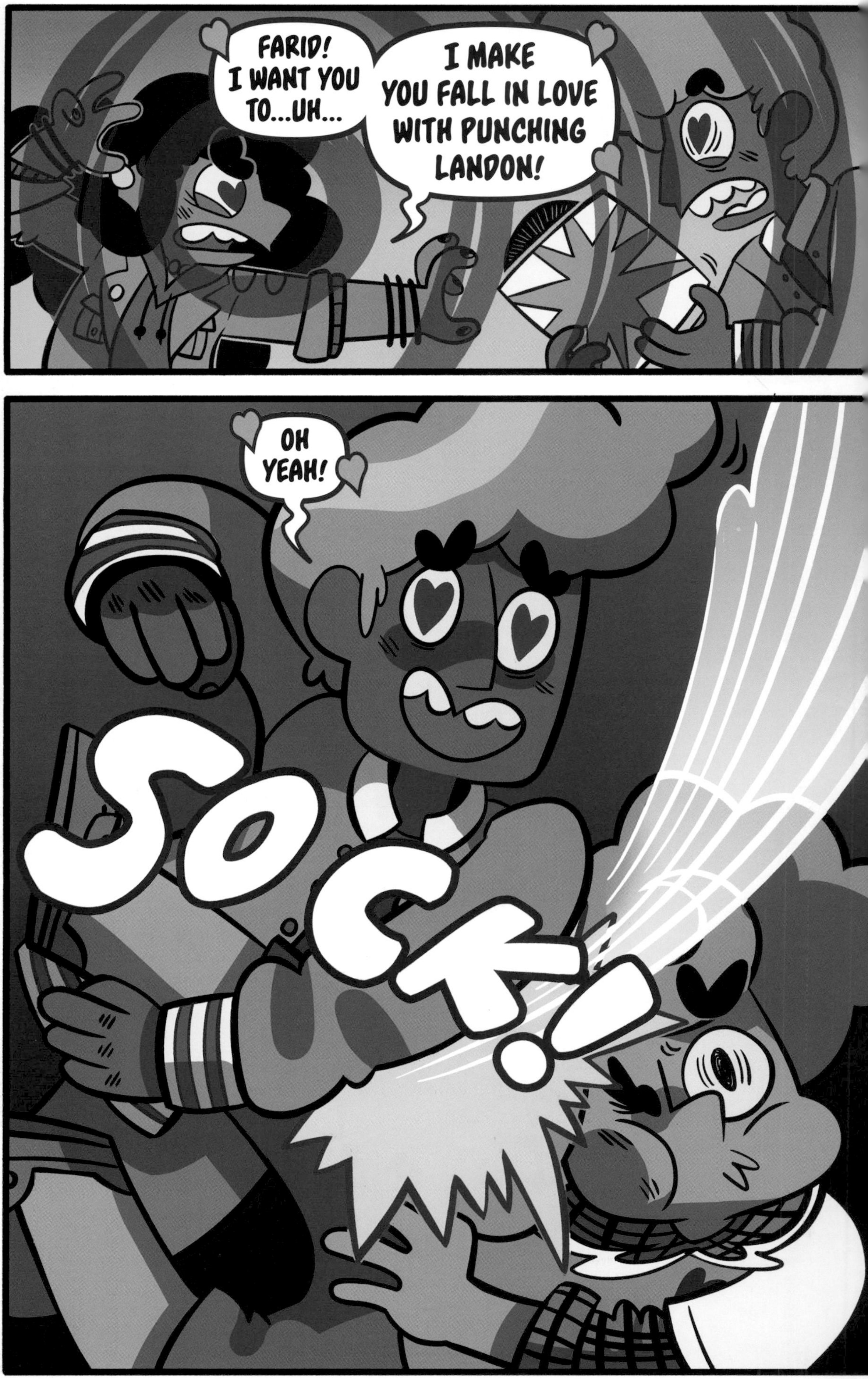
FARID! I WANT YOU TO...UH...
I MAKE YOU FALL IN LOVE WITH PUNCHING LANDON!
OH YEAH!
SOCK!

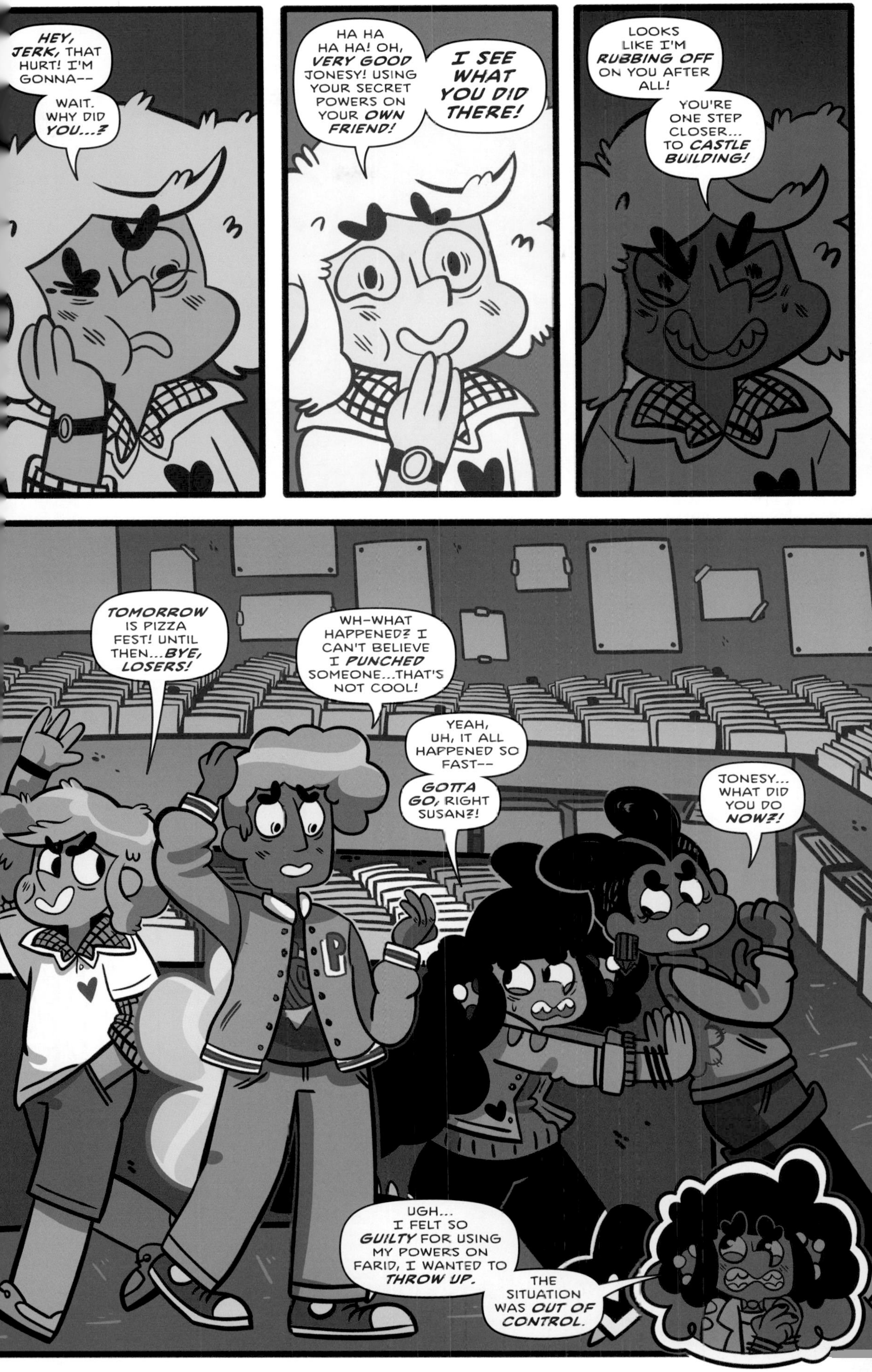

HEY, JERK, THAT HURT! I'M GONNA--
WAIT. WHY DID YOU...?
HA HA HA HA! OH, VERY GOOD JONESY! USING YOUR SECRET POWERS ON YOUR OWN FRIEND!
I SEE WHAT YOU DID THERE!
LOOKS LIKE I'M RUBBING OFF ON YOU AFTER ALL!
YOU'RE ONE STEP CLOSER... TO CASTLE BUILDING!
TOMORROW IS PIZZA FEST! UNTIL THEN...BYE, LOSERS!
WH-WHAT HAPPENED? I CAN'T BELIEVE I PUNCHED SOMEONE...THAT'S NOT COOL!
YEAH, UH, IT ALL HAPPENED SO FAST--
GOTTA GO, RIGHT SUSAN?!
JONESY... WHAT DID YOU DO NOW?!
UGH... I FELT SO GUILTY FOR USING MY POWERS ON FARID, I WANTED TO THROW UP.
THE SITUATION WAS OUT OF CONTROL.

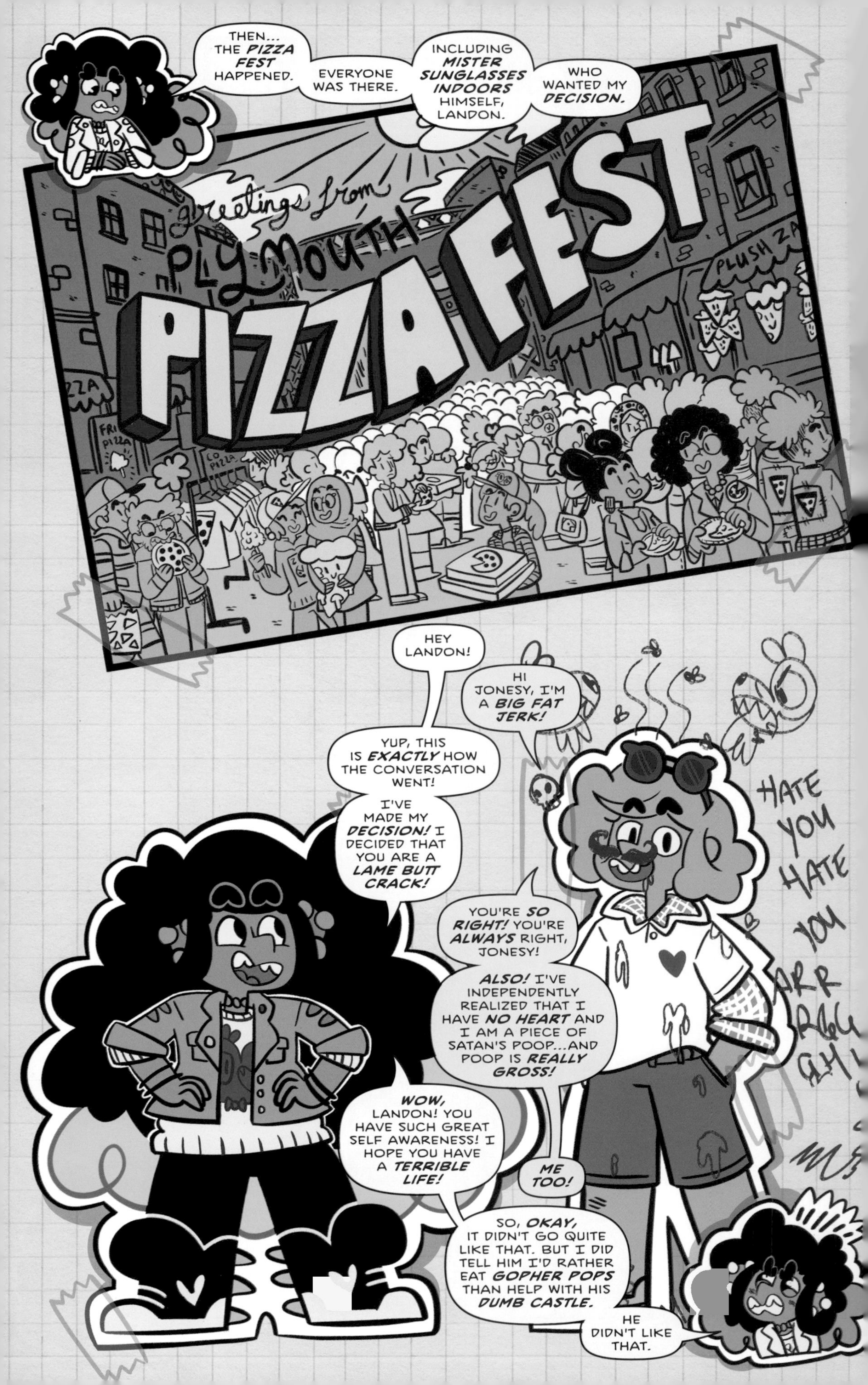
THEN... THE *PIZZA FEST* HAPPENED.
EVERYONE WAS THERE.
INCLUDING *MISTER SUNGLASSES INDOORS* HIMSELF, LANDON.
WHO WANTED MY *DECISION.*
greetings from PLYMOUTH PIZZA FEST
PLUSH ZA
HEY LANDON!
HI JONESY, I'M A *BIG FAT JERK!*
YUP, THIS IS *EXACTLY* HOW THE CONVERSATION WENT!
I'VE MADE MY *DECISION!* I DECIDED THAT YOU ARE A *LAME BUTT CRACK!*
YOU'RE *SO RIGHT!* YOU'RE *ALWAYS* RIGHT, JONESY!
ALSO! I'VE INDEPENDENTLY REALIZED THAT I HAVE *NO HEART* AND I AM A PIECE OF SATAN'S POOP...AND POOP IS *REALLY GROSS!*
WOW, LANDON! YOU HAVE SUCH GREAT SELF AWARENESS! I HOPE YOU HAVE A *TERRIBLE LIFE!*
ME TOO!
HATE YOU HATE YOU
SO, *OKAY,* IT DIDN'T GO QUITE LIKE THAT. BUT I DID TELL HIM I'D RATHER EAT *GOPHER POPS* THAN HELP WITH HIS *DUMB CASTLE.*
HE DIDN'T LIKE THAT.

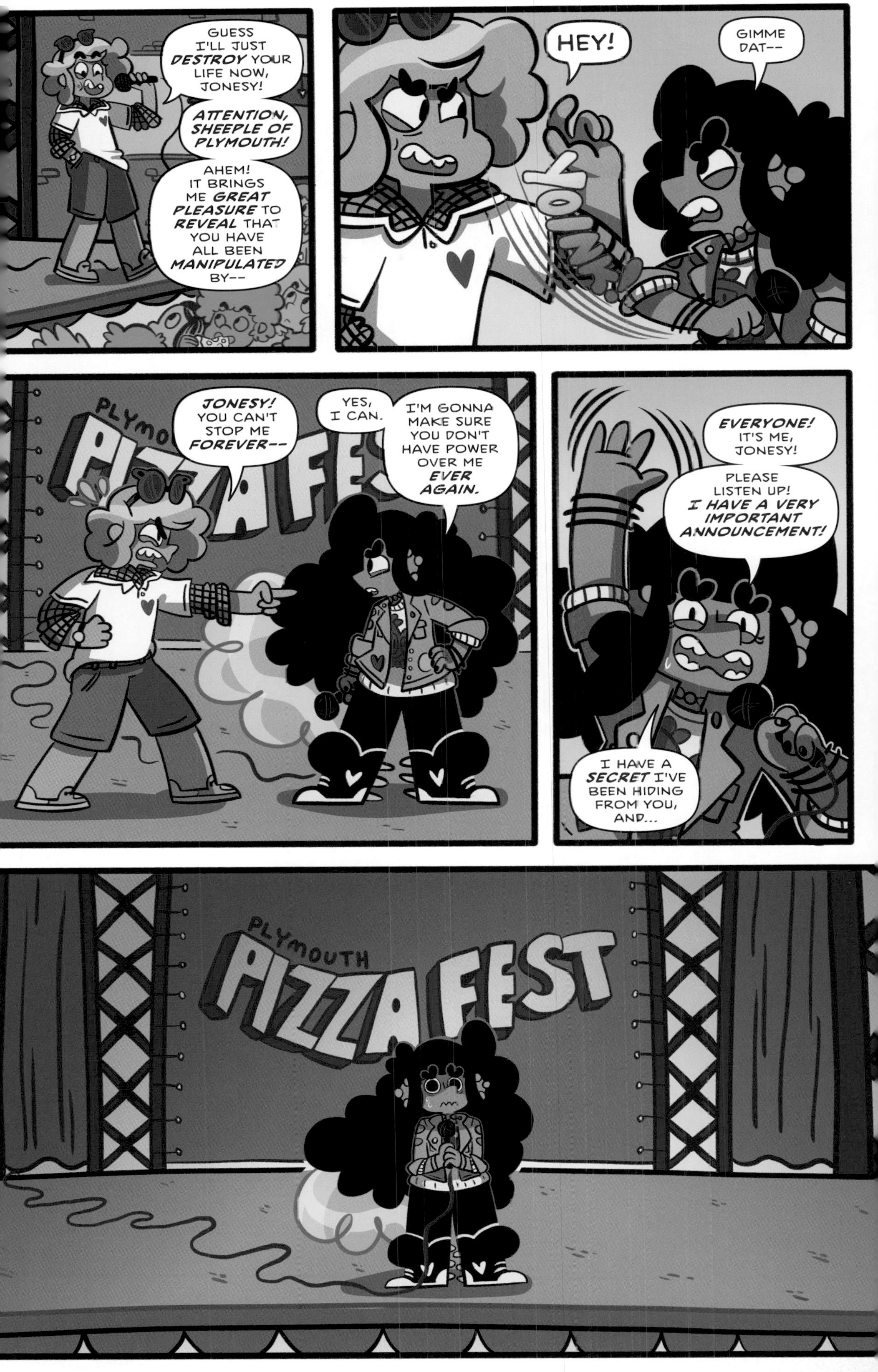
GUESS I'LL JUST DESTROY YOUR LIFE NOW, JONESY!
ATTENTION, SHEEPLE OF PLYMOUTH!
AHEM! IT BRINGS ME GREAT PLEASURE TO REVEAL THAT YOU HAVE ALL BEEN MANIPULATED BY--
HEY!
GIMME DAT--
YOINK!
PLYMOUTH PIZZA FEST
JONESY! YOU CAN'T STOP ME FOREVER--
YES, I CAN.
I'M GONNA MAKE SURE YOU DON'T HAVE POWER OVER ME EVER AGAIN.
EVERYONE! IT'S ME, JONESY!
PLEASE LISTEN UP! I HAVE A VERY IMPORTANT ANNOUNCEMENT!
I HAVE A SECRET I'VE BEEN HIDING FROM YOU, AND...
PLYMOUTH PIZZA FEST

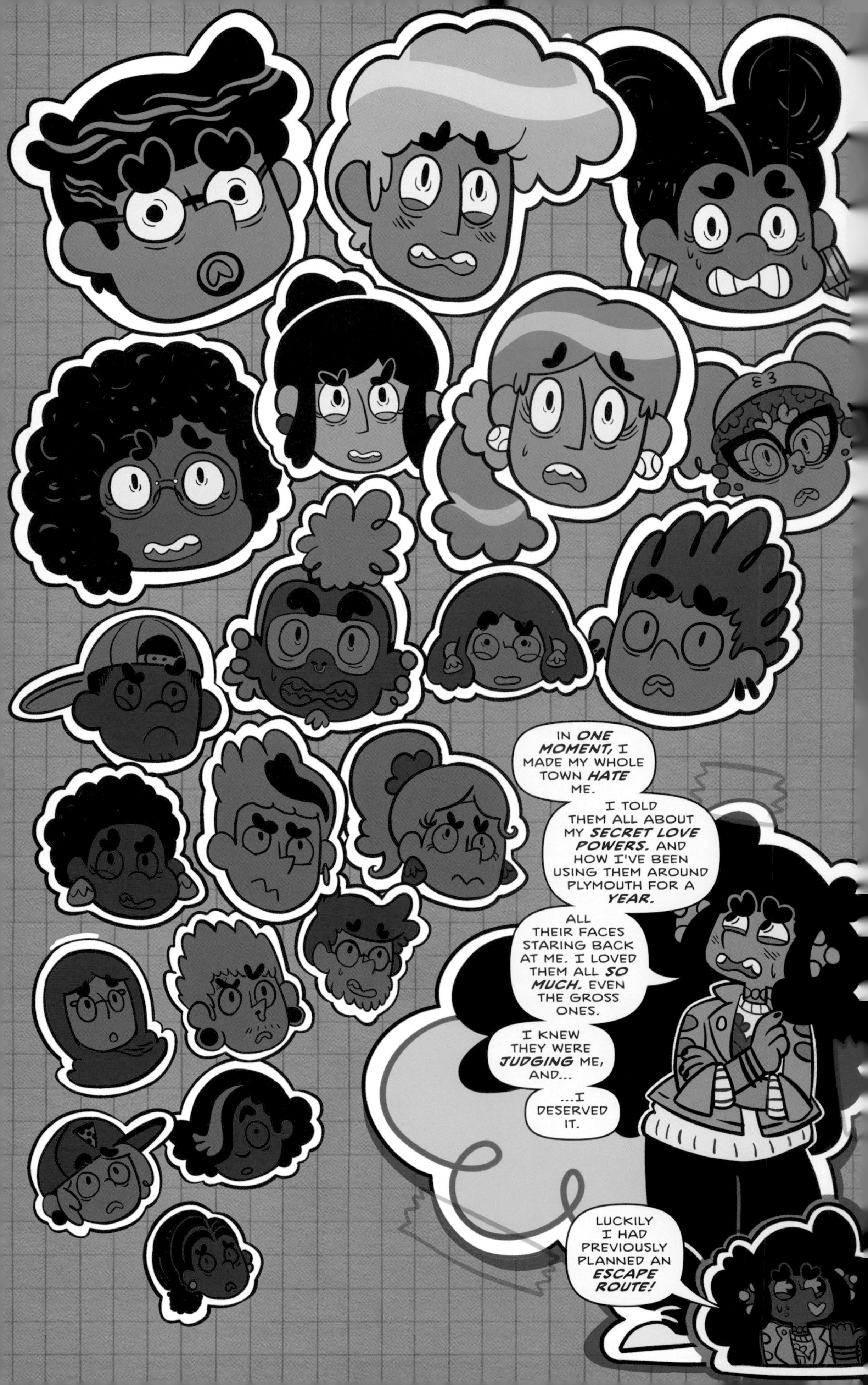

IN ONE MOMENT, I MADE MY WHOLE TOWN HATE ME.
I TOLD THEM ALL ABOUT MY SECRET LOVE POWERS. AND HOW I'VE BEEN USING THEM AROUND PLYMOUTH FOR A YEAR.
ALL THEIR FACES STARING BACK AT ME. I LOVED THEM ALL SO MUCH. EVEN THE GROSS ONES.
I KNEW THEY WERE JUDGING ME, AND...
...I DESERVED IT.
LUCKILY I HAD PREVIOUSLY PLANNED AN ESCAPE ROUTE!

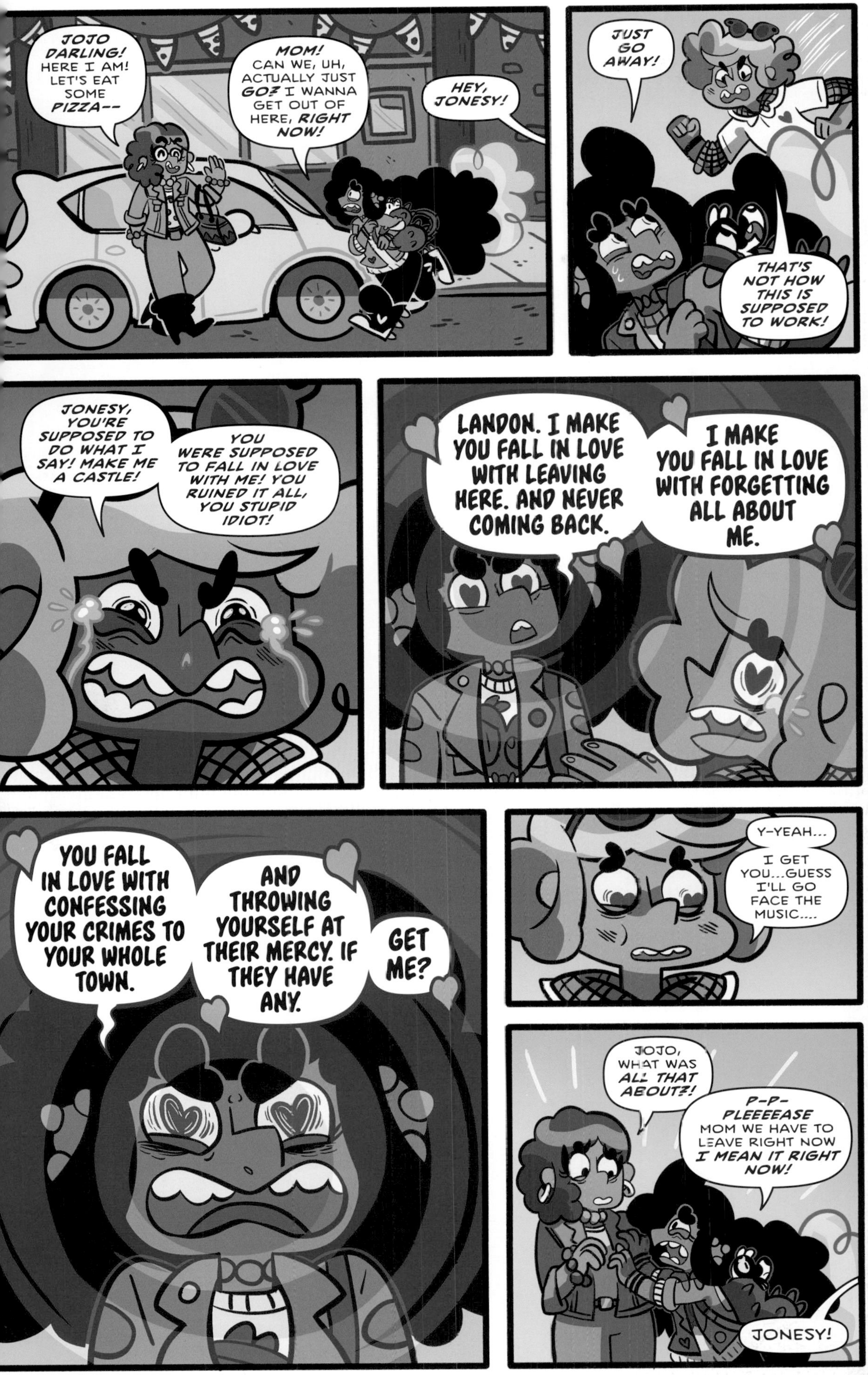
JOJO DARLING! HERE I AM! LET'S EAT SOME PIZZA--
MOM! CAN WE, UH, ACTUALLY JUST GO? I WANNA GET OUT OF HERE, RIGHT NOW!
HEY, JONESY!
JUST GO AWAY!
THAT'S NOT HOW THIS IS SUPPOSED TO WORK!
JONESY, YOU'RE SUPPOSED TO DO WHAT I SAY! MAKE ME A CASTLE!
YOU WERE SUPPOSED TO FALL IN LOVE WITH ME! YOU RUINED IT ALL, YOU STUPID IDIOT!
LANDON. I MAKE YOU FALL IN LOVE WITH LEAVING HERE. AND NEVER COMING BACK.
I MAKE YOU FALL IN LOVE WITH FORGETTING ALL ABOUT ME.
YOU FALL IN LOVE WITH CONFESSING YOUR CRIMES TO YOUR WHOLE TOWN.
AND THROWING YOURSELF AT THEIR MERCY. IF THEY HAVE ANY.
GET ME?
Y-YEAH...
I GET YOU...GUESS I'LL GO FACE THE MUSIC....
JOJO, WHAT WAS ALL THAT ABOUT?!
P-P-PLEEEEASE MOM WE HAVE TO LEAVE RIGHT NOW I MEAN IT RIGHT NOW!
JONESY!

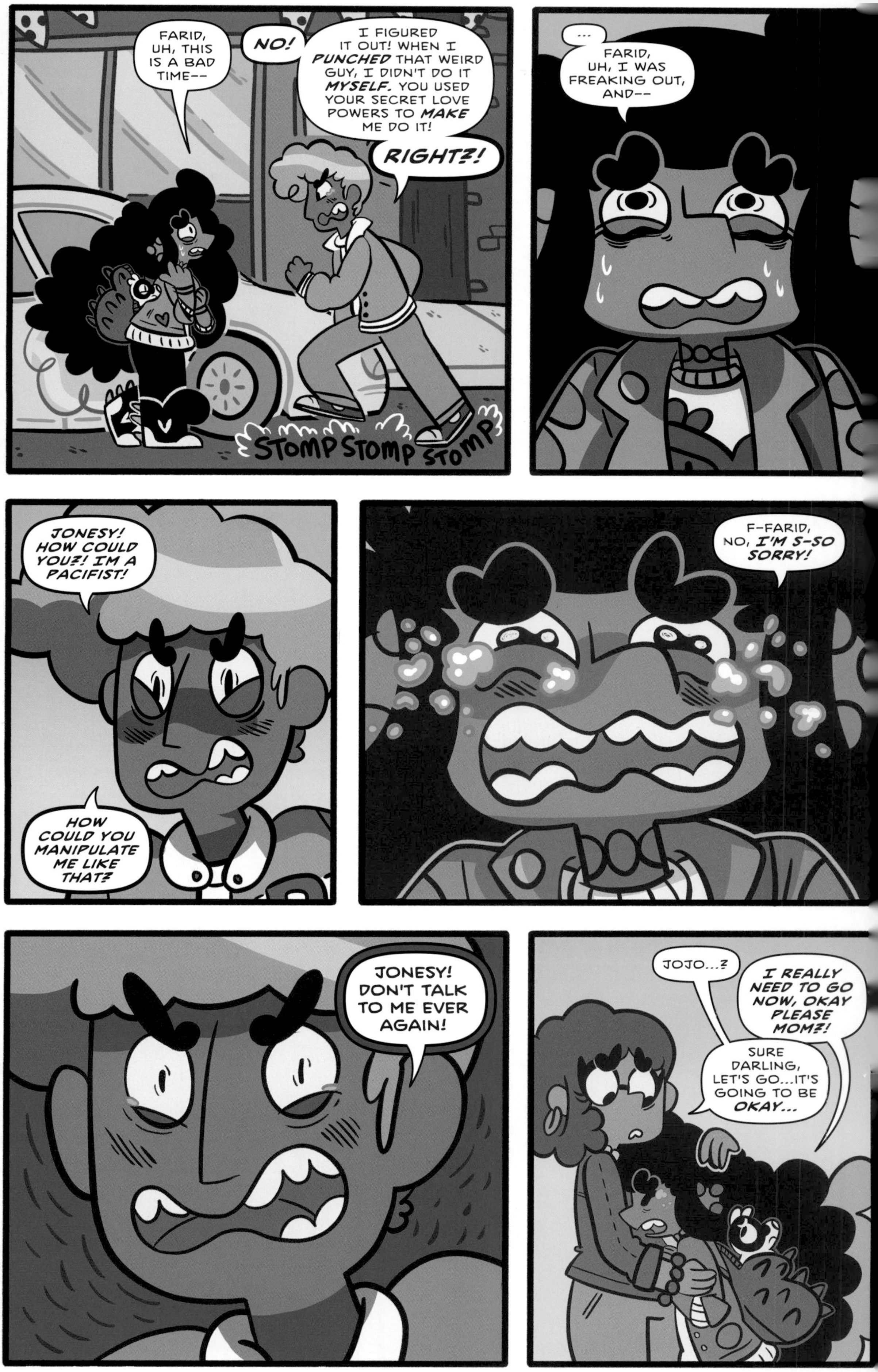
FARID, UH, THIS IS A BAD TIME--
NO!
I FIGURED IT OUT! WHEN I PUNCHED THAT WEIRD GUY, I DIDN'T DO IT MYSELF. YOU USED YOUR SECRET LOVE POWERS TO MAKE ME DO IT!
RIGHT?!
STOMP STOMP STOMP
...
FARID, UH, I WAS FREAKING OUT, AND--
JONESY! HOW COULD YOU?! I'M A PACIFIST!
HOW COULD YOU MANIPULATE ME LIKE THAT?
F-FARID, NO, I'M S-SO SORRY!
JONESY! DON'T TALK TO ME EVER AGAIN!
JOJO...?
I REALLY NEED TO GO NOW, OKAY PLEASE MOM?!
SURE DARLING, LET'S GO...IT'S GOING TO BE OKAY...

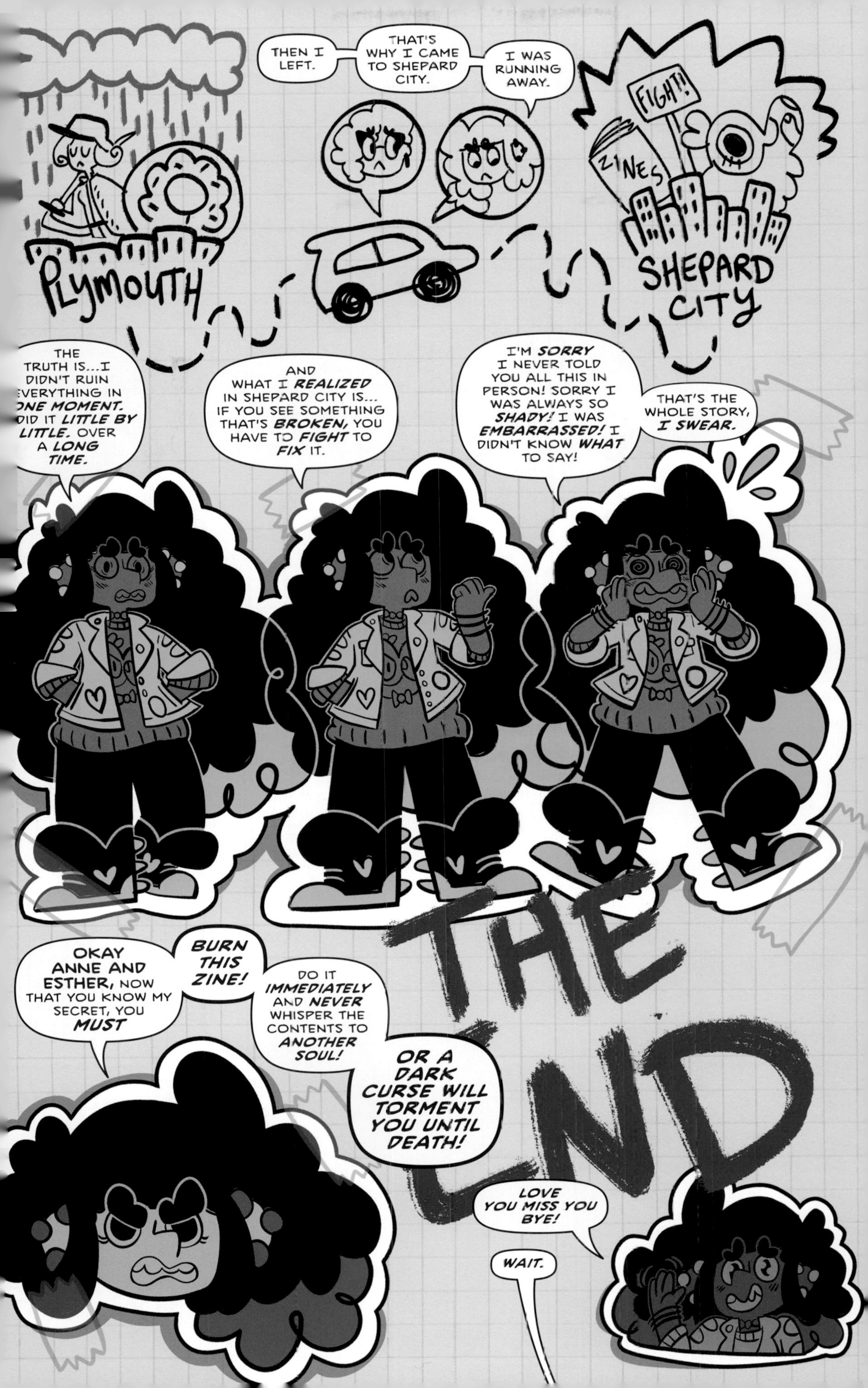
THEN I LEFT.
THAT'S WHY I CAME TO SHEPARD CITY.
I WAS RUNNING AWAY.
PLYMOUTH
FIGHT!
ZINES
SHEPARD CITY
THE TRUTH IS... I DIDN'T RUIN EVERYTHING IN ONE MOMENT. I DID IT LITTLE BY LITTLE. OVER A LONG TIME.
AND WHAT I REALIZED IN SHEPARD CITY IS... IF YOU SEE SOMETHING THAT'S BROKEN, YOU HAVE TO FIGHT TO FIX IT.
I'M SORRY I NEVER TOLD YOU ALL THIS IN PERSON! SORRY I WAS ALWAYS SO SHADY! I WAS EMBARRASSED! I DIDN'T KNOW WHAT TO SAY!
THAT'S THE WHOLE STORY, I SWEAR.
OKAY ANNE AND ESTHER, NOW THAT YOU KNOW MY SECRET, YOU MUST
BURN THIS ZINE!
DO IT IMMEDIATELY AND NEVER WHISPER THE CONTENTS TO ANOTHER SOUL!
OR A DARK CURSE WILL TORMENT YOU UNTIL DEATH!
THE END
LOVE YOU MISS YOU BYE!
WAIT.

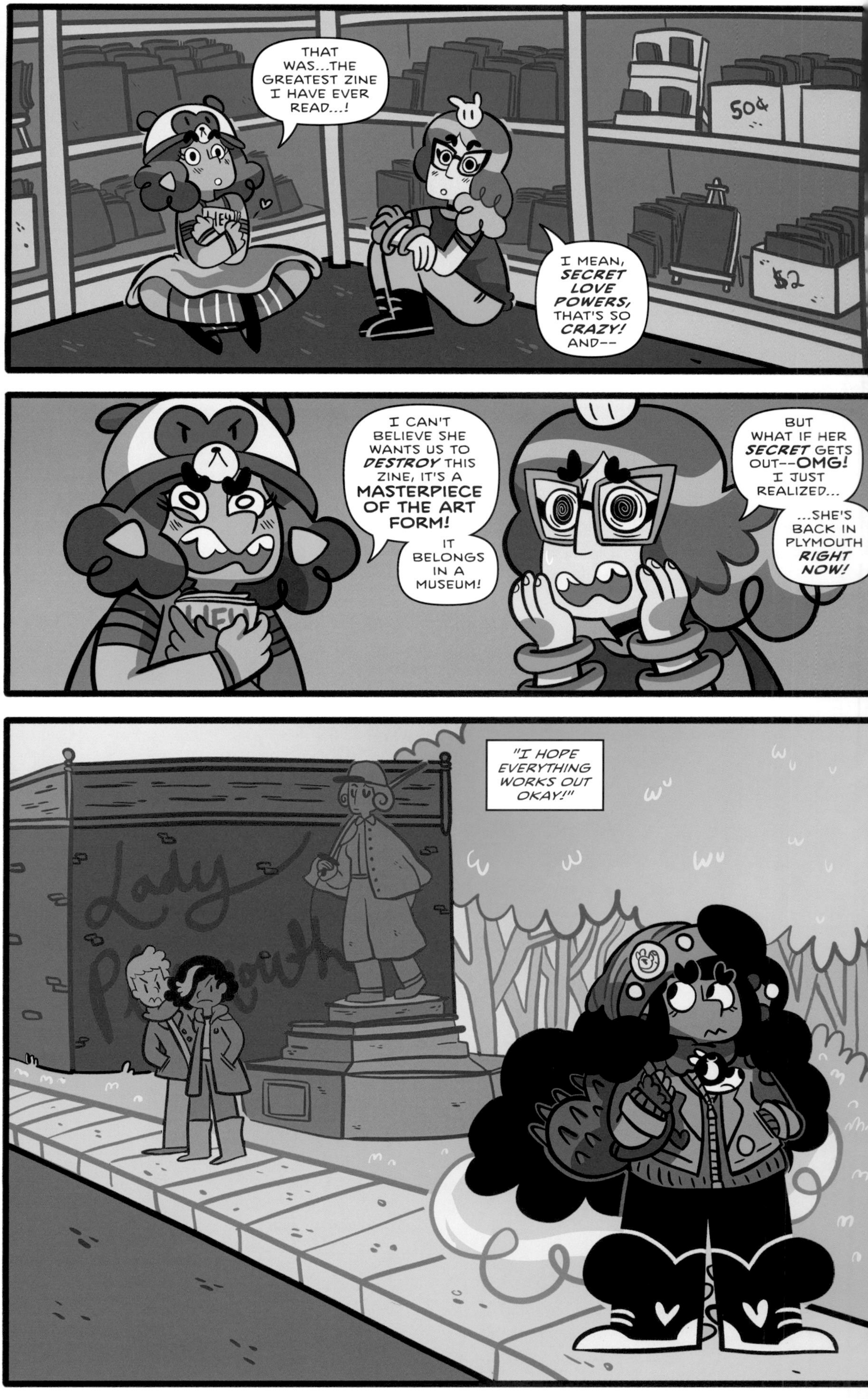
THAT WAS...THE GREATEST ZINE I HAVE EVER READ...!
50¢
$2
I MEAN, SECRET LOVE POWERS, THAT'S SO CRAZY! AND--
I CAN'T BELIEVE SHE WANTS US TO DESTROY THIS ZINE, IT'S A MASTERPIECE OF THE ART FORM!
IT BELONGS IN A MUSEUM!
BUT WHAT IF HER SECRET GETS OUT--OMG! I JUST REALIZED...
...SHE'S BACK IN PLYMOUTH RIGHT NOW!
"I HOPE EVERYTHING WORKS OUT OKAY!"

CHAPTER FOUR

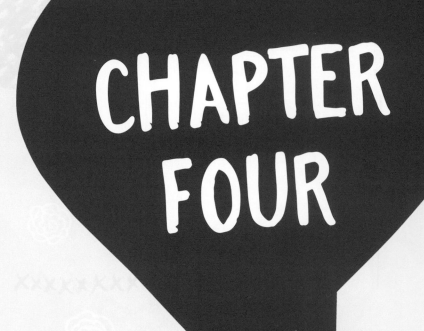

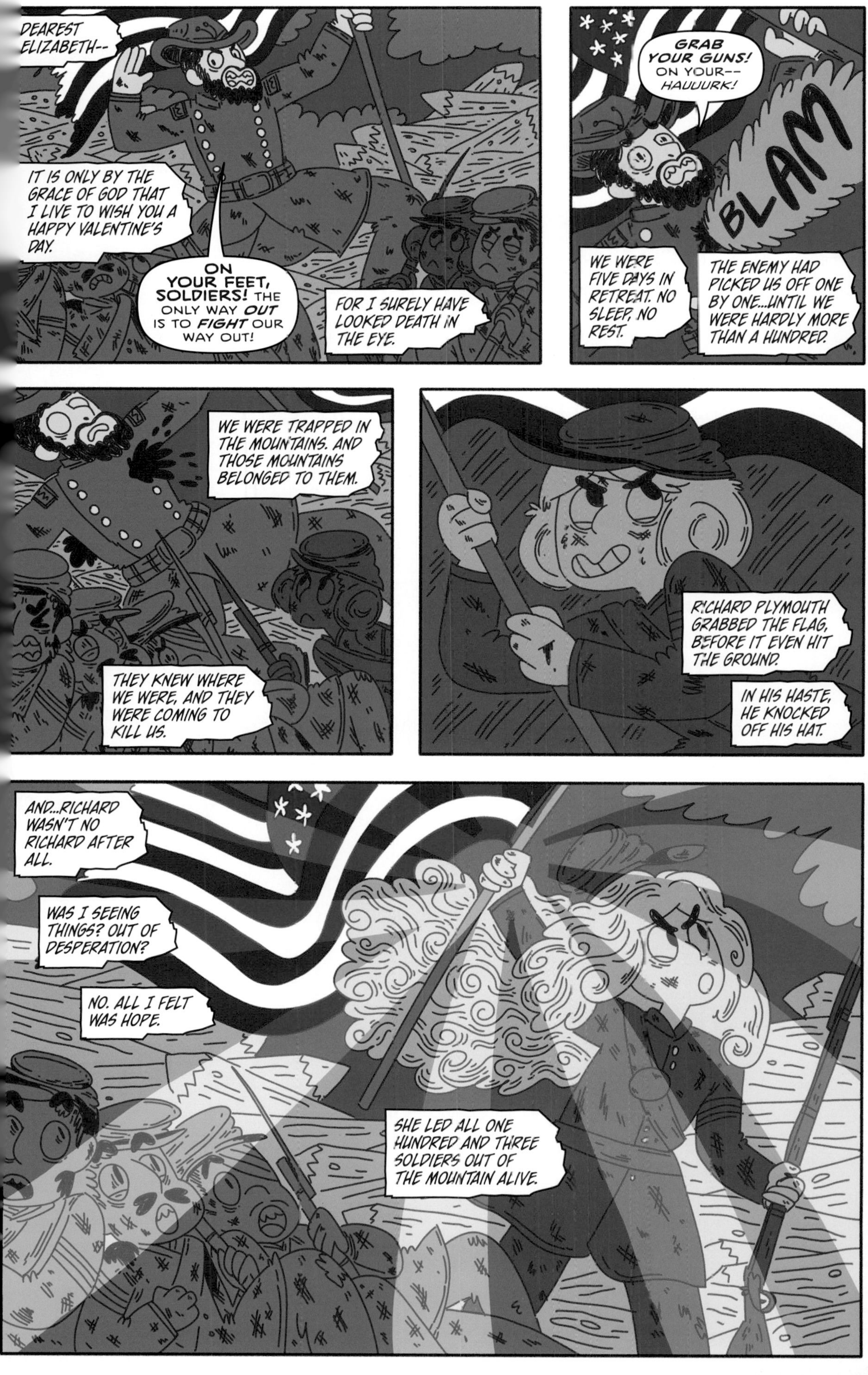
DEAREST ELIZABETH--
IT IS ONLY BY THE GRACE OF GOD THAT I LIVE TO WISH YOU A HAPPY VALENTINE'S DAY.
ON YOUR FEET, SOLDIERS! THE ONLY WAY OUT IS TO FIGHT OUR WAY OUT!
FOR I SURELY HAVE LOOKED DEATH IN THE EYE.
GRAB YOUR GUNS! ON YOUR-- HAUUURK!
BLAM
WE WERE FIVE DAYS IN RETREAT. NO SLEEP, NO REST.
THE ENEMY HAD PICKED US OFF ONE BY ONE...UNTIL WE WERE HARDLY MORE THAN A HUNDRED.
WE WERE TRAPPED IN THE MOUNTAINS. AND THOSE MOUNTAINS BELONGED TO THEM.
THEY KNEW WHERE WE WERE, AND THEY WERE COMING TO KILL US.
RICHARD PLYMOUTH GRABBED THE FLAG, BEFORE IT EVEN HIT THE GROUND.
IN HIS HASTE, HE KNOCKED OFF HIS HAT.
AND...RICHARD WASN'T NO RICHARD AFTER ALL.
WAS I SEEING THINGS? OUT OF DESPERATION?
NO. ALL I FELT WAS HOPE.
SHE LED ALL ONE HUNDRED AND THREE SOLDIERS OUT OF THE MOUNTAIN ALIVE.

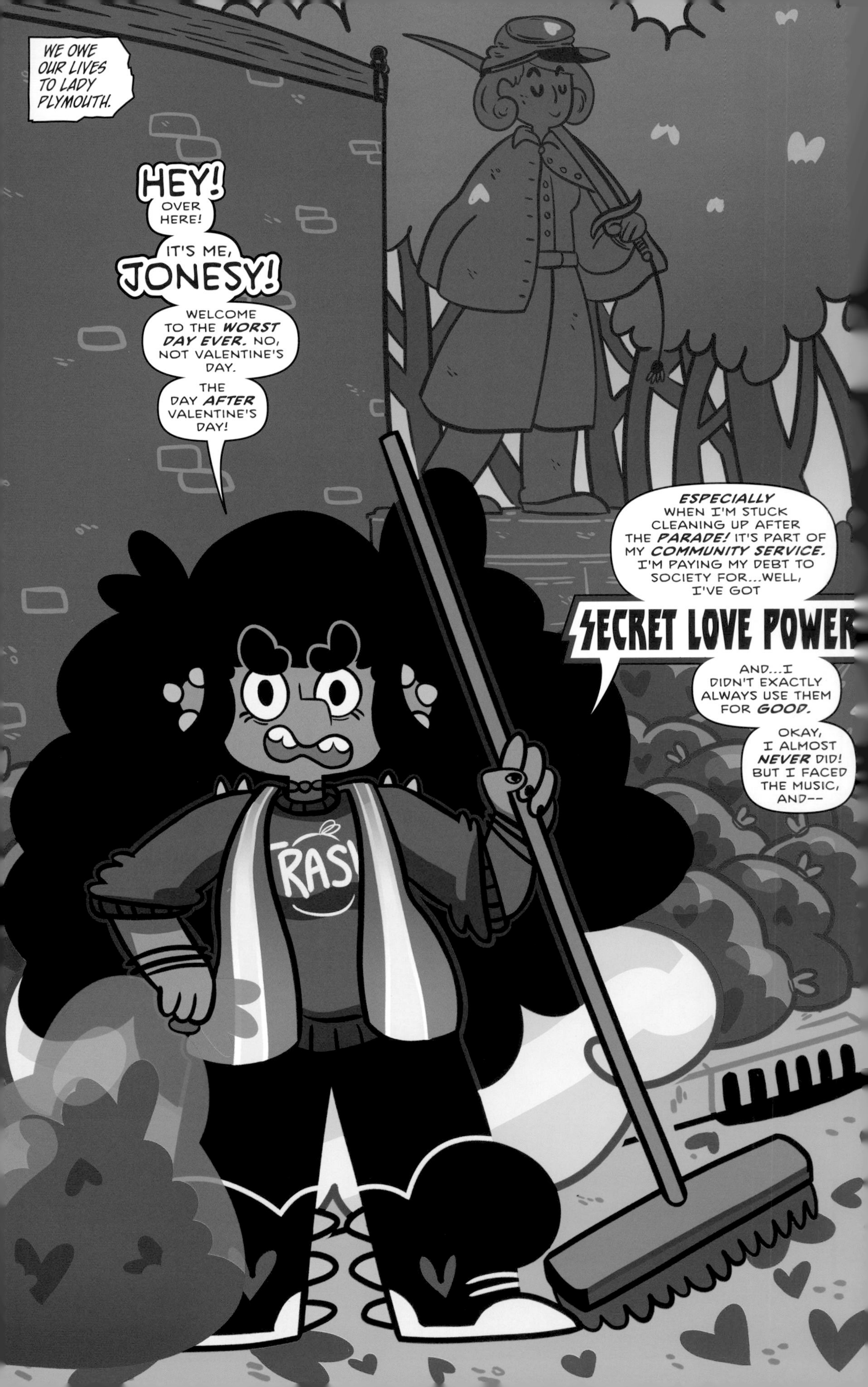

WE OWE OUR LIVES TO LADY PLYMOUTH.
HEY! OVER HERE!
IT'S ME, JONESY!
WELCOME TO THE WORST DAY EVER. NO, NOT VALENTINE'S DAY.
THE DAY AFTER VALENTINE'S DAY!
ESPECIALLY WHEN I'M STUCK CLEANING UP AFTER THE PARADE! IT'S PART OF MY COMMUNITY SERVICE. I'M PAYING MY DEBT TO SOCIETY FOR...WELL, I'VE GOT
SECRET LOVE POWER
AND...I DIDN'T EXACTLY ALWAYS USE THEM FOR GOOD.
OKAY, I ALMOST NEVER DID! BUT I FACED THE MUSIC, AND--
TRASH

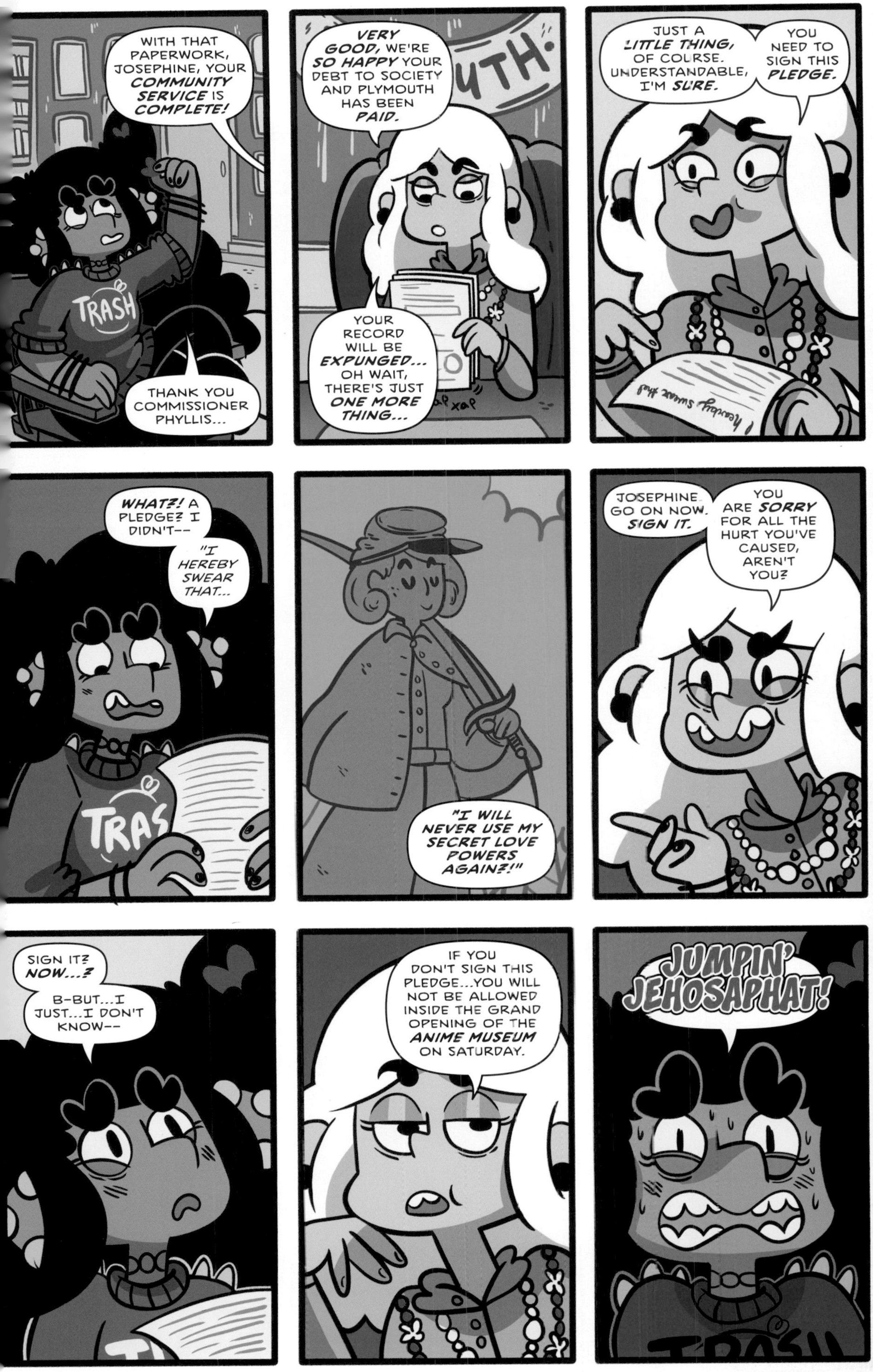
WITH THAT PAPERWORK, JOSEPHINE, YOUR COMMUNITY SERVICE IS COMPLETE!
THANK YOU COMMISSIONER PHYLLIS...
VERY GOOD, WE'RE SO HAPPY YOUR DEBT TO SOCIETY AND PLYMOUTH HAS BEEN PAID.
YOUR RECORD WILL BE EXPUNGED... OH WAIT, THERE'S JUST ONE MORE THING...
JUST A LITTLE THING, OF COURSE. UNDERSTANDABLE, I'M SURE.
YOU NEED TO SIGN THIS PLEDGE.
WHAT?! A PLEDGE? I DIDN'T--
"I HEREBY SWEAR THAT...
"I WILL NEVER USE MY SECRET LOVE POWERS AGAIN?!"
JOSEPHINE. GO ON NOW. SIGN IT.
YOU ARE SORRY FOR ALL THE HURT YOU'VE CAUSED, AREN'T YOU?
SIGN IT? NOW...?
B-BUT...I JUST...I DON'T KNOW--
IF YOU DON'T SIGN THIS PLEDGE...YOU WILL NOT BE ALLOWED INSIDE THE GRAND OPENING OF THE ANIME MUSEUM ON SATURDAY.
JUMPIN' JEHOSAPHAT!

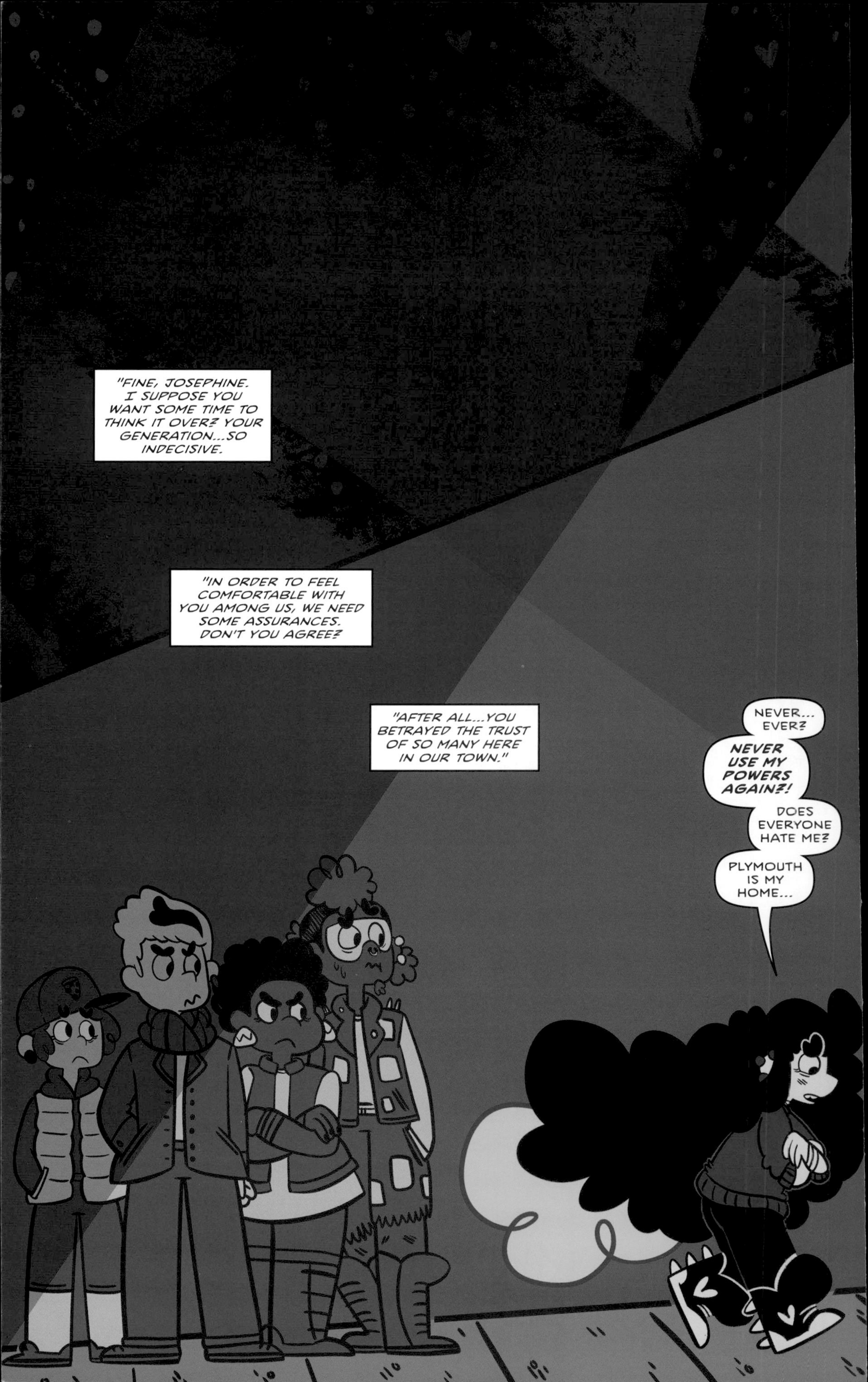
"FINE, JOSEPHINE. I SUPPOSE YOU WANT SOME TIME TO THINK IT OVER? YOUR GENERATION...SO INDECISIVE.
"IN ORDER TO FEEL COMFORTABLE WITH YOU AMONG US, WE NEED SOME ASSURANCES. DON'T YOU AGREE?
"AFTER ALL...YOU BETRAYED THE TRUST OF SO MANY HERE IN OUR TOWN."
NEVER... EVER?
NEVER USE MY POWERS AGAIN?!
DOES EVERYONE HATE ME?
PLYMOUTH IS MY HOME...

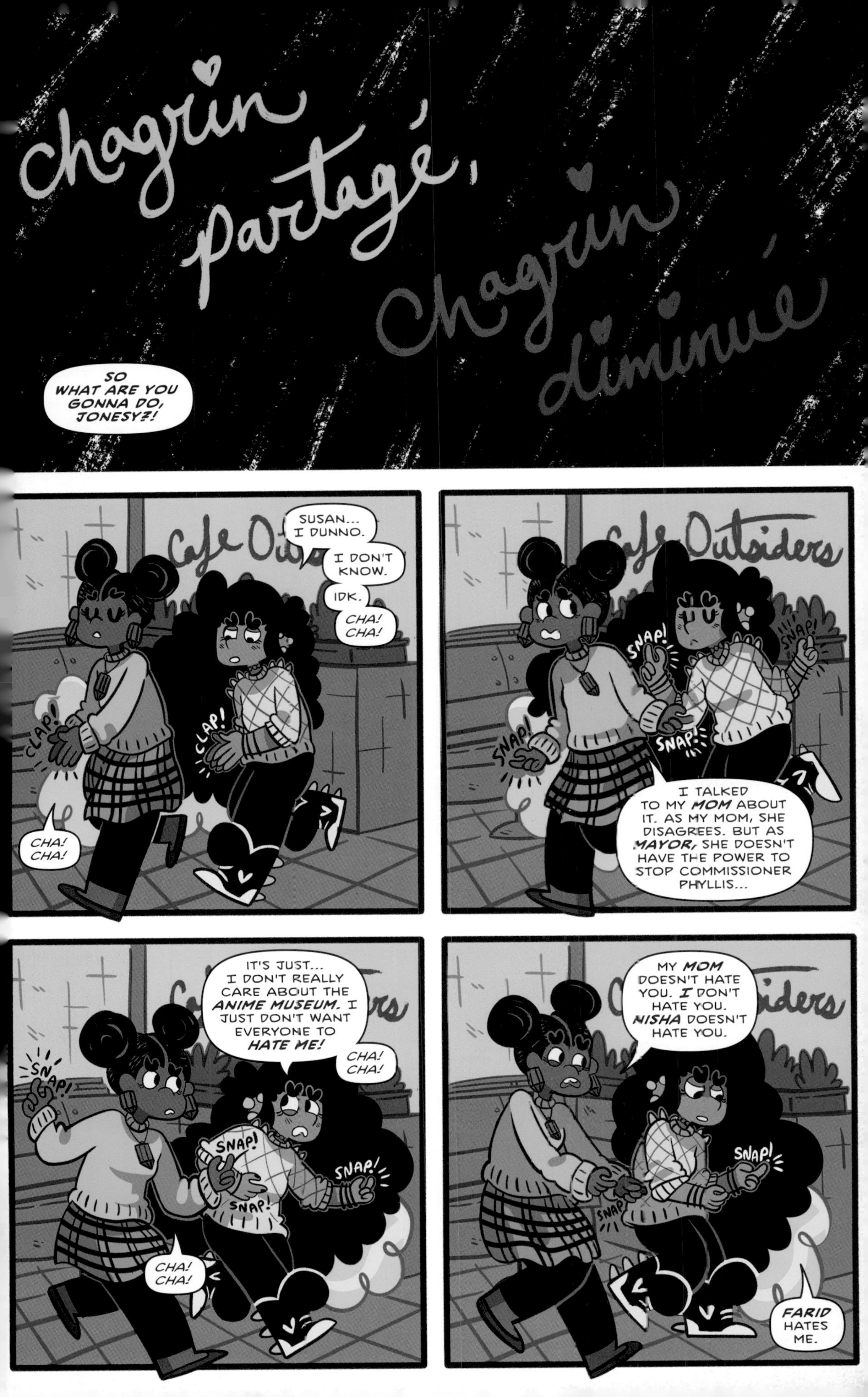
Chagrin partagé, Chagrin diminué
SO WHAT ARE YOU GONNA DO, JONESY?!
SUSAN... I DUNNO.
I DON'T KNOW.
IDK.
CHA! CHA!
CLAP!
CLAP!
CHA! CHA!
Cafe Outsiders
SNAP!
SNAP!
SNAP!
SNAP!
I TALKED TO MY MOM ABOUT IT. AS MY MOM, SHE DISAGREES. BUT AS MAYOR, SHE DOESN'T HAVE THE POWER TO STOP COMMISSIONER PHYLLIS...
SNAP!
IT'S JUST... I DON'T REALLY CARE ABOUT THE ANIME MUSEUM. I JUST DON'T WANT EVERYONE TO HATE ME!
CHA! CHA!
SNAP!
SNAP!
SNAP!
CHA! CHA!
MY MOM DOESN'T HATE YOU. I DON'T HATE YOU. NISHA DOESN'T HATE YOU.
SNAP!
SNAP!
FARID HATES ME.

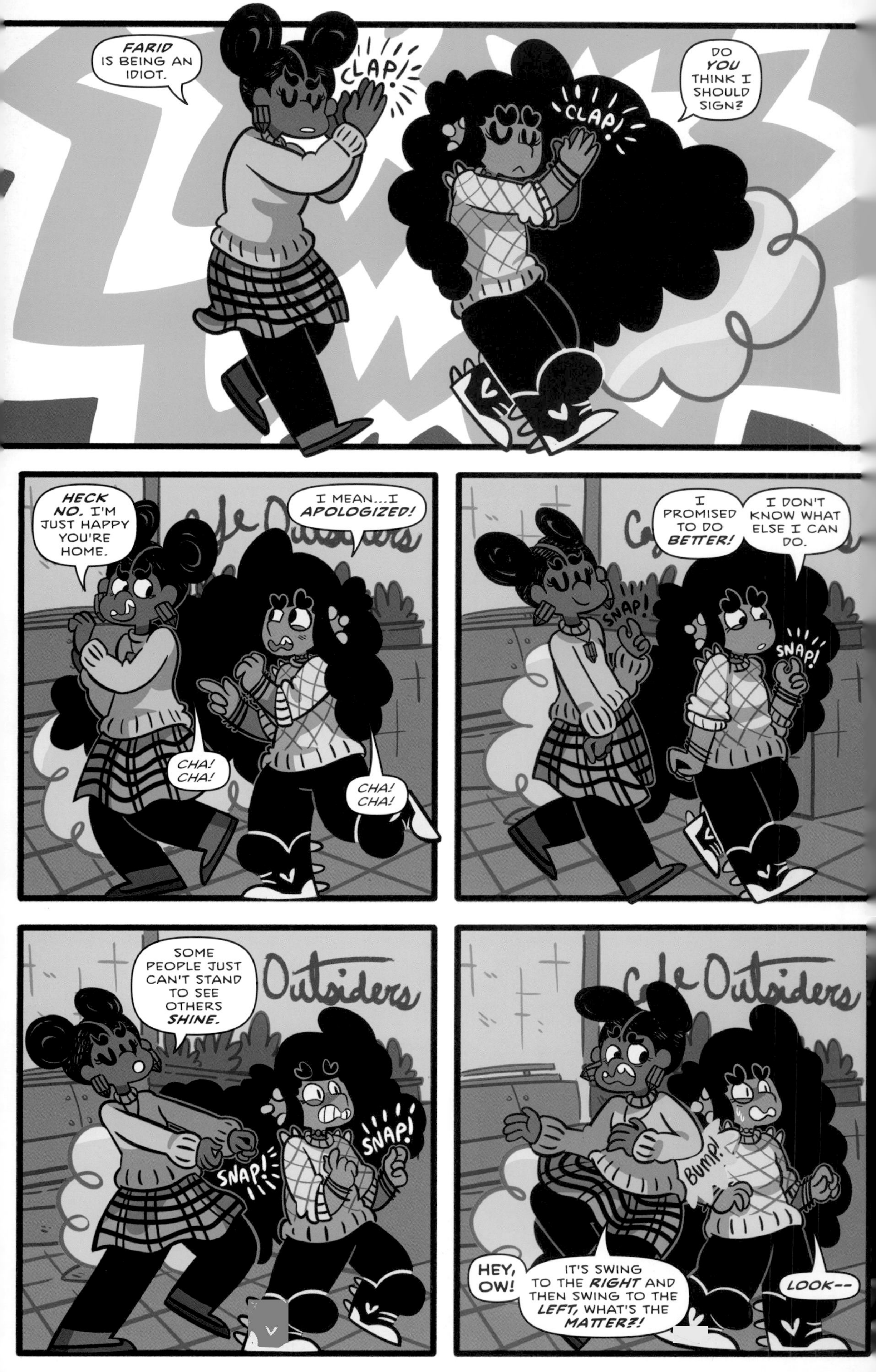
FARID IS BEING AN IDIOT.
CLAP!
CLAP!
DO YOU THINK I SHOULD SIGN?
HECK NO. I'M JUST HAPPY YOU'RE HOME.
I MEAN...I APOLOGIZED!
Cafe Outsiders
CHA! CHA!
CHA! CHA!
I PROMISED TO DO BETTER!
I DON'T KNOW WHAT ELSE I CAN DO.
SNAP!
SNAP!
SOME PEOPLE JUST CAN'T STAND TO SEE OTHERS SHINE.
Outsiders
SNAP!
SNAP!
Cafe Outsiders
BUMP!
HEY, OW!
IT'S SWING TO THE RIGHT AND THEN SWING TO THE LEFT, WHAT'S THE MATTER?!
LOOK--

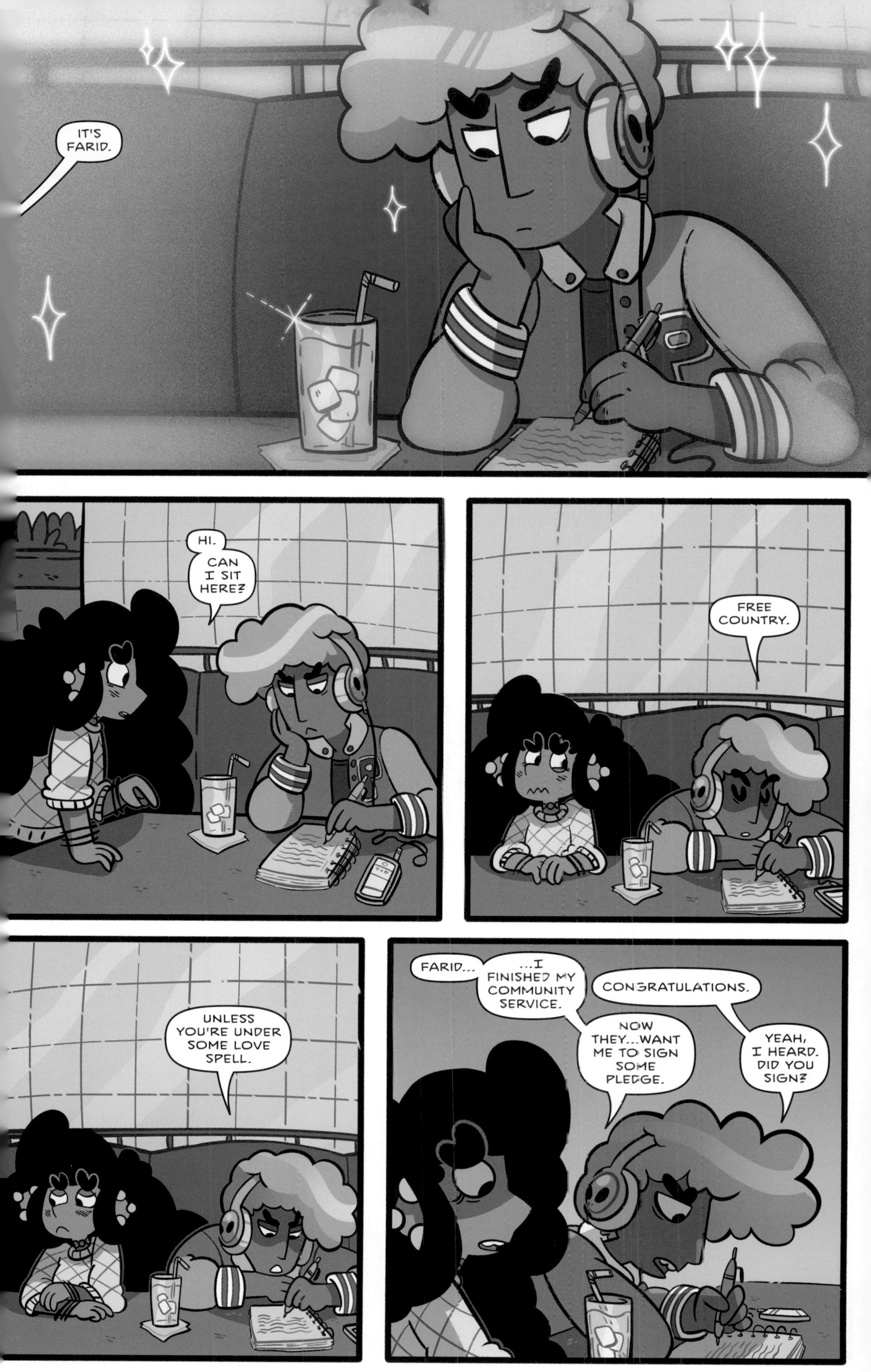
IT'S FARID.
HI.
CAN I SIT HERE?
FREE COUNTRY.
UNLESS YOU'RE UNDER SOME LOVE SPELL.
FARID...
...I FINISHED MY COMMUNITY SERVICE.
NOW THEY...WANT ME TO SIGN SOME PLEDGE.
CONGRATULATIONS.
YEAH, I HEARD. DID YOU SIGN?

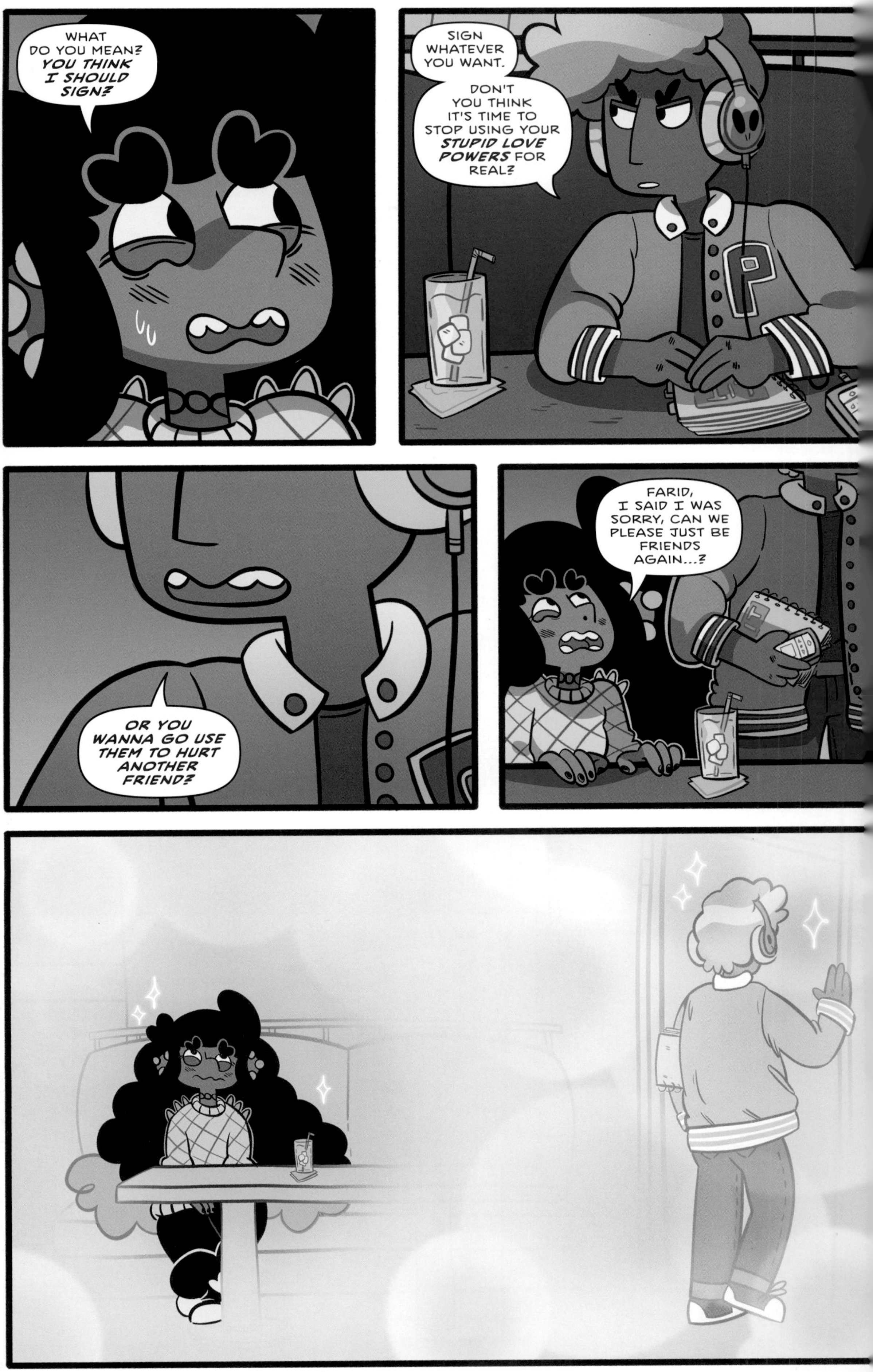

WHAT DO YOU MEAN? YOU THINK I SHOULD SIGN?
SIGN WHATEVER YOU WANT.
DON'T YOU THINK IT'S TIME TO STOP USING YOUR STUPID LOVE POWERS FOR REAL?
OR YOU WANNA GO USE THEM TO HURT ANOTHER FRIEND?
FARID, I SAID I WAS SORRY, CAN WE PLEASE JUST BE FRIENDS AGAIN...?

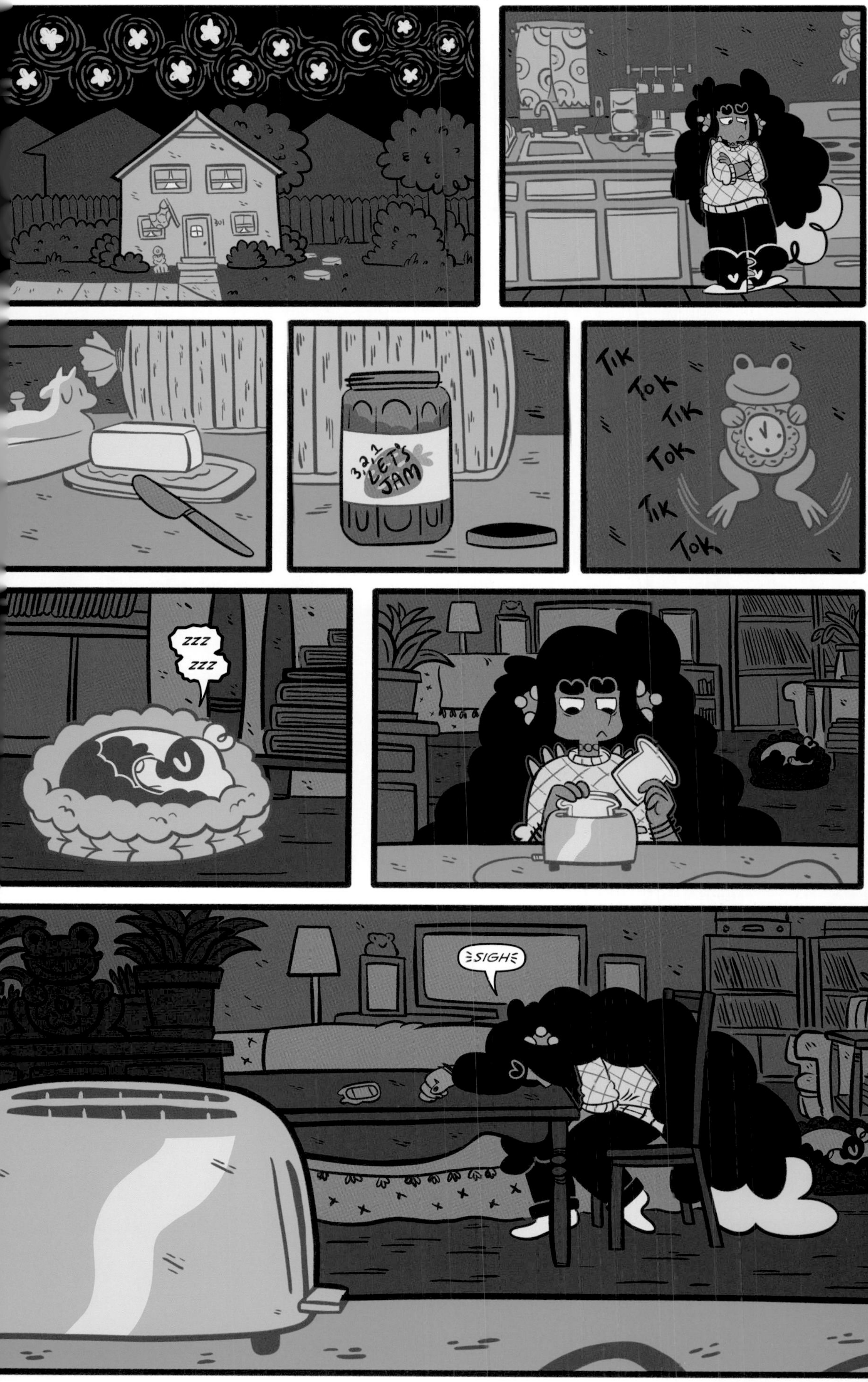
3,2,1 LET'S JAM
TIK
TOK
TIK
TOK
TIK
TOK
ZZZ
ZZZ
SIGH

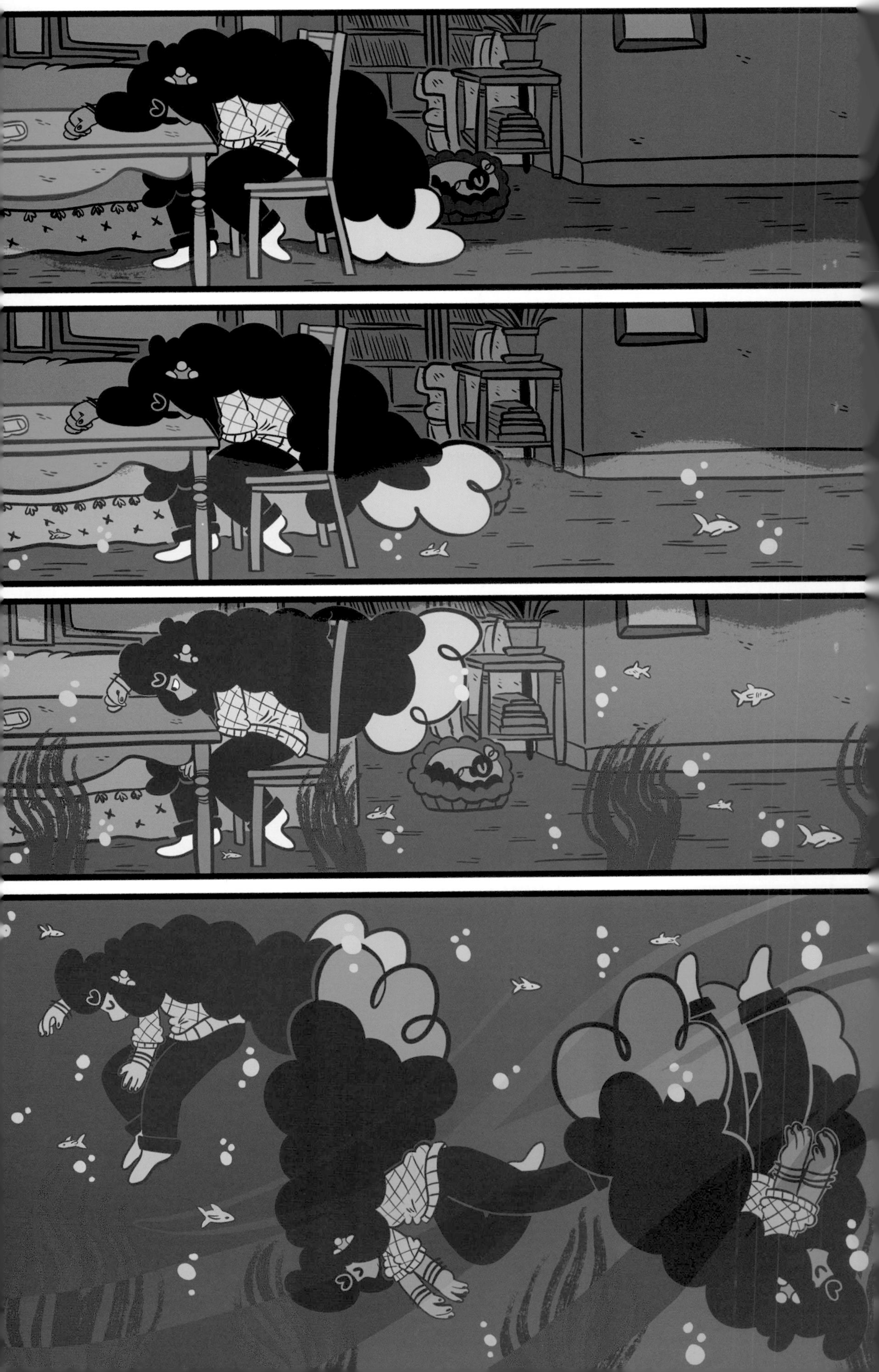

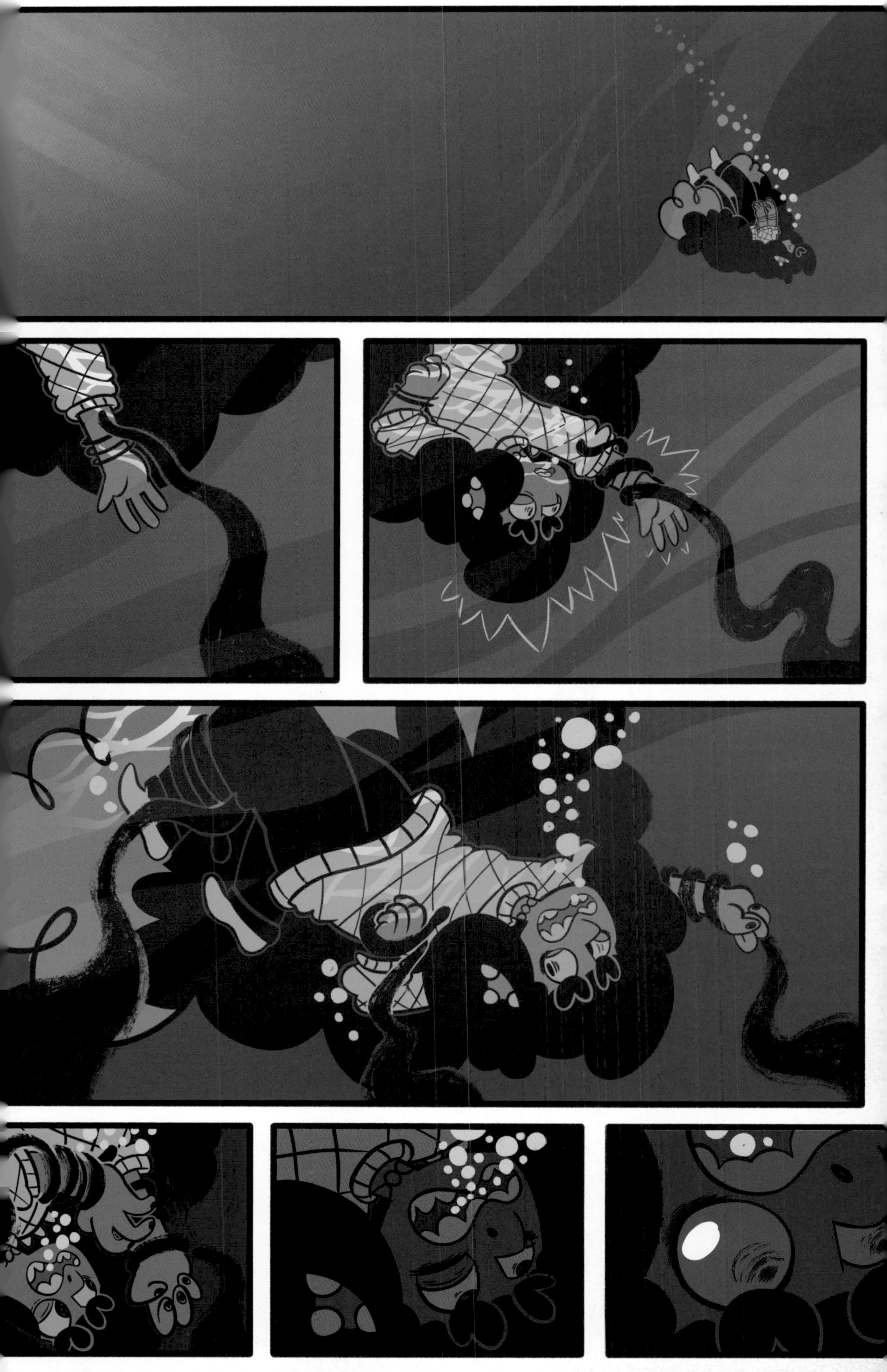

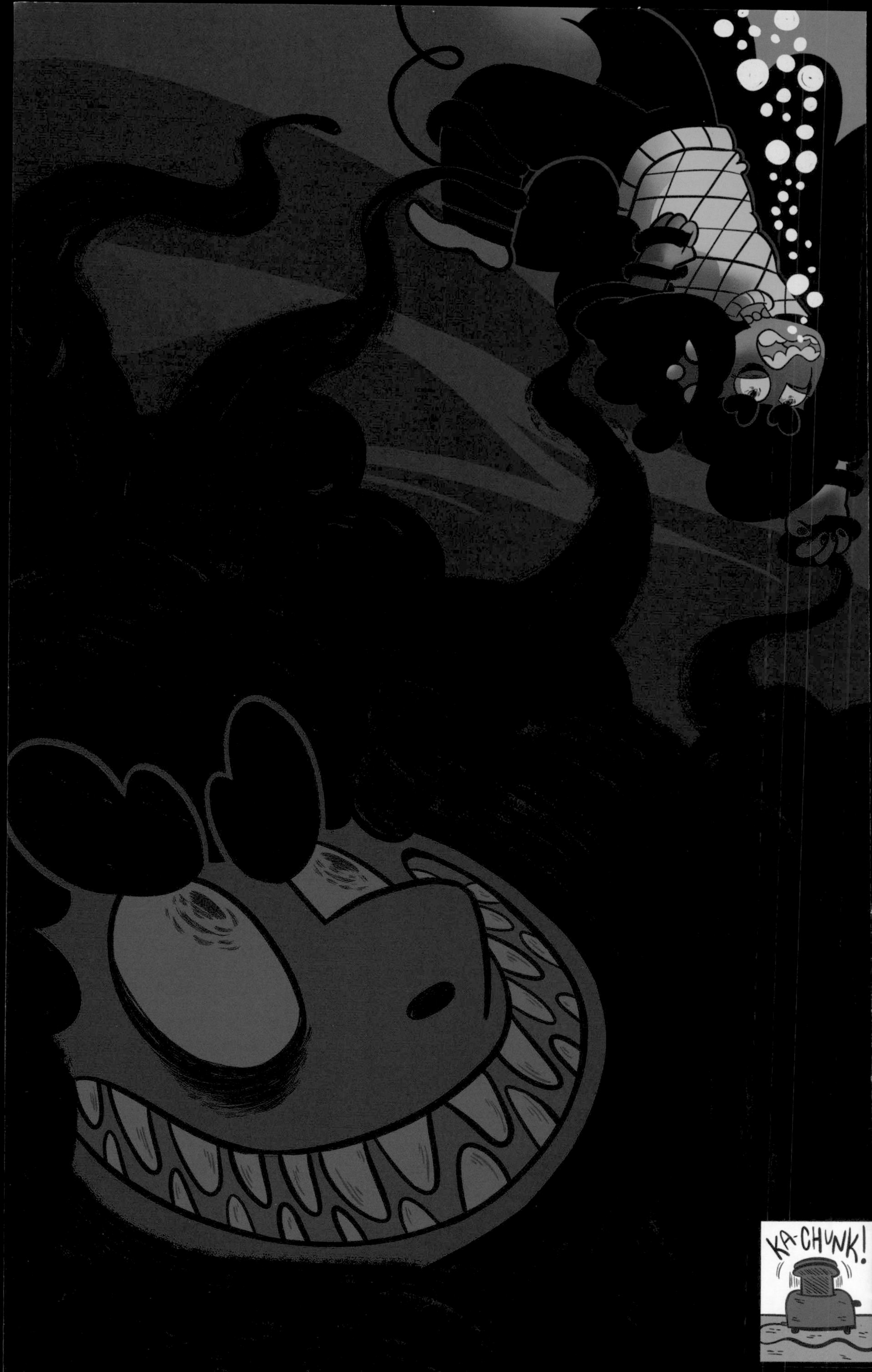
KA-CHUNK!

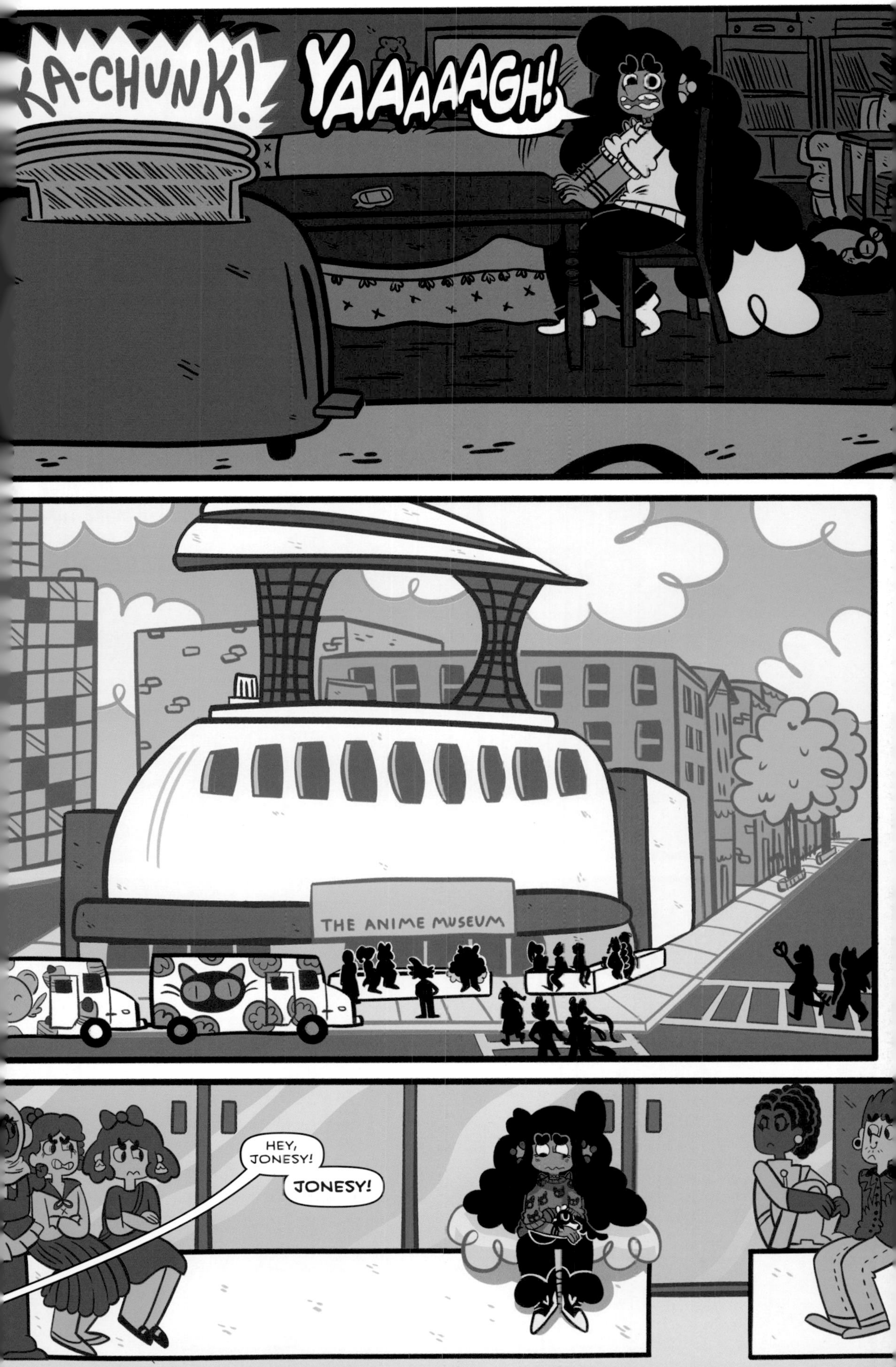
KA-CHUNK!
YAAAAAGH!
THE ANIME MUSEUM
HEY, JONESY!
JONESY!

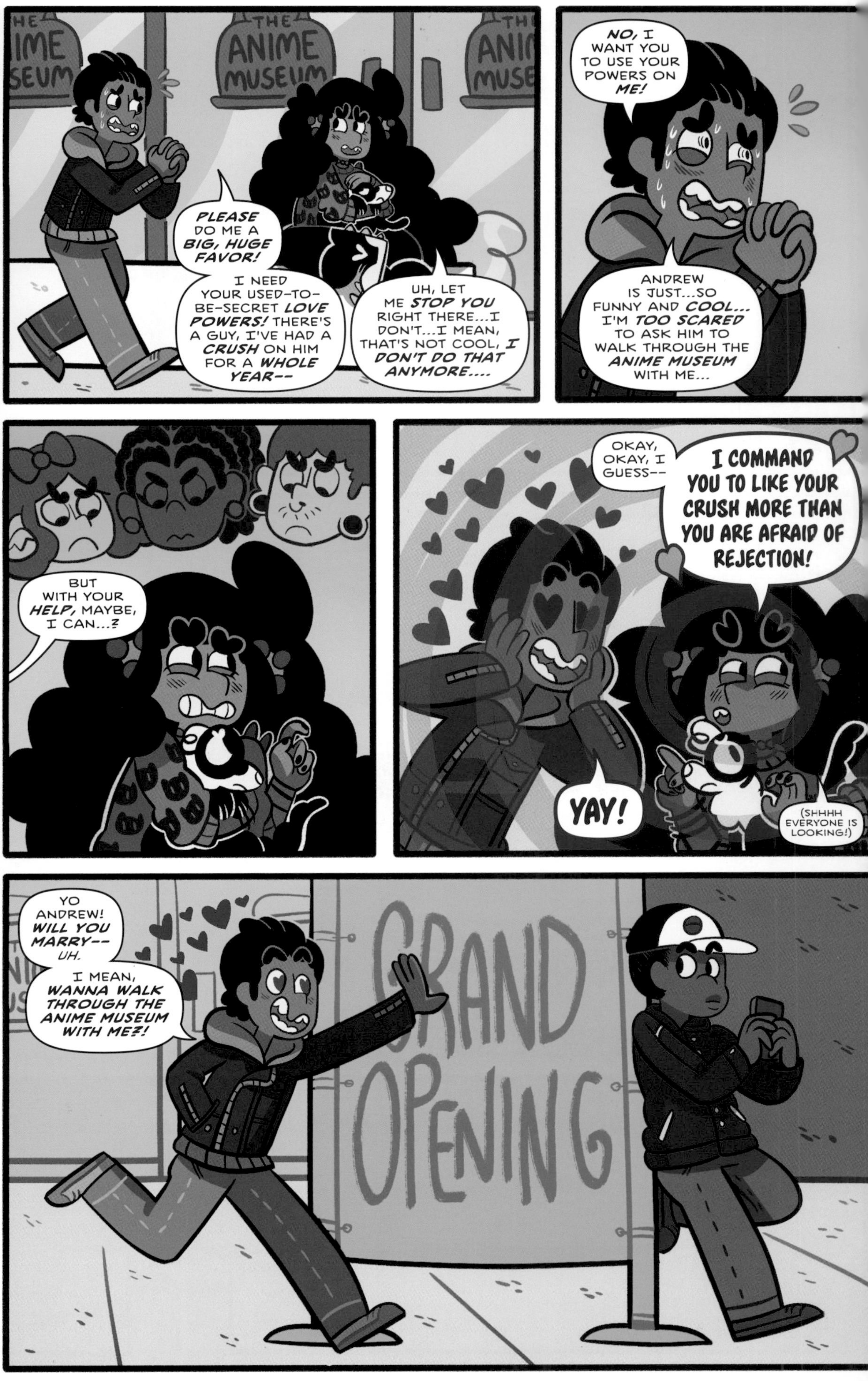

PLEASE DO ME A BIG, HUGE FAVOR!
I NEED YOUR USED-TO-BE-SECRET LOVE POWERS! THERE'S A GUY, I'VE HAD A CRUSH ON HIM FOR A WHOLE YEAR--
UH, LET ME STOP YOU RIGHT THERE...I DON'T...I MEAN, THAT'S NOT COOL, I DON'T DO THAT ANYMORE....
NO, I WANT YOU TO USE YOUR POWERS ON ME!
ANDREW IS JUST...SO FUNNY AND COOL... I'M TOO SCARED TO ASK HIM TO WALK THROUGH THE ANIME MUSEUM WITH ME...
BUT WITH YOUR HELP, MAYBE, I CAN...?
OKAY, OKAY, I GUESS--
I COMMAND YOU TO LIKE YOUR CRUSH MORE THAN YOU ARE AFRAID OF REJECTION!
YAY!
(SHHHH EVERYONE IS LOOKING!)
YO ANDREW! WILL YOU MARRY-- UH.
I MEAN, WANNA WALK THROUGH THE ANIME MUSEUM WITH ME?!
GRAND OPENING

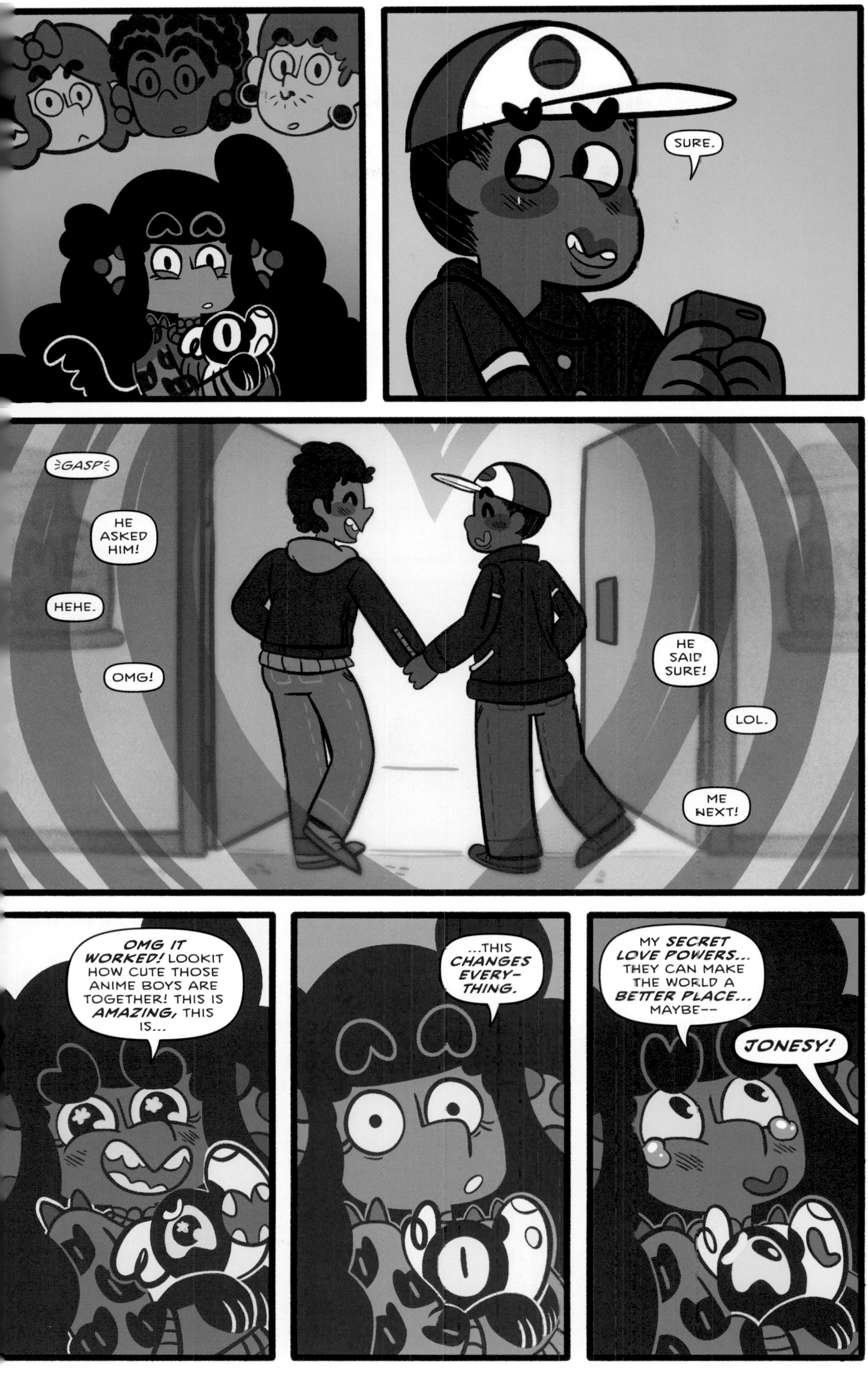
SURE.
GASP
HE ASKED HIM!
HEHE.
OMG!
HE SAID SURE!
LOL.
ME NEXT!
OMG IT WORKED! LOOKIT HOW CUTE THOSE ANIME BOYS ARE TOGETHER! THIS IS AMAZING, THIS IS...
...THIS CHANGES EVERY-THING.
MY SECRET LOVE POWERS... THEY CAN MAKE THE WORLD A BETTER PLACE... MAYBE--
JONESY!

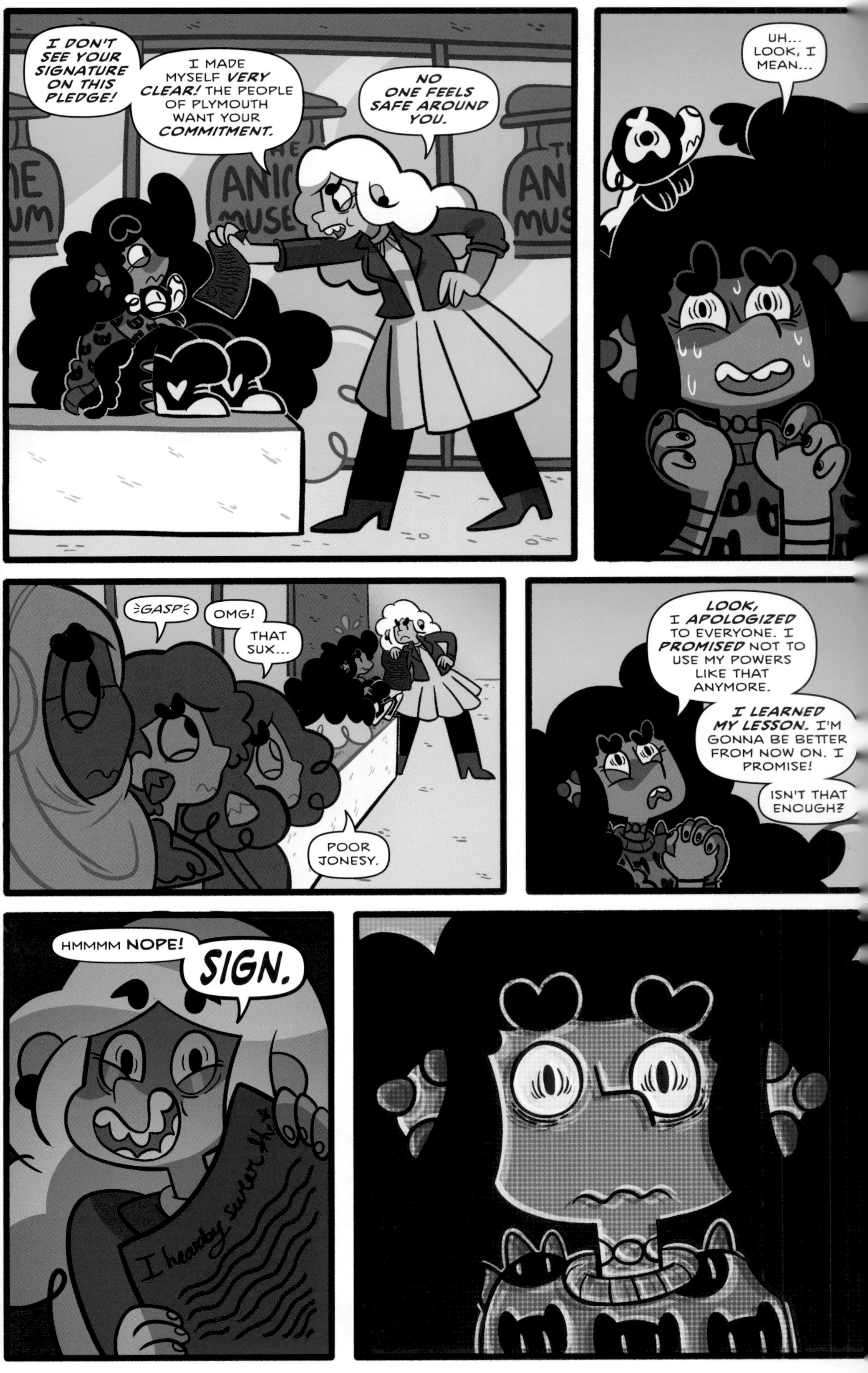
I DON'T SEE YOUR SIGNATURE ON THIS PLEDGE!
I MADE MYSELF VERY CLEAR! THE PEOPLE OF PLYMOUTH WANT YOUR COMMITMENT.
NO ONE FEELS SAFE AROUND YOU.
UH... LOOK, I MEAN...
GASP
OMG!
THAT SUX...
POOR JONESY.
LOOK, I APOLOGIZED TO EVERYONE. I PROMISED NOT TO USE MY POWERS LIKE THAT ANYMORE.
I LEARNED MY LESSON. I'M GONNA BE BETTER FROM NOW ON. I PROMISE!
ISN'T THAT ENOUGH?
HMMMM NOPE!
SIGN.
I hearby swear

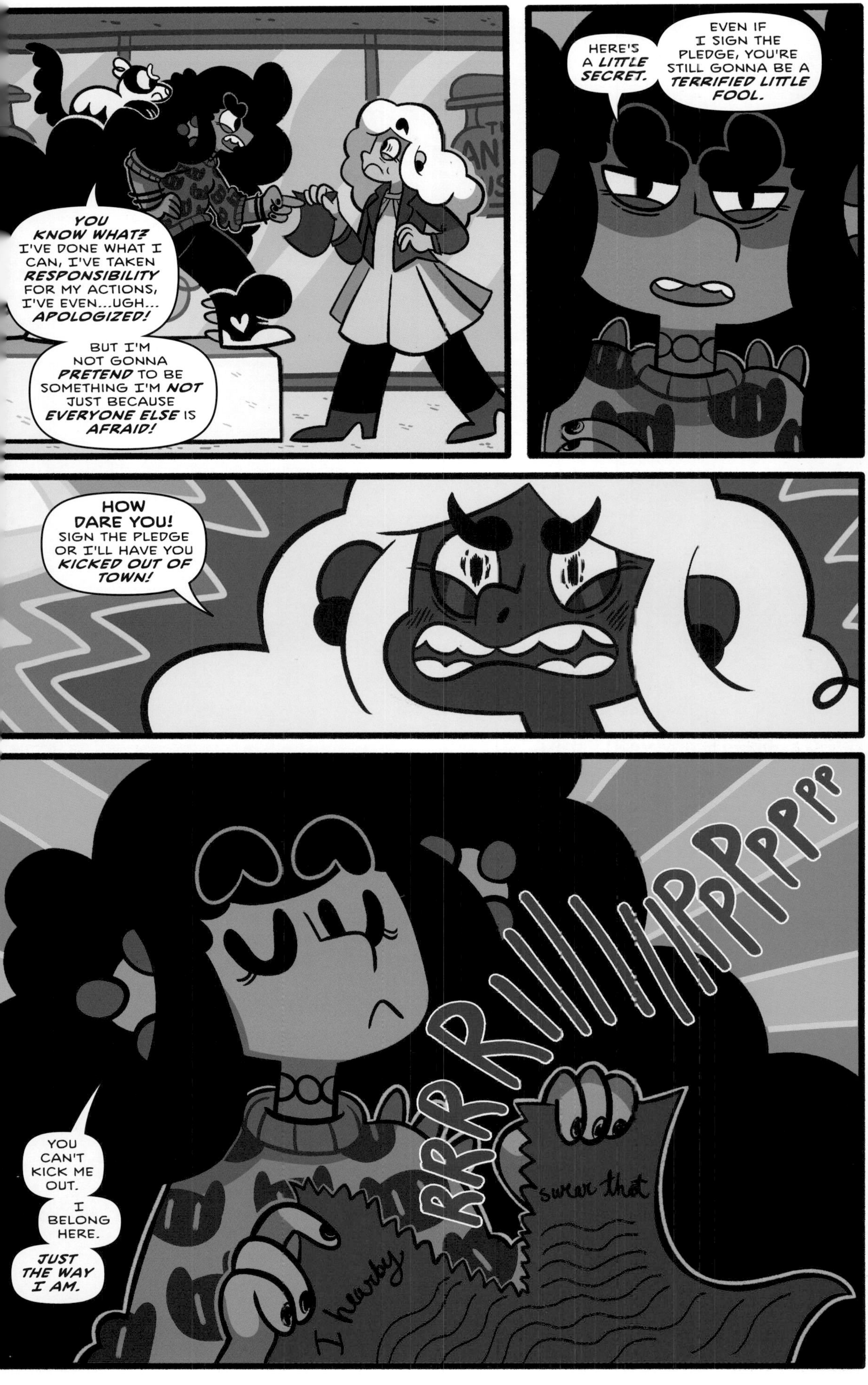

YOU KNOW WHAT? I'VE DONE WHAT I CAN, I'VE TAKEN RESPONSIBILITY FOR MY ACTIONS, I'VE EVEN...UGH... APOLOGIZED!
BUT I'M NOT GONNA PRETEND TO BE SOMETHING I'M NOT JUST BECAUSE EVERYONE ELSE IS AFRAID!
HERE'S A LITTLE SECRET.
EVEN IF I SIGN THE PLEDGE, YOU'RE STILL GONNA BE A TERRIFIED LITTLE FOOL.
HOW DARE YOU! SIGN THE PLEDGE OR I'LL HAVE YOU KICKED OUT OF TOWN!
RRRRIIIIIIPPPPPPPPP
I hearby
swear that
YOU CAN'T KICK ME OUT.
I BELONG HERE.
JUST THE WAY I AM.

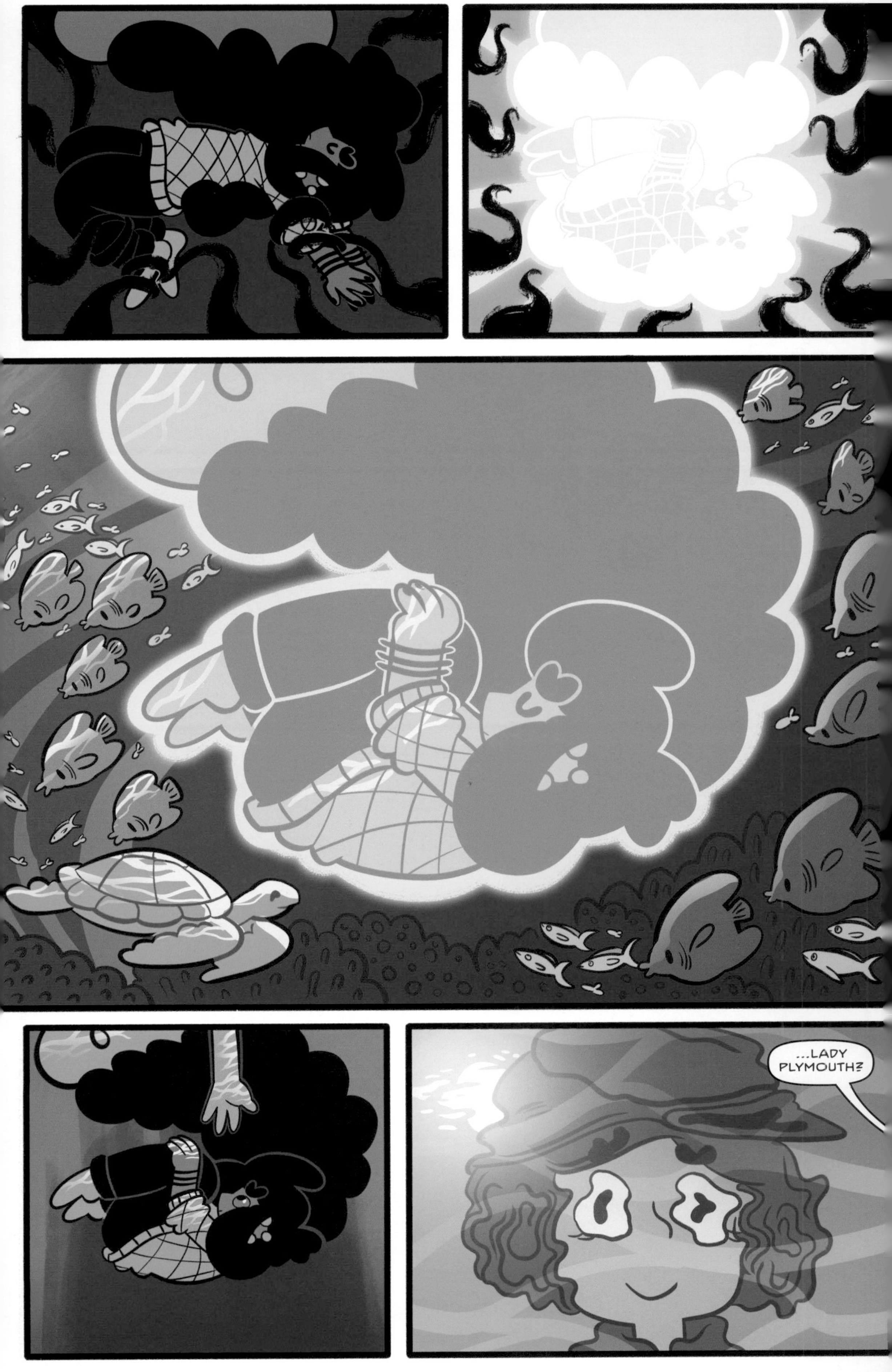
...LADY
PLYMOUTH?

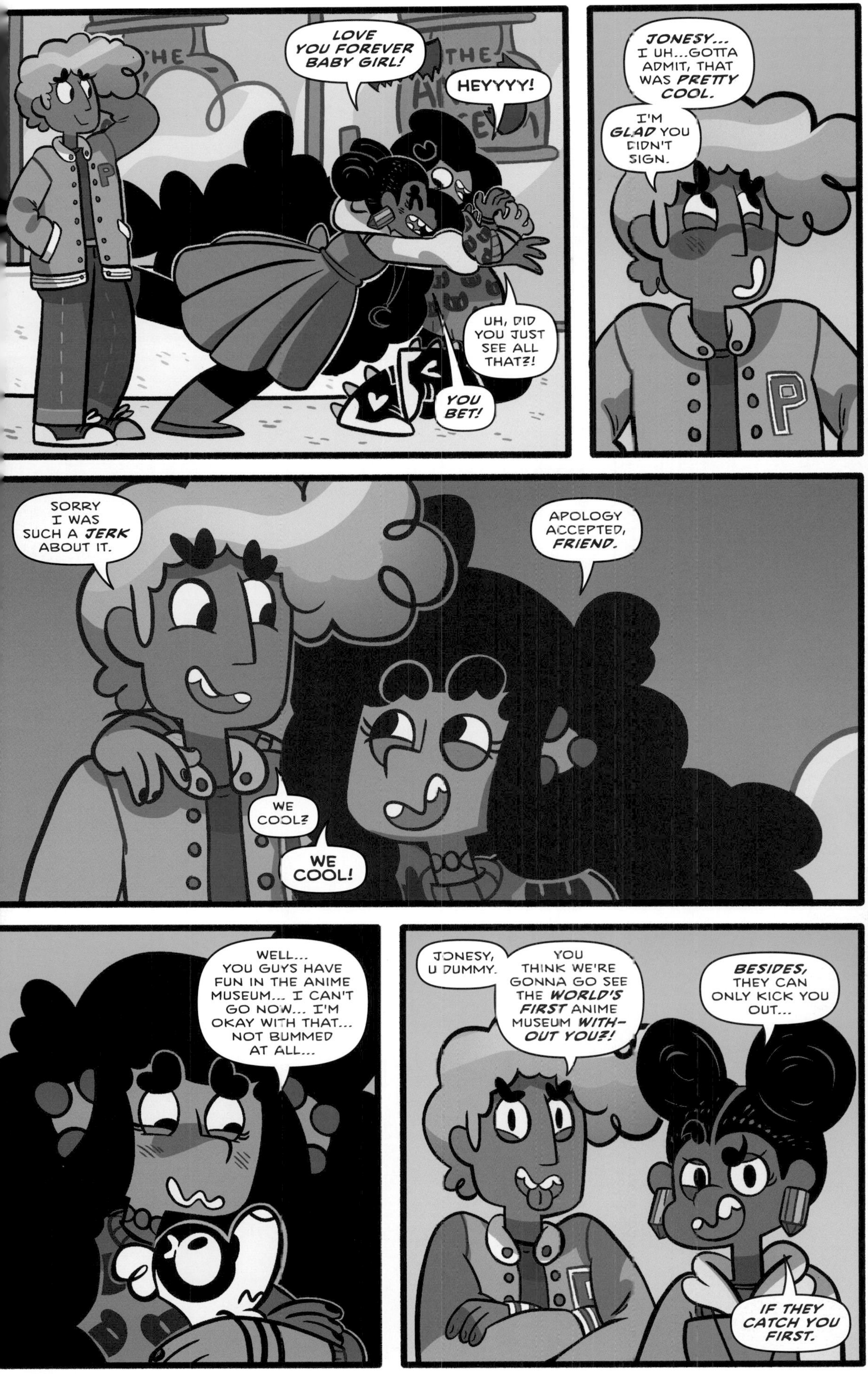
LOVE YOU FOREVER BABY GIRL!
HEYYYY!
UH, DID YOU JUST SEE ALL THAT?!
YOU BET!
JONESY... I UH...GOTTA ADMIT, THAT WAS PRETTY COOL.
I'M GLAD YOU DIDN'T SIGN.
SORRY I WAS SUCH A JERK ABOUT IT.
APOLOGY ACCEPTED, FRIEND.
WE COOL?
WE COOL!
WELL... YOU GUYS HAVE FUN IN THE ANIME MUSEUM... I CAN'T GO NOW... I'M OKAY WITH THAT... NOT BUMMED AT ALL...
JONESY, U DUMMY.
YOU THINK WE'RE GONNA GO SEE THE WORLD'S FIRST ANIME MUSEUM WITHOUT YOU?!
BESIDES, THEY CAN ONLY KICK YOU OUT...
IF THEY CATCH YOU FIRST.

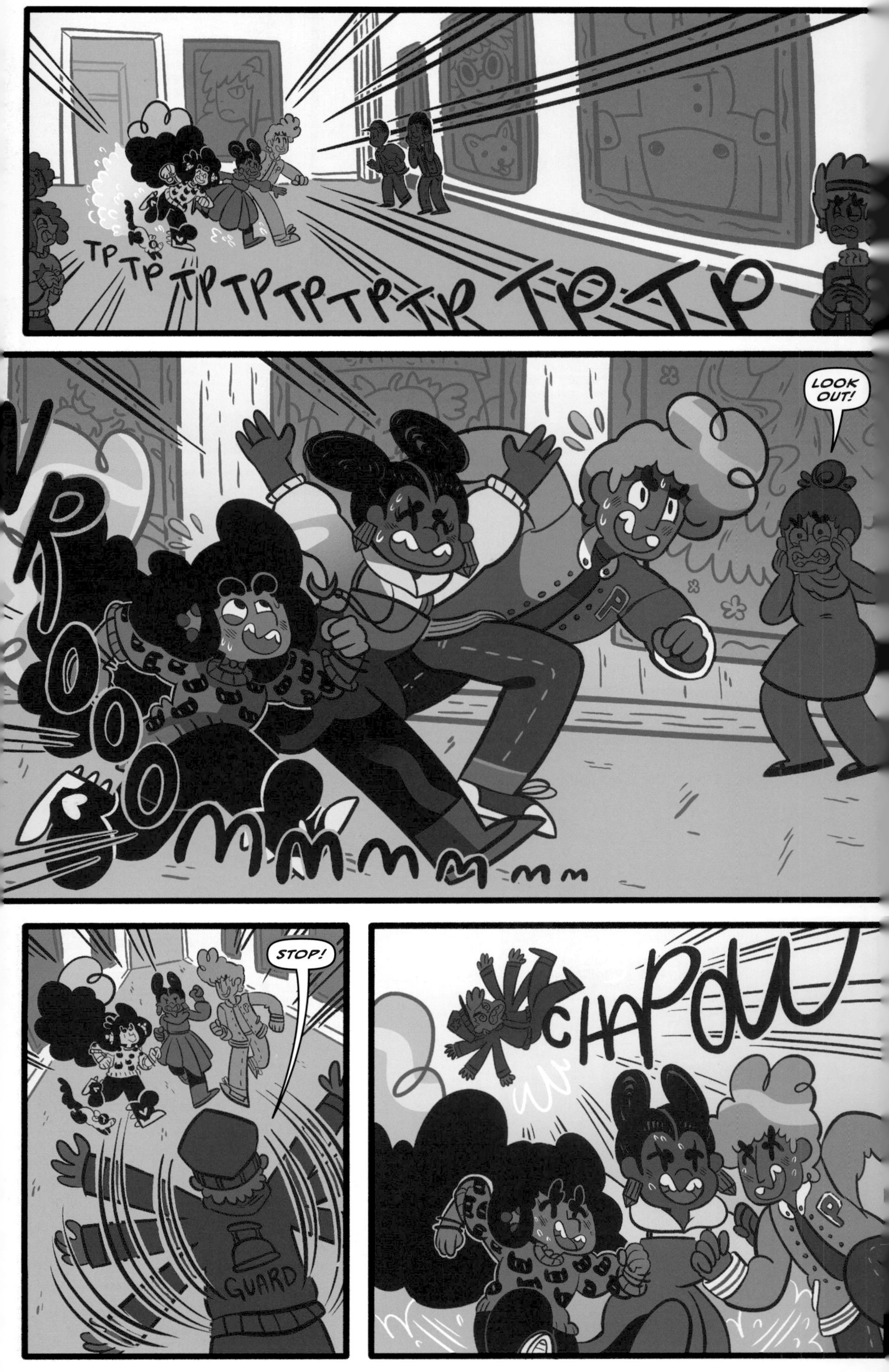
TP TP TP TP TP TP TP TP TP TP TP
LOOK OUT!
VROOOOOMMMMMMMM
STOP!
GUARD
CHAPOW

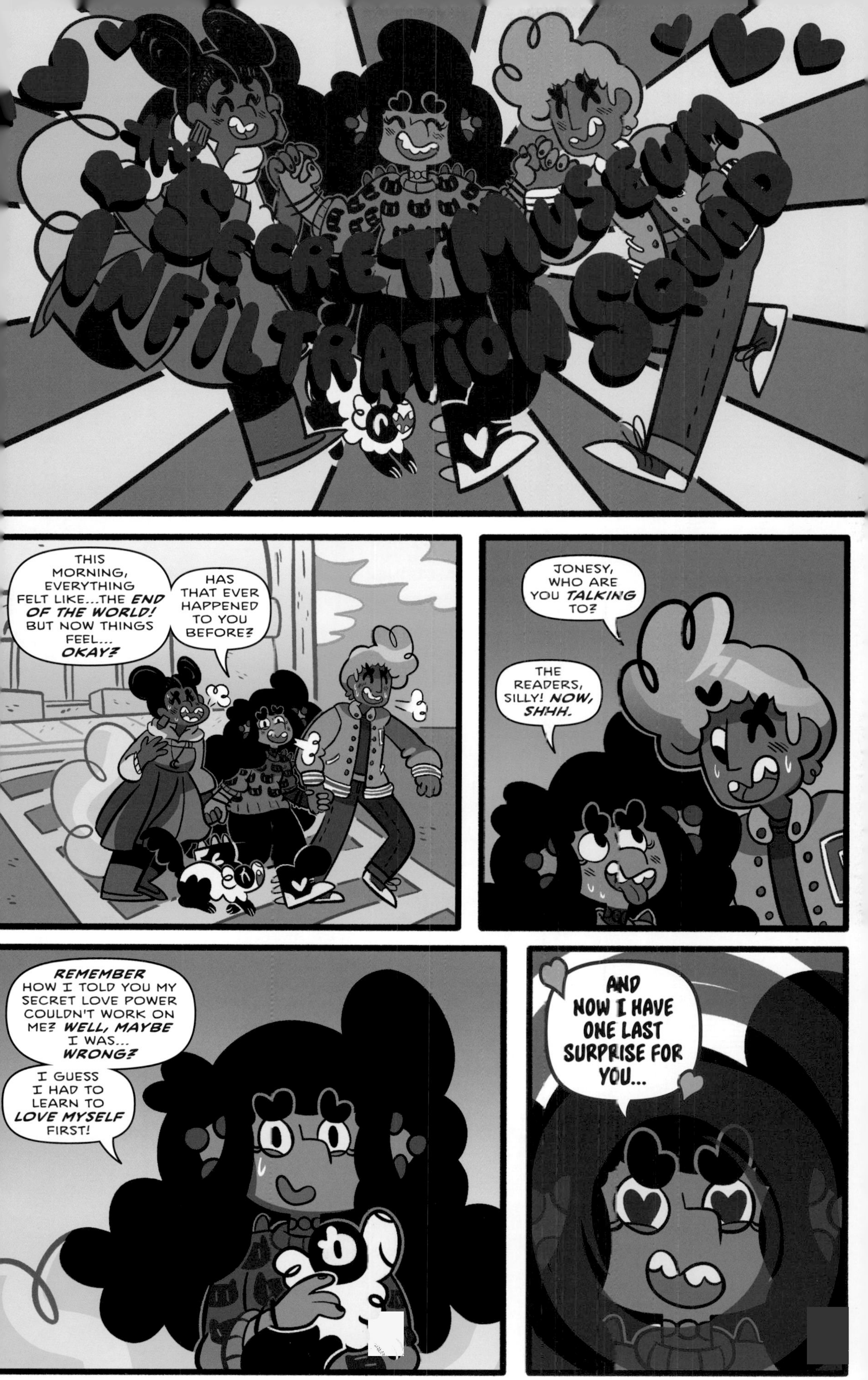
The Secret Museum Infiltration Squad
THIS MORNING, EVERYTHING FELT LIKE...THE END OF THE WORLD! BUT NOW THINGS FEEL... OKAY?
HAS THAT EVER HAPPENED TO YOU BEFORE?
JONESY, WHO ARE YOU TALKING TO?
THE READERS, SILLY! NOW, SHHH.
REMEMBER HOW I TOLD YOU MY SECRET LOVE POWER COULDN'T WORK ON ME? WELL, MAYBE I WAS... WRONG?
I GUESS I HAD TO LEARN TO LOVE MYSELF FIRST!
AND NOW I HAVE ONE LAST SURPRISE FOR YOU...

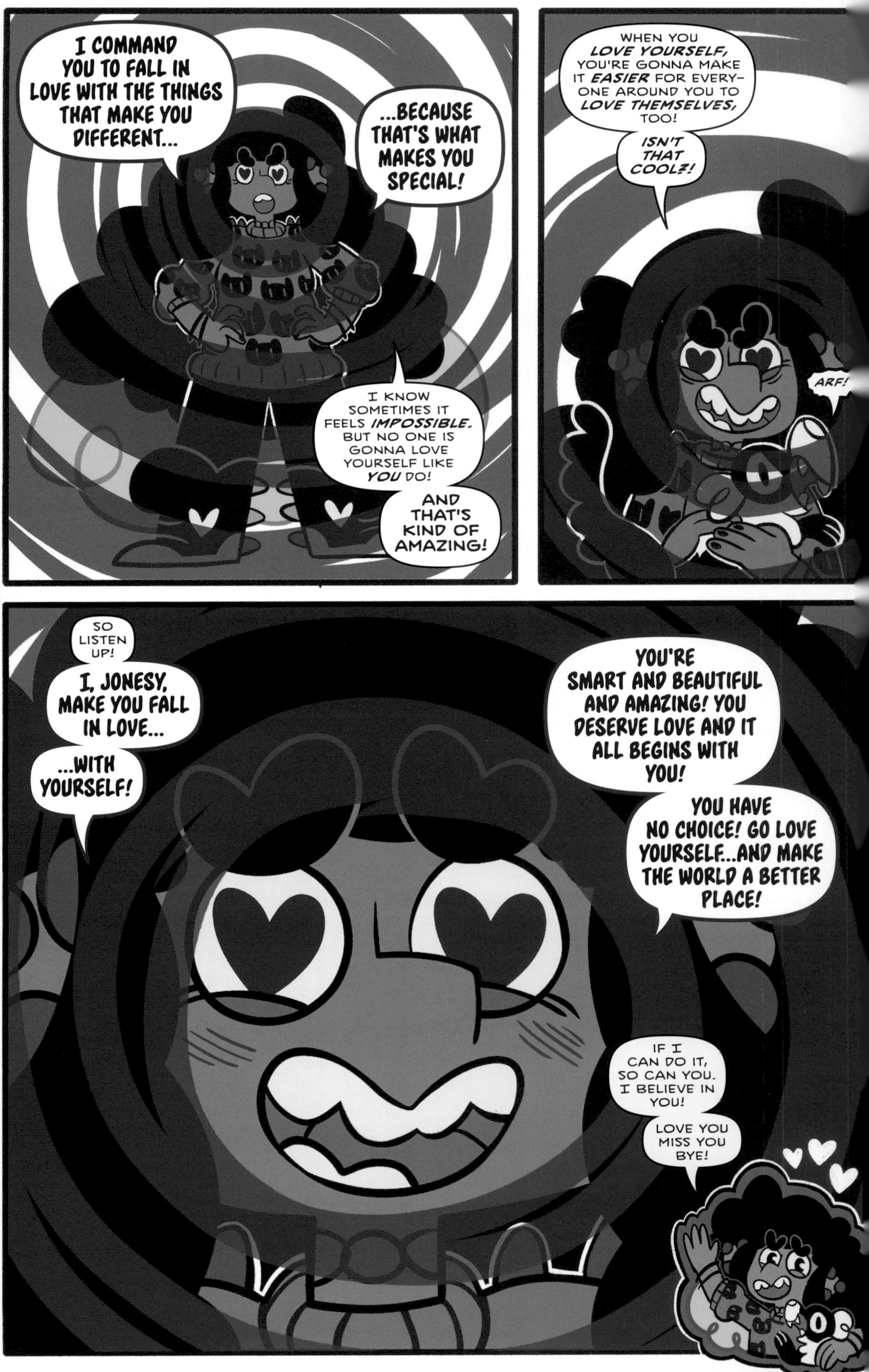
I COMMAND YOU TO FALL IN LOVE WITH THE THINGS THAT MAKE YOU DIFFERENT...
...BECAUSE THAT'S WHAT MAKES YOU SPECIAL!
I KNOW SOMETIMES IT FEELS IMPOSSIBLE. BUT NO ONE IS GONNA LOVE YOURSELF LIKE YOU DO!
AND THAT'S KIND OF AMAZING!
WHEN YOU LOVE YOURSELF, YOU'RE GONNA MAKE IT EASIER FOR EVERY-ONE AROUND YOU TO LOVE THEMSELVES, TOO!
ISN'T THAT COOL?!
ARF!
SO LISTEN UP!
I, JONESY, MAKE YOU FALL IN LOVE...
...WITH YOURSELF!
YOU'RE SMART AND BEAUTIFUL AND AMAZING! YOU DESERVE LOVE AND IT ALL BEGINS WITH YOU!
YOU HAVE NO CHOICE! GO LOVE YOURSELF...AND MAKE THE WORLD A BETTER PLACE!
IF I CAN DO IT, SO CAN YOU. I BELIEVE IN YOU!
LOVE YOU MISS YOU BYE!

COVER GALLERY

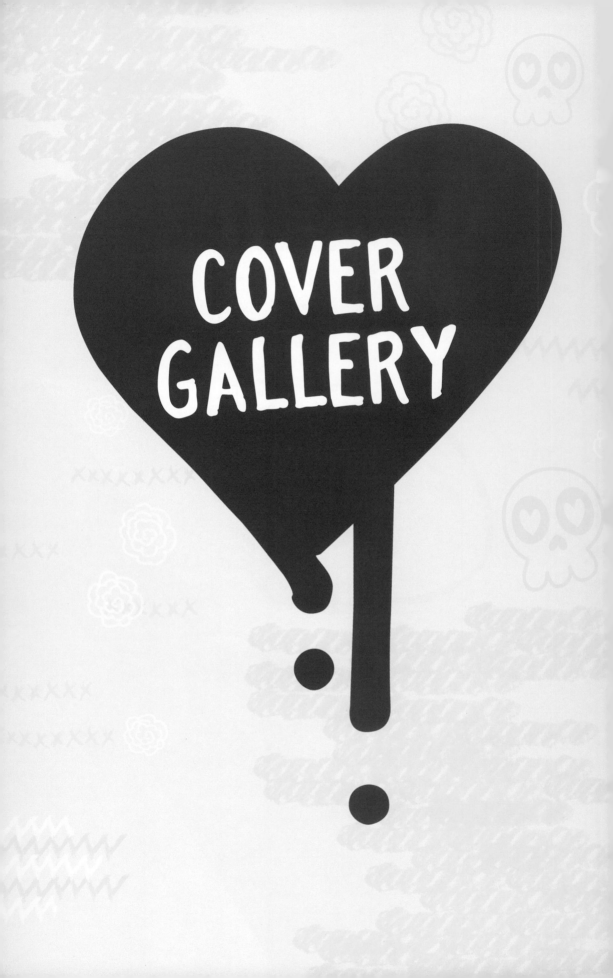

ISSUE NINE COVER BY
CAITLIN ROSE BOYLE
COLORS BY FRED C. STRESING

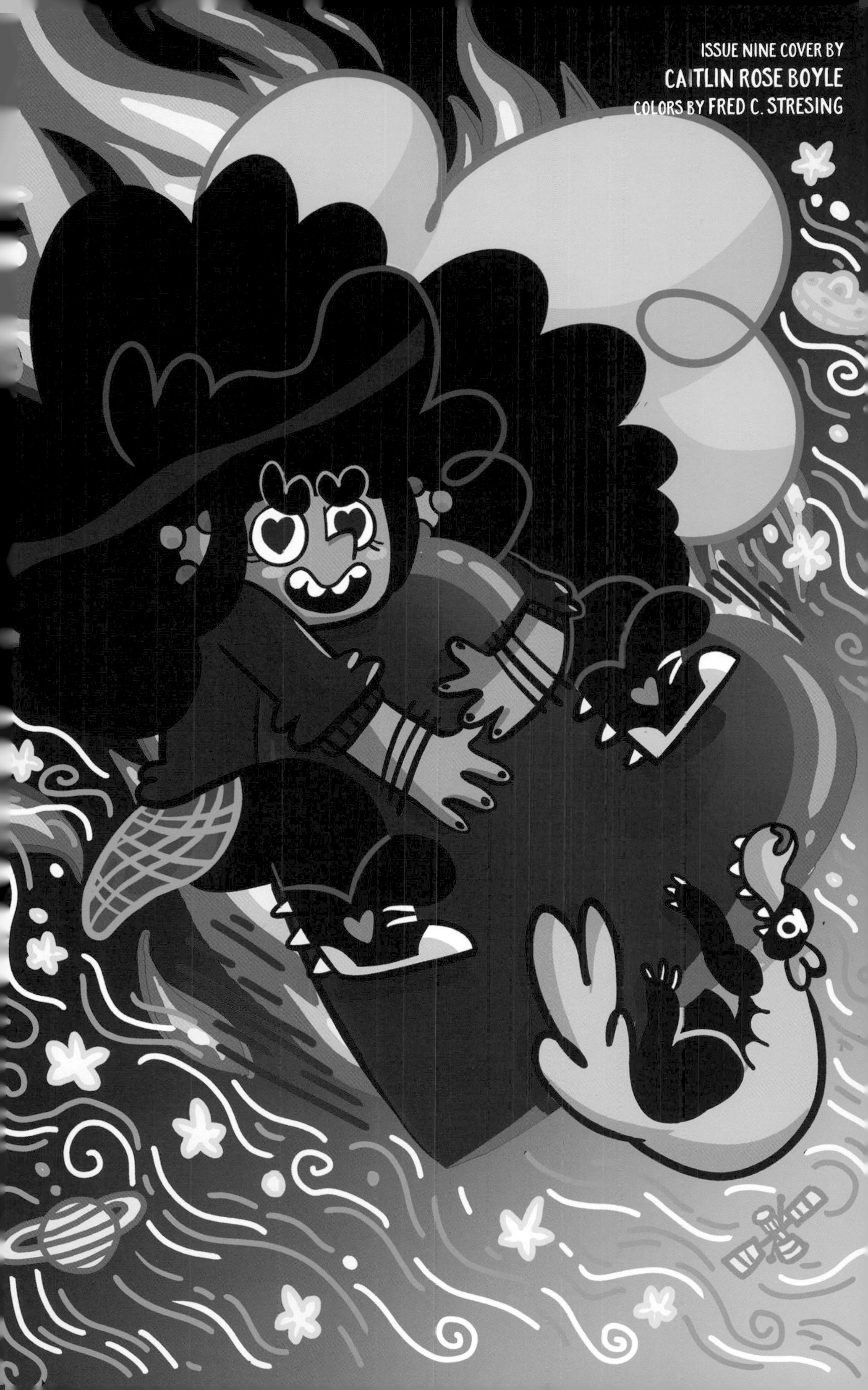

ISSUE TEN COVER BY
CAITLIN ROSE BOYLE
COLORS BY BRITTANY PEER

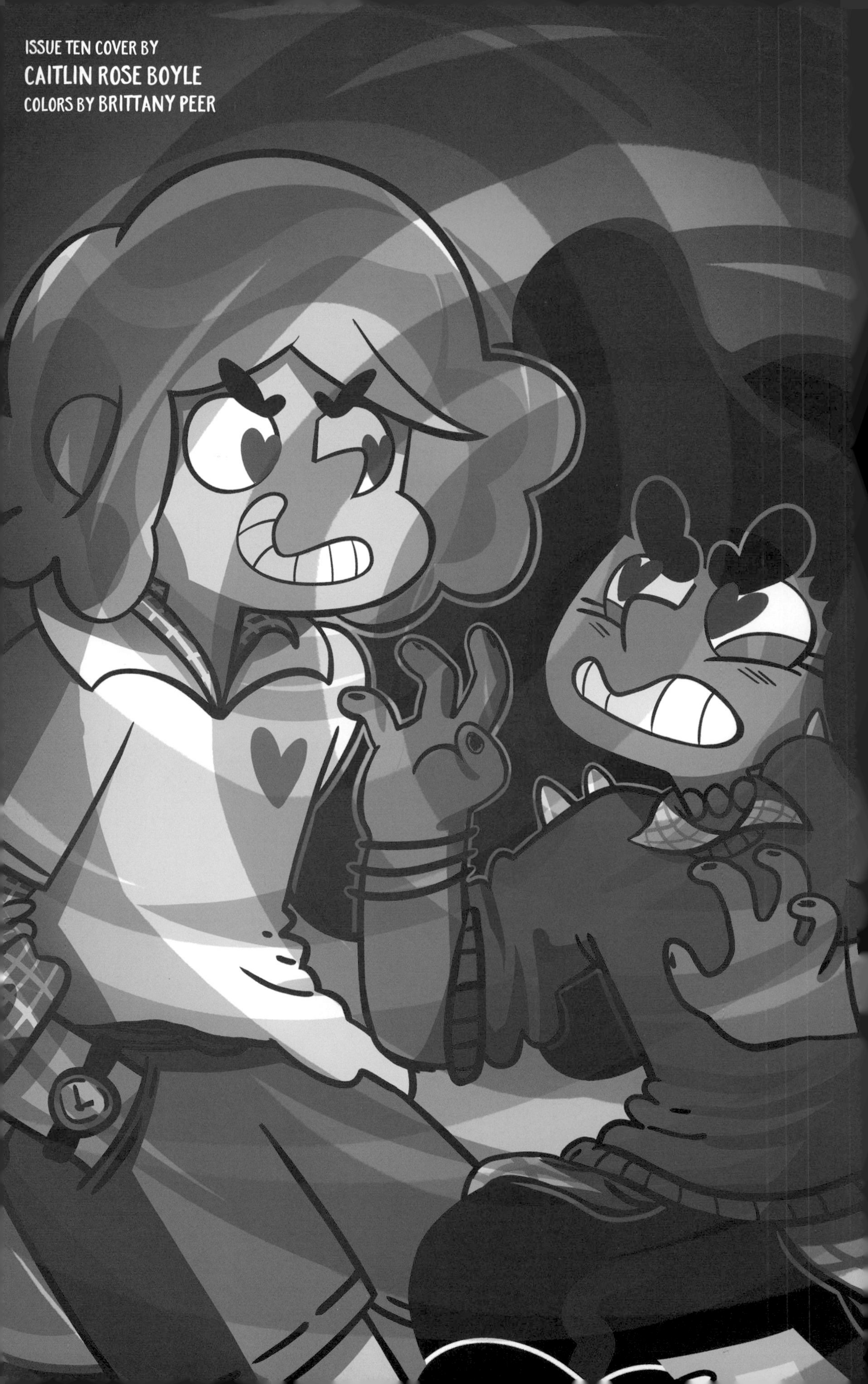

ISSUE ELEVEN COVER BY
CAITLIN ROSE BOYLE
COLORS BY BRITTANY PEER

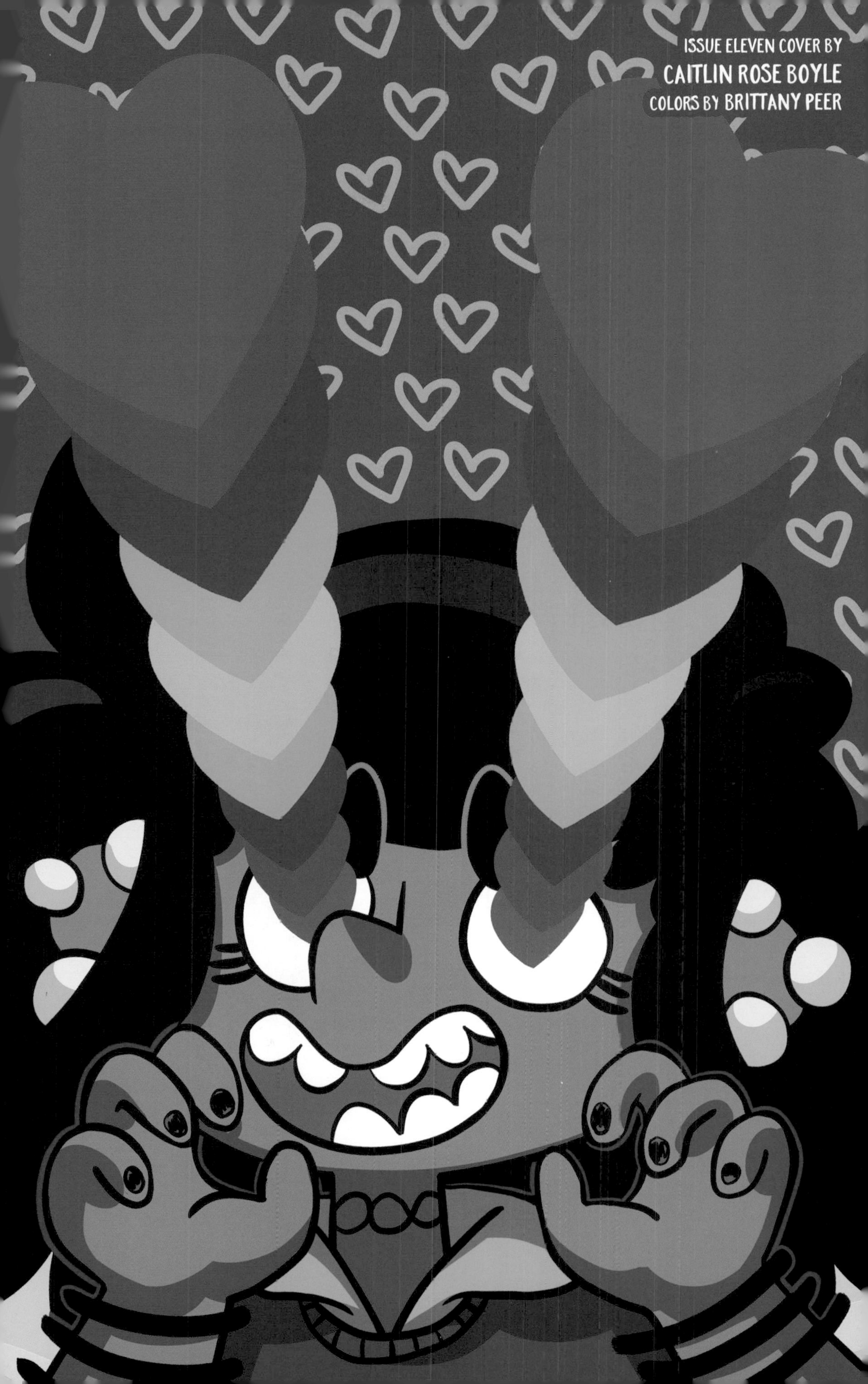

ISSUE TWELVE COVER BY
CAITLIN ROSE BOYLE
COLORS BY BRITTANY PEER

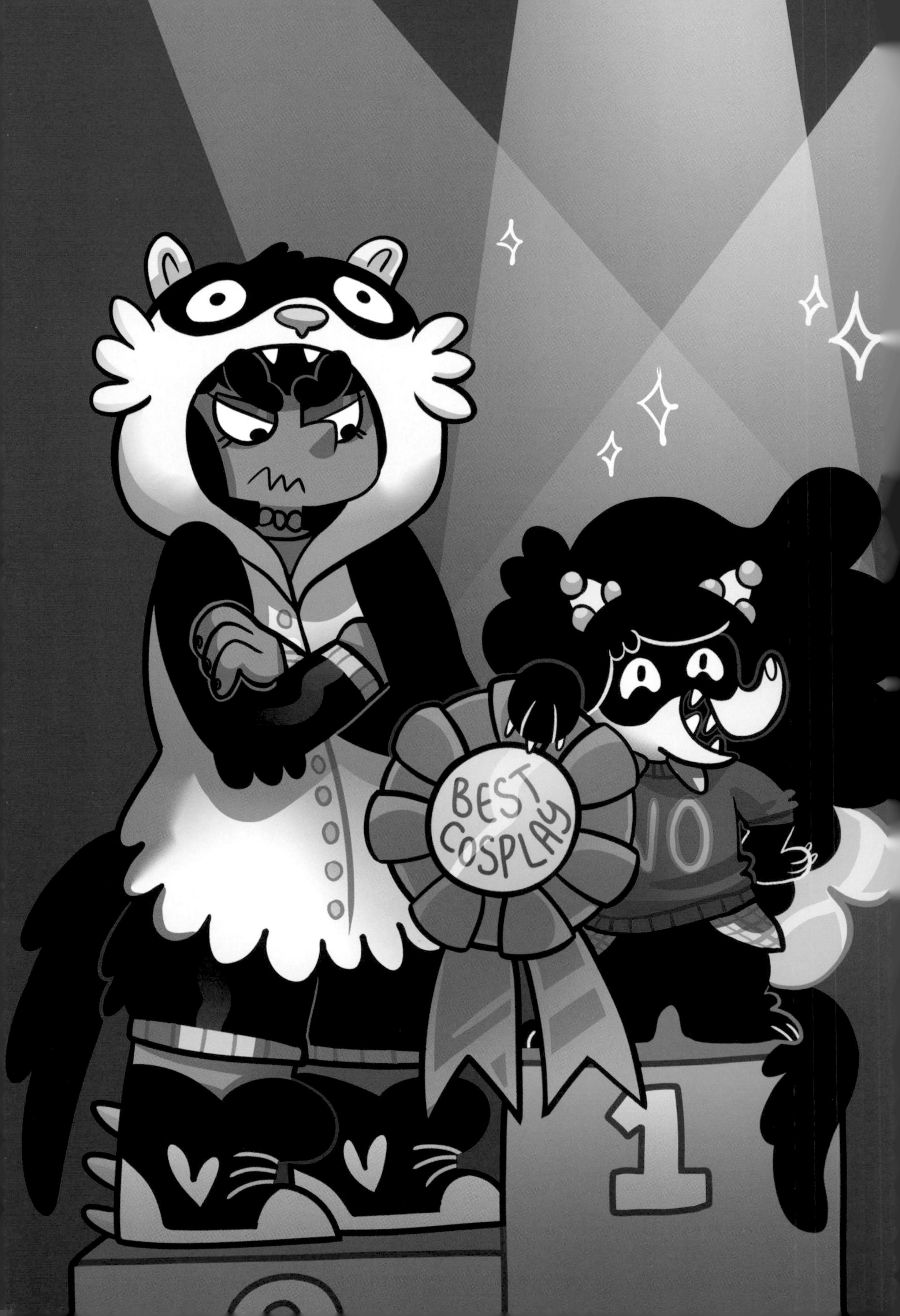
BEST COSPLAY
NO
1

CREATOR BIOS

SAM HUMPHRIES is a comic book writer. He broke into comics with the self-published runaway hits *Our Love Is Real* and *Sacrifice*. Since then, he has written high profile books such as *Legendary Star-Lord* for Marvel, *Green Lanterns* for DC Comics, and *Citizen Jack* for Image Comics. He lives in Los Angeles with his girlfriend and their cats, El Niño and Hopey.

CAITLIN ROSE BOYLE is a cartoonist who spends way too much time on the internet. Like way, way, way too much time. She co-created the Short Toon *Buck N' Lou & The Night Crew* for Nickelodeon's 2014 Shorts Program. Jonesy is her first comic book series, and now the longest running project she's ever worked on! Caitlin currently resides in Pittsburgh.

BRITTANY PEER is a colorist who spends most of her free time laying on the floor of her office with her cat. She has worked on IDW's *TMNT Casey & April*, quite a few indie projects, and has been featured in various anthologies.

COREY BREEN has been a professional in the comic book industry for over fifteen years, thirteen of which were for DC Entertainment. As a Sr Pre-Press Artist, he has contributed art, lettering, color and more to thousands of comic books and other media. Having left DC Entertainment in 2013 to move down to Virginia, Corey is now a superhero in his own right. He is a head designer at a top investment firm company by day, and continues to work in the comic book industry as a freelancer by night. He currently enjoys lettering some of DC and BOOM! Studios' fan favorite books. Corey lives with his loving wife, Kristy, toddler son Tyler, and three cats.

MATTHEW LEVINE is an assistant editor at BOOM! Studios who appreciates the art of a well made deli sandwich. He's worked in television as a writer's assistant and has self published his own comic. He lives in Los Angeles, where he's also from.

JEANINE SCHAEFER has been editing comics for over ten years. She's worked at both Marvel and DC, and her current titles include the upcoming *Motor Crush* and *Prima* from Image Comics. She founded *Girl Comics*, an anthology celebrating the history of women at Marvel, and edited the Eisner-nominated Marvel YA title *Mystic*. She lives in Los Angeles with her husband and two kids, and sporadically runs a tumblr celebrating the special relationship between nerds and cats.

SHANNON WATTERS is an editor at BOOM! Studios and the head of its BOOM! Box and KaBOOM! imprints. She is also the co-creator and co-writer of the Eisner Award-winning comic book series *Lumberjanes*. She lives in Los Angeles with her beautiful Canadian wife and their exceptionally adorable dog.

SCRIPT TO PAGE

THE EVOLUTION OF *JONESY*, FROM ORIGINAL SCRIPT TO FINAL ILLUSTRATION

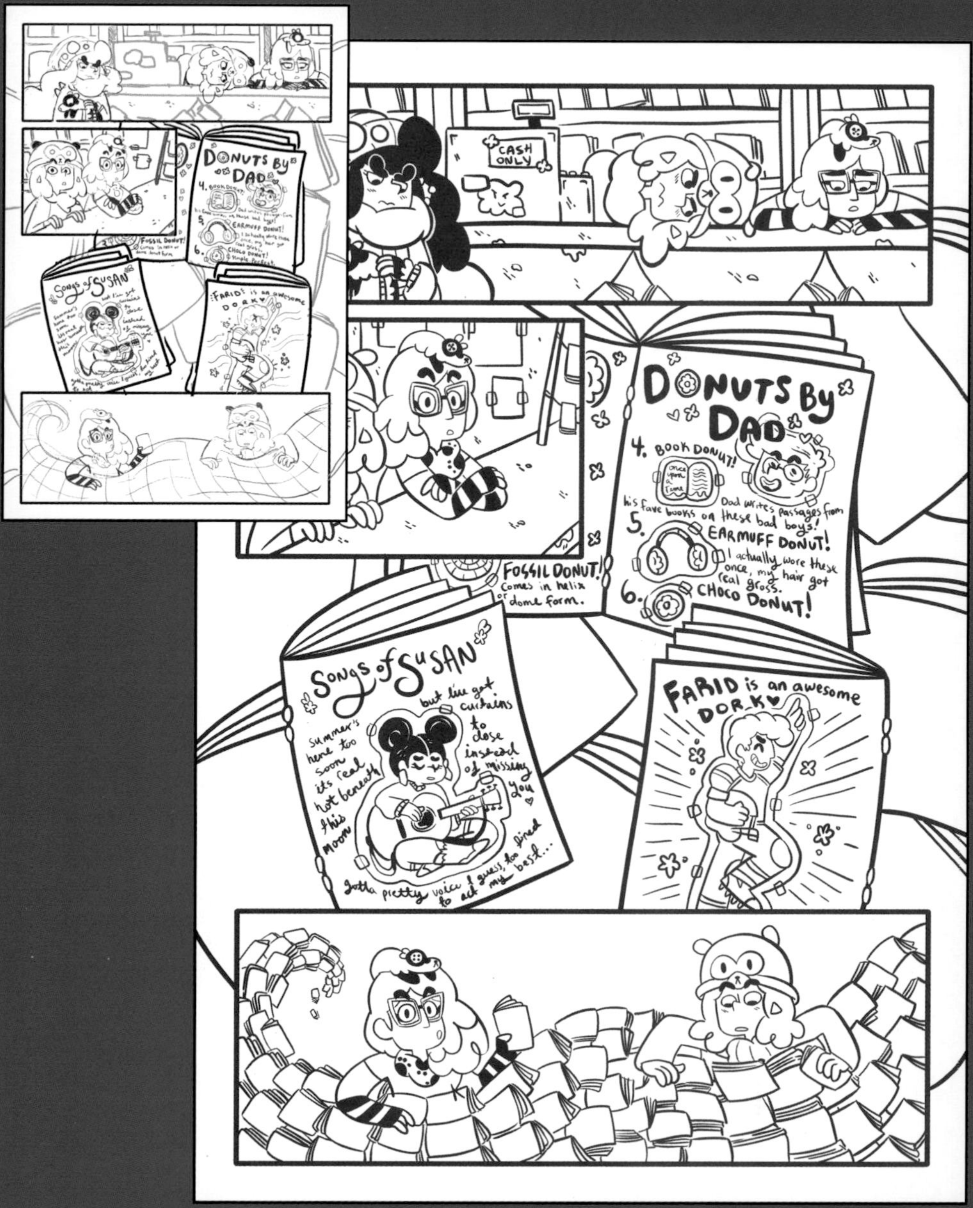

CASH ONLY
DONUTS By DAD
4. BOOK DONUT!
Dad writes passages from his fave books on these bad boys!
5. EARMUFF DONUT!
I actually wore these once, my hair got real gross.
6. CHOCO DONUT!
FOSSIL DONUT! Comes in helix or dome form.
Songs of SuSAN
summer's here too soon its real hot beneath this moon
but i've got curtains to close instead of missing you
Gotta pretty voice I guess, too tired to act my best...
FARID is an awesome DORK♥

ISSUE TEN, PAGE FOUR

PANEL ONE: Establishing shot. Inside the zine store. It is NOT a triumphant mood. Each girl is kinda stewing in their own frustration, sitting apart from each other, looking in opposite directions. But -- it's quiet. They've had the fire taken out from them... for now. Esther on the far right.

ESTHER: Hey, Jonesy...

PANEL TWO: Two shot on Anne and Esther.

ANNE: You never **really** told us why you moved here to Shepard City.

ESTHER: **Yeah**, what happened to you back in **Plymouth**?
I mean, we know a lot from your zines...

Panel Three: ZINES! ZINE PAGE! It's like a scrapbook of dad and donuts. Maybe Jonesy's five (four, three, whatever) of her favorite donuts?

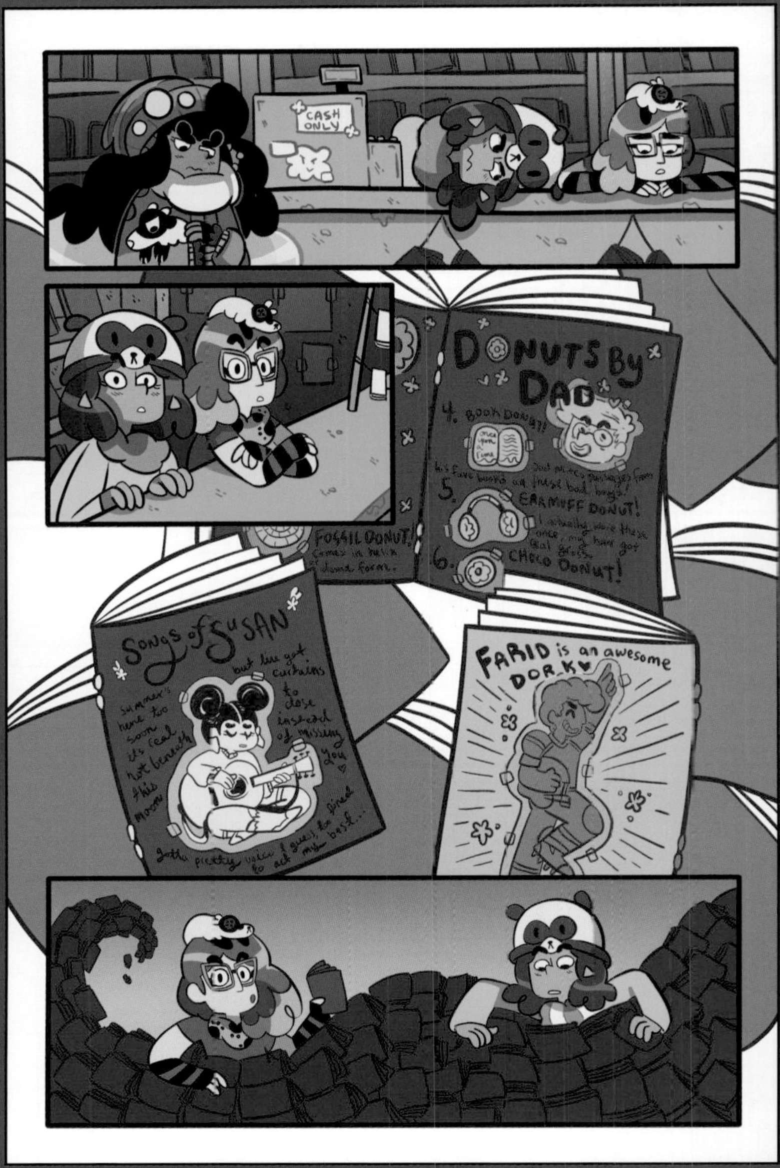
CASH ONLY
DONUTS By DAD
4. Book Donut!
5. EARMUFF DONUT!
6. CHOCO DONUT!
FOSSIL DONUT!
Songs of Susan
FARID is an awesome DORK

ANNE(no tails): I can practically recite the menu of your **dad's donut restaurant**!

ESTHER(no tails): I know all the lyrics to the songs by **your bestie, Susan**!

ANNE(no tails): And I feel like I know everything about Farid!

PANEL SIX: Esther and Anne, in a sea of Jonesy zines, as if trying to put them in chronological order.

ESTHER: We, like, know **all about** your life in Plymouth!
It **inspired** us to open our zine store!

ANNE: But we don't know why you **left**?
Unless we're **missing** a zine...)

ESTHER: (**Shut up**, you said we had them **all**!)

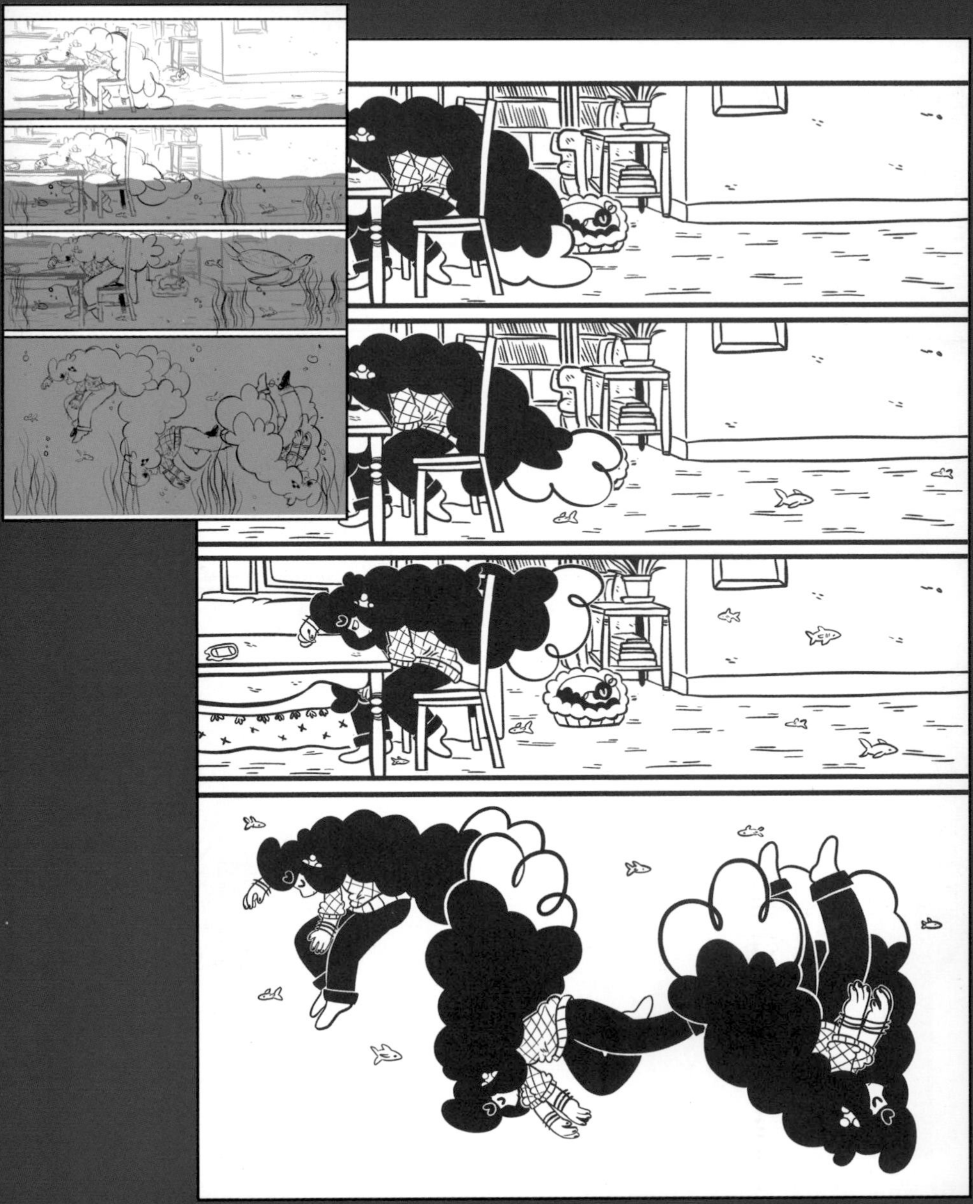

ISSUE TWELVE, PAGE TEN

Start with three same sized panels across the page.

PANEL ONE: Jonesy at the table. We notice water pooling at the bottom of the panel. Like the kitchen is beginning to flood. Jonesy doesn't move or acknowledge it in any way. She's wrapped up in her anxiety, depression.

PANEL TWO: Same shot. Jonesy doesn't move. The water is now mid-way up the page. Now we see some indications...this isn't a flood. It's the ocean. Some fish, maybe seaweed, bubbles, etc.

PANEL THREE: Same shot. The water is almost to the top of the panel. Jonesy is now UNDERWATER. She still hasn't acknowledged the water or moved to do anything about it, altho her arms/head/hair are now "weightless" under the water.

PANEL FOUR: BIG PANEL! No more kitchen. Just ocean.

Remember those panels where we have Jonesy in three different full body poses across the page? Like when she's apologizing to Susan at the end of issue 2?

Similar idea here, but with a twist. The first pose is upper left, the second pose is middle-center, and the last pose is bottom right, as if she is SLOWLY SINKING.

And (HI BRITTANY!) the ocean gets darker, and murkier the more we go down.

But Jonesy's poses here...they're not manic, as we've seen before. They're GRACEFUL, like she is FLOATING down, twisting as she falls, swirling in the water. It's like unintentional ballet. It's peaceful, but...it is also SURRENDER. Her eyes closed. Limbs flowing, but without control. She is GIVING UP. She could even be TUMBLING so that in the last pose she is UPSIDE DOWN...

DISCOVER
ALL THE HITS

STEVENSON · ELLIS · WATTERS · ALLEN
LUMBERJANES
BEWARE THE KITTEN HOLY
NEW YORK TIMES BESTSELLING SERIES

Allison + Treiman + Cogar
GIANT DAYS
VOLUME ONE

JONESY
HUMPHRIES · BOYLE · QUINN
"A SPIRITUAL SUCCESSOR TO SCOTT PILGRIM" —NERDIST
"PURE CUTE" —TEEN VOGUE
VOLUME ONE

Hope Larson · Brittney Williams · Sarah Stern
GOLDIE VANCE
Volume One

JAMES TYNION IV · RIAN SYGH · WALTER BAIAMONTE
THE BACKSTAGERS

TYSON HESSE'S
DIESEL
IGNITION

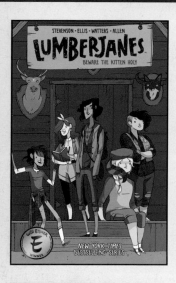

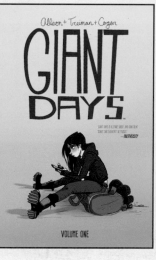

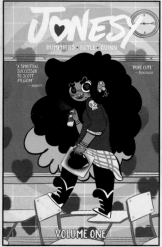

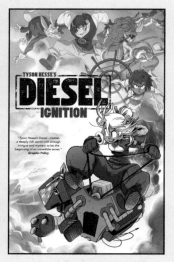

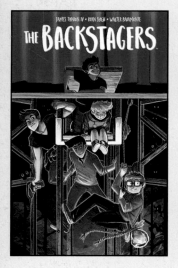

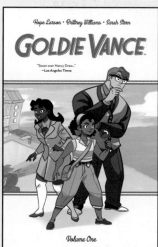

Lumberjanes
Noelle Stevenson, Shannon Watters, Grace Ellis, Brooke Allen, and Others
Volume 1: Beware the Kitten Holy
ISBN: 978-1-60886-687-8 | $14.99
Volume 2: Friendship to the Max
ISBN: 978-1-60886-737-0 | $14.99
Volume 3: A Terrible Plan
ISBN: 978-1-60886-803-2 | $14.99
Volume 4: Out of Time
ISBN: 978-1-60886-860-5 | $14.99
Volume 5: Band Together
ISBN: 978-1-60886-919-0 | $14.99

Giant Days
John Allison, Lissa Treiman, Max Sarin
Volume 1
ISBN: 978-1-60886-789-9 | $9.99
Volume 2
ISBN: 978-1-60886-804-9 | $14.99
Volume 3
ISBN: 978-1-60886-851-3 | $14.99

Jonesy
Sam Humphries, Caitlin Rose Boyle
Volume 1
ISBN: 978-1-60886-883-4 | $9.99
Volume 2
ISBN: 978-1-60886-999-2 | $14.99

Goldie Vance
Hope Larson, Brittney Williams
Volume 1
ISBN: 978-1-60886-898-8 | $9.99
Volume 2
ISBN: 978-1-60886-974-9 | $14.99

The Backstagers
James Tynion IV, Rian Sygh
ISBN: 978-1-60886-993-0 | $29.99

Tyson Hesse's Diesel: Ignition
Tyson Hesse
ISBN: 978-1-60886-907-7 | $14.99

Power Up
Kate Leth, Matt Cummings
ISBN: 978-1-60886-837-7 | $19.99

Teen Dog
Jake Lawrence
ISBN: 978-1-60886-729-5 | $19.99

Midas Flesh
Ryan North, Braden Lamb, Shelli Paroline
ISBN: 978-1-60886-455-3 | $14.99

Help Us! Great Warrior
Madeline Flores, Trillian Gunn
ISBN: 978-1-60886-802-5 | $19.99

BOOM! BOX™

AVAILABLE AT YOUR LOCAL COMICS SHOP AND BOOKSTORE
To find a comics shop in your area, call 1-888-266-4226
WWW.**BOOM-STUDIOS**.COM